LINGUISTICA ANTVERPIENSIA NEW SERIES

Themes in Translation Studies

10/2011

LINGUISTICA ANTVERPIENSIA

NEW SERIES

Themes in Translation Studies

10/2011

ARTESIS UNIVERSITY COLLEGE ANTWERP
DEPARTMENT OF TRANSLATORS & INTERPRETERS

TRANSLATION AS A SOCIAL ACTIVITY

Edited by

Minako O'Hagan

Contents

Community Translation: Translation as a social activity and its possible consequences in the advent of Web 2.0 and beyond

Minako O'Hagan

Dublin City University

This introduction to the 10th issue of Linguistica Antverpiensia New Series – Themes in Translation Studies (LANS-TTS) begins by discussing the central concept of community translation, highlighting its terminological ambiguity. This is in part due to the already well-established field of community interpreting where the term is often used to mean the written translation of public information for immigrants. It is also an indication of the terminological instability typical of an emerging paradigm. For example, community translation is used more or less synonymously with such terms as translation crowdsourcing, user-generated translation and collaborative translation. The meaning of the term as we discuss in this issue can be best specified when the concept is anchored in the context of Web 2.0 (second generation web-technologies). This in turn acknowledges its intrinsic tie to online communities and directs us to new dynamics resulting from general Internet users acting as translators. While participants in community translation are not necessarily all unpaid, untrained volunteers community translation is used by some organisations as a mechanism to obtain free translations by going outside the professional translation sphere. To this end the ethical question of profit-making enterprises accessing free labour on the pretext of openness and sharing remains. That said, the author believes community translation is far more than a dilettante, anti-professional movement. Building on the emerging picture from the contributions in this volume, the author suggests some of the future directions that research on community translation might take, emphasising the need to reflect on the current translation practices and be open to the new developments and opportunities arising from the free and social Internet.

1. Background

Focusing on increasingly visible and somewhat controversial translation practices typically performed by unspecified individuals on the Internet, this tenth edition of *Linguistica Antverpiensia New Series – Themes in Translation Studies* explores key issues arising from the emerging translation phenomenon of community translation.

Due partly to the existing concept and practice of *community interpreting* which has become well established in Translation Studies (TS), the term *community translation* is not entirely transparent. As commented by Pym (2011), the term's usage by some authors especially in Australia and the US is closely associated with community interpreting, referring mainly to the written translation of public information for an immigrant population. Over the last decade, community interpreting has become more and more professionalised but it still frequently involves "untrained individuals" and is often associated with "amateurism and ad hoc solutions" (Wadensjö, 2009, p. 43). Perhaps it is in the latter sense of involvement of non-professionals that community translation and community interpreting may point to some conceptual overlap. However, at least according to our usage in this volume, the key difference is that unlike community interpreting, community translation is tied to the online community particularly in the specific context of Web 2.0. As such it signifies specific translation practices that are unfolding on the Internet as the central foci. Nevertheless, given the inherent difficulty in defining *community* due to its multiplicity as more recently highlighted by Internet researchers (Kendall, 2011), community translation calls for further explanation.

First used at the O'Reilly and Associates conference in 2004, the slogan Web 2.0 has become an influential concept (Barry, 2008), if at times somewhat over-hyped. The second generation web technologies have become strongly identified with such key words as user-generated content and social networking. However, Nancy Baym (2011) reminds us that user-generated content is in fact not new as "all of the content on the Internet was generated by people, for people" from the start (p.384). According to Baym (2011), the development of "professionally provided content" for profit is newly brought about by Web 2.0 as an alternative to free user-generated content which dominated the Internet until 1994. She highlights how the free user-generated content is now often destined for profit-making enterprises such as Facebook and YouTube. Furthermore, the dimension of social networking has become the most distinctive feature of Web 2.0 platforms as the "participative web" (OECD, 2007) where people exchange ideas, collaborate and share with others their own user-generated content, thus leading to a web of social interactions that generate business.

It is this broad technological milieu in which community translation is couched with the implied meaning of a community of Internet users. For example, Google valued YouTube at $1.65 billion at the time of its acquisition, not for the company of 67 employees but "for the community – the people who use it" that are in the multimillions (Howe, 2008, p. 109). In this way the concept of community in the era of Web 2.0 has acquired a specific meaning, which warrants the term *community translation* despite the problems mentioned at the beginning. When Facebook filed a patent for its purpose-built translation application in August 2009 at the US Patent & Trademark Office, the invention was named *Community Translation On A Social Network* and described as:[1] "embodiments of the invention provide techniques for translating text in a social network". Not surprisingly, the

Facebook example best illustrates how community translation is tightly woven into social networking. As mentioned by several contributors in this volume, the Facebook user translation initiatives became the most publicised early example of community translation, where a group of self-selected Internet users translate fragments of text to be used on the Facebook website in different language versions. These translators are mostly already Facebook members familiar with the environment; if not, volunteers need to be registered with Facebook in order to use its own purpose-built translation platform. The proposed translations are in turn voted on by other Facebook users. Translators who contribute well in terms of quantity and quality appear on the leader board. Added to the social networking flavour are discussions in which such community translators often passionately engage, debating translation-related issues. As illustrated by Facebook, community translation in general incorporates social dimensions where the participants interact, for example, in deciding the quality of a translation (Jiménez-Crespo in this volume). There is also clear intervention by paid professional translators in the Facebook example to maintain quality as explained by Kelly et al. in this volume.

In general, participants in community translation settings are not all untrained volunteers; professional translators also respond to a particular call which they consider worthwhile, despite a lack of remuneration. These calls for participation are usually made directly by content owners as in Facebook, making the entire exercise legally legitimate, i.e., no copyright infringement in terms of the use of the content. This contrasts with cases where individuals or groups of individuals take the liberty of carrying out their own unsolicited translation of content they themselves choose, and then share the translation on the Internet. An example of this is fan translation, notably of fansubs of Japanese anime, and now extended to a wider range of digital content, which essentially appropriates the copyrighted source material. Kageura et al. in this volume make a specific reference to copyright issues in relation to the Minna no Hon'yaku (MNH) platform, which they describe as "a translation hosting site with rich translation-aid functions". MNH only publishes materials with copyright permission, otherwise storing the materials in the users' private space while the site as a whole generally promotes Creative Commons licenses.

As is evident in the terminology usage by contributors in this volume, labels other than *community translation* are used more or less synonymously. A closer look indicates that terms such as *translation crowdsourcing, user-generated translation* (O'Hagan, 2009; Perrino, 2009) and *CT³* in reference to *community, crowdsourced* and *collaborative translation* (DePalma & Kelly, 2008) are often used with some slight differences in meaning, depending on the author. Désilets and van der Meer in this volume use *collaborative translation* as an umbrella term encompassing approaches such as "agile translation teamware, collaborative terminology resources, translation memory sharing, online translation marketplaces, post-editing by the crowd, and […] translation crowdsourcing". From a TS perspective, Pym (2011) in turn suggests that terms such as community translation, crowdsourcing and collaborative translation "seem shot through with activist ideologies" (p. 97). Similarly Cronin (2010) finds "the subversive potential of the crowd" useful in framing crowdsourcing practices. I would argue that instances of community translation that are embedded in strict commercial contexts applied by for-profit organisations are generally devoid of such political agenda, which cannot be said of cases of fan translation and its variants. On the assumption that the key difference at stake is the remuneration, Pym (2011) recommends *volunteer translation* as a preferred term. Here too, as observed in contributions in this volume, a lack of monetary reward is not an essential characteristic of community translation although the act of volunteering may aptly describe the self-initiated action typical of community translation. Key common characteristics shared in the above terms highlight that it is translation performed voluntarily by Internet users and is usually produced in some form of collaboration often on specific platforms by a group of people forming an online community.

In particular, the term *crowdsourcing* has captured the imagination of the business world as a means of leveraging the potential capacity of the bourgeoning number of Internet users who participate en masse in various online activities in the spirit of openness, sharing and collaboration. In an analogy to the concept of outsourcing, Jeff Howe (2006) coined the term, highlighting an unknown yet potentially significant power of a crowd organically formed to perform a given task. Earlier James Surowiecki (2005) had shown how the opinions of a large number of sufficiently diverse groups of people tend to converge on the right answer, which he theorised as "the wisdom of crowds". Exploiting the potential of the Internet crowd to solve otherwise intractable problems, crowdsourcing has entered into business discourses and practices as a mechanism of distributed problem solving in the age of Web 2.0 (Tapscott & Williams, 2006). Clay Shirky (2010), in turn, treats crowdsourcing as a manifestation of the "cognitive surplus"—the title of his book—of the vast population of Internet users who generate content in their spare time with the intention that it be shared by other users, suggesting this social dimension as a critical motivator.

Since the most high-profile early example of Facebook Translations began in the end of 2007, the crowdsourcing concept has been applied by different organisations as a means to obtain translation by reaching out to the vast resources of Internet users. However, exploitation of the Internet crowd to obtain free translations in these initiatives, in particular by 'for-profit' entities, antagonised professional translators as a development which could threaten their livelihood. When Facebook called on its users to help translate its website, various protest groups sprouted, including the 7,000-strong "Leave Translation to Translators!" deriding the Facebook translation community as "people who think they can do it" (cited in Keegan, 2009). A subsequent similar protest by translator members of LinkedIn against what appeared to be a free ride for a for-profit company saw the formation of "Translators against Crowdsourcing for Commercial Business" (Kelly, 2009). Concerns raised by professional translators are understandable on the grounds of the likely threat to their jobs and the risk that such movements may lead to a further devaluation of what is involved in translation work (Kelly, 2009). The ethical question of profit-making enterprises exploiting free labour, no matter how willing are the volunteers, also remains. Yet the other side of the coin is that every day most remunerated translators rely on the vast amount of free user-generated content and information available on the Internet, be it glossaries of terms or technical information of all kinds in a given language. Placed in the bigger picture of the powerful trends of Internet technologies advocating openness and sharing, which is feeding through also to the design of translation tools, community translation is far too complex to be treated simply as a dilettante, anti-professional movement.

While the whole practice of translation outside the strictly professional sphere seems to have sprung up suddenly, this is not the case. Open source software under the banner of FLOSS (Free/Libre Open Source) developed a large contingency of volunteers who were often well versed in the open source domain. This group collaborated with some professional translators who were happy to be involved in these translation projects mainly without monetary compensation. Even before the FLOSS activities, fans of certain media products, as mentioned earlier, were engaged in the practice known as fan translation in order to share content with fellow fans (Díaz Cintas & Muños Sánchez, 2007). Curiously there have been few, if any, official complaints raised by professional translators about these fan activities although there has been increasingly less tolerance demonstrated by copyright holders who had once turned a blind eye towards these mostly illegal translation activities (Leonard, 2005). The unease expressed by the professional translator community about crowdsourcing (Kelly, 2009) relates to a concern about the rise of "the cult of the amateur" (Keen, 2007). Here the term *amateur* has a distinctively pejorative undertone rather than the original meaning of a person who loves something.

In the meantime the trend of crowdsourcing is already clearly on the radar screen of the localisation industry, which is embracing the model (Schäler, 2008). Similarly, among those who saw scope in the emerging practice and have been working for some time to facilitate a diverse group of individuals engaged in translation were researchers with a particular interest in collaborative translation and translation technology tools (e.g., Bey et al., 2006; Désilets, 2007). At this current junction, however, for most translation professionals and scholars alike, translation practices involving the Internet crowd are still an emerging phenomenon with even its label yet to be agreed upon. This makes the topic ripe for discussion, especially to bridge a relative paucity of views from the Translation Studies perspective.

2. Contributions in this volume

This tenth edition of *Linguistica Antverpiensia new Series – Themes in Translation Studies* presents nine contributions, intended to provide a snapshot of different perspectives on community translation in the context of Translation Studies and from the wider circle of the industry and platform designers.

The first section, *the State of Play*, presents two invited papers from contributors who have been working in the field for some time. Both papers represent practically-oriented research undertaken in partnership with industry links. *Alain Désilets* and *Jaap van der Meer* first provide a detailed survey and a critical analysis of the key community translation developments to date. Among the common issues highlighted in current practices are quality control, crowd motivation and the role of professionals, which touch on themes picked up by other contributors. Grounded in current approaches, which are diverse and complex, Désilets and van der Meer attempt to capture the key essence of best practice. They aim to develop design patterns that are context-sensitive and elicit the core elements of what makes successful collaborative translation. The resultant design pattern repository, placed in a freely accessible wiki site, is intended to provide an up-to-date practical design descriptor in support of those who are implementing community translation and the initiatives in themselves demonstrate an example of the collaborative and sharing spirit. *Kageura et al.* in turn share a rich set of observations based on three different types of community translation platforms, which they designed and implemented. Addressing underreported issues of community translation from platform designers' perspectives, they provide a fine-grained analysis on user behaviours on each platform examining issues ranging from volunteer motivations to units of translation affected by different document types and the specific characteristics of the given translation activities. One of the platforms, *Kotoba no Volunteer* [Volunteers of Words], was specifically prompted by the Great East Japan Earthquake which occurred in March 2011. Its purpose is to prepare for future natural disasters by pooling useful terms and expressions which can be deployed for translating information in timely fashion by online volunteers. On the basis of the authors' experience in designing, operating and observing the different types of community translation platforms, they arrive at a big question: has translation truly gone online and collaborative involving the masses on the Internet—as much as some of us believe? It remains an open question which readers are encouraged to explore.

The next section, *Findings from Commercial Market Research Perspectives*, presents research outcomes based on large-scale commercial market studies conducted by *Kelly et al.* who maintain that a major shift is taking place in the translation process. This involves a departure from the traditional linear model based on TEP (Translate, Edit and Publish) by a project team to a parallel translation model by a more organically formed "project community". Drawing on a large number of case studies that they have conducted, the paper highlights the way in which the TEP model is giving way to a new model not solely based on collaborative translation but with multiple approaches, implementing a suite of translation technologies and in some cases employing additional in-house translators. On the basis of their studies on community translation, the authors point out that it usually exploits an already existing community as illustrated in the Facebook example (also mentioned in *Kageura et al.* in this volume), thus naturally rendering itself to the formation of a collaborative translation group. While the TEP model is likely to decrease in importance, the authors observe that the adoption of translation crowdsourcing by language service providers is still rare. Their observations show that organisations using the community translation model are discovering a benefit in the way it allows them "to engage meaningfully with potential customers and constituencies on a long-term basis". Having illustrated some of the deficiencies of the current translation process, the authors offer their perspective on the new community translation trend: Collaborative translation should be viewed, not as a dangerous development that threatens the profession of translation, but rather, for what it is—the market's response to specific challenges that are not being satisfactorily addressed through traditional TEP models.

The two papers presented in the third section, *Ethical Implications*, address ethical issues arising from community translation. By examining different types of initiatives of translation crowdsourcing, *Julie McDonough Dolmaya* provides a critical examination of issues that are often considered contentious by translation professionals and scholars alike, focusing on the question of remuneration, the public perception of translation and the impact on minority languages. The findings show that impacts of community translation are determined by how they are organised and communicated to the public, regardless of whether they are intended for-profit or non-profit activities. While community translation can make more visible the value of translation work to society as well as bring benefits by enhancing the presence of minority languages online, the status of translators as trained professionals may be compromised, causing devaluation of the profession overall. McDonough Dolmaya finds that the volunteers can gain satisfaction by participating in these initiatives despite not being remunerated but suggests that they are perhaps not always empowered as purported to be but may be at risk of being exploited. As such, her study leads to nuanced observations on the yet unanswered questions. Also addressing ethical issues, *Joanna Drugan* examines and compares professional codes of practice and their equivalents in community translation. She highlights some useful and original aspects of the latter codes, while clearly indicating the different priorities between the two. Her findings point to specific aspects such as "self-regulation, community policing [...] shared values rather than individual rights, and strong mentoring" as characteristics of community translation codes which at the same time seem to lack concerns about "exploitation, abuse and driving down quality standards". Drugan's suggestion that both translation groups can learn from each other is a refreshing point of view and can potentially facilitate a way forward for a profession facing a drastic change of rules affecting some fundamental and perhaps tacit work ethics.

The fourth section, *Change in Norms of TQA and Language Use in Subtitling for Internet Content*, focuses on the impact of community translation on translation quality assessment (TQA) norms and those of subtitle language in the advent of the gradual spread of the so-called txt lingo—also known as squeeze text—frequently used in electronically mediated communication. Taking the case of Facebook approach to TQA based on user-voting, *Miguel Jiménez-Crespo* argues how this "novel method", often used by community translation, embodies elements of previously proposed but largely unrealised TQA approaches in professional settings, namely "reader-based, functionalist and corpus assisted approaches". The author maintains how new online environments have made relevant and practical these earlier proposals by Translation Studies (TS) scholars that were previously believed difficult to implement. In the advent of new genre conventions such as those applicable to websites, he questions if it is "more productive to enlist large numbers of non-professional uses who have a deep knowledge of digital genre", as opposed to relying on professional translators who may lack such a knowledge. With the increasing translation data which organisations can now collect through community translation, Jiménez-Crespo further sees a new role of academic TS research, able to contribute to developments in the practice in the industry by providing a solid analytical basis. Also challenging existing norms and conventions, this time in the area of subtitling, *Alina Secară* proposes the strategic use of txt lingo in subtitles for carefully selected online materials based on initial supporting evidence from her pilot eye-tracker experiments. The tests involving a set of subtitles with and without such creative spelling indicate not only no detrimental impact on viewers from the use of non-standard spelling but a benefit suggesting that the viewers were able to gain a fuller experience from the film by allowing them to fixate longer outside the subtitled area with the use of txt lingo. Secară draws attention to the widespread impact of new social media promoting txt lingo and suggests that audiovisual translation needs to move on with the new context of the new media landscape as also advocated by "the abusive turns" (Nornes, 2007, pp. 176-187).

The final section, *Implication of Web 2.0 for Translation Teaching and Training*, addresses the impact of Web 2.0 on translator training on the basis of the author's experience using Facebook in the translation classroom and findings from an awareness survey of professional translators on changing technological environments. Reflecting on his experiences over the past few years using Facebook in the translation classroom *Renée Desjardins* advocates the merit of social networking platforms, in which contemporary students are increasingly well versed. He maintains that dimensions such as collaboration and peer-reviewing embraced by social networking platforms are increasingly essential to prepare translators-to-be to operate in the pervasive virtual environment. In relation to a more conventional approach using virtual learning environments, Desjardins argues that the benefits of social networking platforms outweigh potential threats such as security issues. His experience in using Facebook leads him to believe that it allows a more wholehearted shift from teacher-centred to learner-centred training, while helping students "navigate the social, academic and professional spheres, physical and virtual, in which they invariably interact". While a cautious approach is required to implement popular social networking platforms in learning environments, it could arguably help ensure that translation students are better informed of the context in which the new forms of social translation practice are developing.

Also seeking questions arising from technological changes in the context of Web 2.0 and beyond *Joanna Gough*'s contribution derives from her 2010 Master's dissertation, which allowed her to survey over 200 translators at varying stages of their profession to reveal their awareness of state-of-the-art technology developments. Her focus was to understand specifically how well practising translators are informed of macro technological trends harnessing openness, sharing and collaborating characteristic of Web 2.0 as well as the more micro context of translation tools that in turn reflect the macro developments. Gough's findings indicate a relatively low awareness of these trends by the respondents, which leads to their lack of uptake, for example, of open tools or engagement in collaborative translation processes. Furthermore, the survey data demonstrate that the deciding factor in translators' awareness of technological changes is the translators' general attitudes towards adopting new technologies. In relation to community translation, the surveyed translators are found to strongly favour a peer-review quality evaluation approach. At the same time, in other related questions concerning crowdsourcing, they are still largely undecided mainly because they have insufficient knowledge on the topic. Gough suggests that the survey findings also indicate that recent graduates are not necessarily well-informed of the pertinent technological developments and that their main source of technology information was the Internet rather than translation schools, even among relatively recent graduates. Gough sees the need for formal translator education to reflect more closely the technological changes, ideally to influence their fundamental attitudes towards technology which is so profoundly affecting the profession. These findings may tie in with the observations by *Kelly et al.* in this volume for the lack of initiatives by the existing language service providers to integrate an element of community translation. Such evidence indeed calls for an increased awareness of technological developments in academia, especially in translation schools that may tend to consider technology to be a somewhat lesser concern, set aside from the main agenda of translator education.

3. Future direction of research on community translation

Community translation is continuously evolving and it is probable that neither professional translators nor scholars in TS are fully informed of all dimensions of the phenomenon. The contributions in this volume begin to locate the emerging practices in the discipline by relating some of the key issues to its concerns. As evident in this volume of *Linguistica Antverpiensia New Series – Themes in Translation Studies* focused on *Community Translation*, interest in this domain has already inspired research initiatives in close link with industry partners; the invited contributions by *Désilets* and *van der Meer* and *Kageura et al.* shed light onto the nature of the phenomenon by their significant empirical investigations. Such initiatives will likely contribute to further research interest in TS addressing current issues arising from the wider technological trends. As well as working with industry players who are actually organising and implementing community translation, interaction with practising community participants would also allow translation scholars to gain new theoretical and methodological inspiration. The nature of the topic highlights the increasingly important role of translation technology in translation theory, which has so far failed to make a major epistemic impact (see Jiménez-Crespo). The issues raised in this volume are only the tip of the iceberg, yet they indicate seeds for further avenues of research for readers to take up.

While sharing and collaborating evoke the image of co-operative citizens living convivially together, the translation profession may have sensed the dark side of such trends appearing to somewhat privilege non-professionals as dedicated community translators. Technology is often a two-edged sword, bringing both convenience and danger. Translators have benefited greatly from the vast range of multilingual information available on the Internet without which most could not perform their task to satisfaction today. That being the case, one might argue that the new mode of procuring translation via community translation is an inevitable consequence of the free and open Internet harnessing the same spirit which has otherwise served translators well. As often implied by the observations made by the contributors in this volume, this new phenomenon provides us with fresh opportunities to reflect on current practices of professional translation, be it its codes of practice, TQA or subtitling norms. Today's translation practices are by no means all ideal. Translators may be given too little time or context to research and translate adequately or may become too norm-driven to experiment with new approaches, thus ignoring the changing face of the various texts and their end use. It is tempting for translation professionals to condemn the emergence of community translation as "the rise of the amateur" but it may actually be pointing to "the crisis of the experts" who "undervalue what they do not know and overvalue what they do" (Gee & Hayes, 2011, p. 44). While professional translators generally do a wonderful job, it is time to recognise that their operating environments are significantly shifting, giving rise to new ways of working. By being better informed of the nature of the change and by becoming more reflective of current practices, the translation profession will be better served and more likely to survive and flourish in the long run.

Acknowledgements

I would like to thank all the authors for their contributions and their perseverance through several revision steps. This in turn could not have been possible without the assistance of expert reviewers who went through the articles with fine-toothed combs. Last but not least I would like to express my sincere gratitude to Aline Remael for accommodating this new topic for the journal and both Aline Remael and Iris Schrijver for the ensuing support, including the last intensive stage of editing.

References

Barry, D. M. (2008). *Copy, rip, burn: The politics of copyleft and open source.* London: Pluto Press.

Baym, N. (2011). Social Networks 2.0 In M. Consalvo & C. Ess (Eds), *The handbook of Internet studies* (pp. 384-405). Malden, MA: Wiley-Blackwell.

Bey, Y., Boitet, C. & Kageura, K. (2006). The TRANSBey prototype: An online collaborative Wiki-based CAT environment for volunteer translators. In E. Yuste (Ed.), *Proceedings of the Third International Workshop on Language Resources for Translation Work, Research & Training (LR4Trans-III)*, pp. 49-54.

Cronin, M. (2010). The translation crowd. *Revista tradumàtica, 8.* Retrieved from http://www.fti.uab.cat/tradumatica/revista/num8/articles/04/04.pdf

DePalma, D. A. & Kelly, N. (2008). *Translation of, by, and for the people.* Lowell, Mass: Common Sense Advisory.

Désilets, A. (2007). Translation Wikified: How will massive online collaboration impact the world of translation? *ASLIB Translating and the computer 29 Conference Proceedings,* London: ASLIB, n.p.

Díaz Cintas, J. & Muños Sánchez, P. (2007). Fansubs: Audiovisual translation in an amateur environment, *The Journal of Specialised Translation,* 6, 37-52.

Gee, J. P., & Hayes, E. (2011). *Language and learning in the digital age.* London: Routledge.

Howe, J. (2006). The rise of crowdsourcing. *Wired* 14 (6).

Howe, J. (2008). *Crowdsourcing.* New York: Random House.

Keegan, N. (2009). Crowdsourcing: Using cross-cultural competency gained from the global proficiency programme to better understand Facebook's Spanish Translation. Retrieved from http://www.bc.edu/offices/international/gp/meta-elements/pdf/PDF/2009_Reflection_Projects/Keegan,%20Nathan.pdf.

Keen, A. (2007). *The cult of the amateur.* New York: Dubleday.

Kelly, N. (2009). Freelance translators clash with LinkedIn over crowdsourced translation. Retrieved from http://www.commonsenseadvisory.com/ Default.aspx?Contenttype=ArticleDetAD&tabID=63&Aid=591&moduleId=391

Kendall, L. (2011). Community and the Internet. In M. Consalvo & C. Ess (Eds.), *The handbook of Internet studies* (pp. 309-325). Malden, MA: Wiley-Blackwell.

Leonard, S. (2005). Progress against the law: Anime and fandom, with the key to the globalization of culture. *International Journal of Cultural Studies,* 8(3), 281-305.

Nornes, M. (2007). *Cinema Babel: Translating global cinema.* Minneapolis:University of Minesota Press.

OECD (2007). *Participative web and user-created content: Web 2.0 wikis and social networking.* Paris: OECD Pubishing.

O'Hagan, M. (2009). Evolution of user-generated translation: Fansubs, translation hacking and crowdsourcing. *The Journal of Internationalization and Localization,* 1(1), 94-121.

Perrino, S. (2009). User-generated translation: The future of translation in a Web 2.0 environment. *The Journal of Specialised Translation,* 12, http://www.jostrans.org/issue12/artperrino.php.

Pym, A. (2011). Translation research terms: a tentative glossary for moments of perplexity and dispute. In Pym, A (ed.). *From Translation Research Projects 3,* Tarragona: Intercultural Studies Group, pp. 75-110. http://isg.urv.es/publicity/isg/publications/trp_3_2011/index.htm

Schäler, R. (2008). Localisation. In M. Baker, & G. Saldanha (Eds.), *Routledge encyclopedia of Translation Studies* (pp. 157-161). London: Routledge,.

Shirky, C. (2010). *Cognitive surplus: Creativity and generosity in a connected age.* London: Allen Lane.

Surowiecki, J. (2005). *The wisdom of the crowd: Why the many are smarter than the few.* London: Abacus.

Tapscott, D., & Williams, A. (2006). *Wikinomics: How mass collaboration change everything.* New York: Portfolio.

Wadensjö, C. (2009). Community interpreting. In M. Baker, & G. Saldanha (Eds.), *Routledge encyclopedia of Translation Studies (*pp. 43-48). London: Routledge,.

---

[1] The patent application filed at the US Patent & Trademark Office is available at: http://appft.uspto.gov/netacgi/nph-Parser?Sect1=PTO2&Sect2=HITOFF&p=1&u=/ netahtml/PTO/search-bool.html&r=1&f=G&l=50&co1=AND&d=PG01&s1= facebook.AS.&s2=translation.AB.&OS=AN/facebook+AND+ABST/translation&R S=AN/facebook+AND+ABST/translation

I. INVITED CONTRIBUTIONS: THE STATE OF PLAY

Co-creating a repository of best-practices for collaborative translation

Alain Désilets

National Research Council of Canada

Jaap van der Meer

Translation Automation Users Society

Collaborative translation has the potential for significantly changing how we translate content. However, successful deployment of this kind of approach is far from trivial, as it presents potential adopters with a rich and complex envelope of processes and technologies, whose respective impacts are still poorly understood. The present paper aims at facilitating this kind of decision making, by describing and cataloguing current best-practices in collaborative translation. More precisely, we present a collection of Design Patterns which was created collectively by a small group of practitioners, at a one day roundtable hosted by the Translation Automation Users Society in October of 2011. This collection has been put on an open wiki site (www.collaborative-translation-patterns.com) in the hopes that other practitioners in the field will refine and augment it.

1. Introduction

Collaborative and social networking technologies, as seen on sites like Wikipedia, Facebook and Amazon Mechanical Turk, are having profound effects in many spheres of human activity. Translation is no exception, as evidenced by Facebook's use of crowdsourcing, to co-opt its loyal user base into translating the system's web interface on a volunteer basis (Ellis, 2009). Using this approach, Facebook was able to rapidly recruit 250,000 volunteers, who translated 350,000 words into 70 languages, often with very short lead time (less than two days for high density languages like French) (Baer, 2010).

Highly publicized cases like this caused somewhat of a commotion in the translation industry, as exemplified by the strong negative reaction of professional translators to a similar crowdsourcing attempt by LinkedIn, a professionally-oriented social network (Stejskal, 2009; ATA, 2009). At the time, translation crowdsourcing conjured up a picture where customers could get fast translations at rock-bottom prices, through the work of volunteer or offshore translators and the help of new technology acquired from vendors, while professional translators risked seeing their profit margins shrink drastically. However, two years after the Facebook and

LinkedIn initiatives, one cannot help but notice that the impact of translation crowdsourcing remains marginal, and that successful uses of this paradigm are still few and far between.

This does not mean that collaborative technologies cannot have a major impact on the translation industry. It simply means that the particular model used by Facebook is just one of many ways in which massive online collaboration can be leveraged for translation, and that the applicability of this particular approach may be limited to very specific contexts (for example, situations where there is a community of people with a strong emotional bond to the content being translated).

Indeed, the term collaborative translation can be used to encompass a much wider collection of approaches, such as agile translation teamware, collaborative terminology resources, translation memory sharing, online translation marketplaces, post-editing by the crowd, and of course, translation crowdsourcing (Note: all these terms will be defined more precisely below). At present, selecting and successfully deploying one of those variants is somewhat of a black art, and one must navigate through many challenging issues such as quality assurance, crowd motivation and the dangers of de-contextualization.

While there are many case studies which describe how collaborative translation was successfully implemented in specific organizations (Ambati & Vogel, 2010; Baer, 2010; Baer 2011; Bloodgood & Callison-Burch, 2010; Calvert, 2008; Ellis, 2009; Meyer, 2011; Munro, 2010; Yahaya, 2008), there is a clear need for a more concise, summative body of knowledge that captures recurrent best practices. In this paper, we advocate the building of such a compendium, in the form of a collection of design patterns ("Design pattern", 2011), which could be written collectively by practitioners of collaborative translation.

The remainder of the paper is organized as follows. In Section 2, we provide an overview of the burgeoning field of collaborative translation. In Section 3, we provide an introduction to design patterns, and explain why they seem like a good format for capturing best practices of collaborative translation. Finally, in Section 4 we report on the outcome of a day-long workshop which was hosted by TAUS in October of 2011, with the explicit goal of generating such a collection of patterns. It brought together several leading practitioners of collaborative translation who worked together to create collaborative-translation-patterns.com, a wiki site that captures some of the most successful best-practices in the field today.

2. An overview of Collaborative Translation

2.1. The different flavors of Collaborative Translation

As mentioned in the Introduction, collaborative translation encompasses more than just Facebook-style translation crowdsourcing. Possible uses of collaborative technologies in translation include the following.

- **Agile translation teamware**: wiki-like systems and processes that allow multidisciplinary teams of professionals (translators, terminologists, domain experts, revisers, managers) to collaborate on large translation projects, using an agile, grassroots, parallelized process instead of the more top-down, assembly-line approach found in most translation workflow systems. Examples of this approach can be found in Beninatto & De Palma, 2008; Calvert, 2008; Yahaya, 2008.
- **Collaborative terminology resources**: Wikipedia-like platforms for the creation and maintenance of large terminology resources by a crowd of translators, terminologists, domain experts, and even general members of the public. Examples of this approach include Wiktionary (Wiktionary, 2011), ProZ's Kudoz forum (Goddard, 2010) and the Urban Dictionary (Urban Dictionary, 2011).
- **Translation memory sharing**: platforms for large scale pooling and sharing of multilingual parallel corpora between organisations and individuals. Examples of this approach include the TAUS Data Association (TAUS Data Association, 2011), MyMemory (MyMemory, 2011) and Google Translator Toolkit (Google Translator Toolkit, 2011).
- **Online marketplaces for translators**: eBay-like disintermediated environments for connecting customers and translators directly, with minimal intervention by a middle man. Examples of this include ProZ.com (ProZ.com, 2011), TranslatorsCafe (TranslatorCafe, 2011) and Translated.net (Translated.net, 2011).
- **Translation crowdsourcing**: Mechanical-Turk-like systems to support the translation of content by large crowds of mostly amateurs, through an open-call process. This is by far the most talked about collaborative translation approach. It has been used successfully for translating a variety of content types, including software user interface (Ellis, 2009; Meyer, 2011), technical documentation (Meyer, 2011), transcripts of videos of an "inspirational" nature (Ted Open Translation Project, 2011; Meyer, 2011) and humanitarian aid content (Munro, 2010; Baer, 2010; Baer & Nagle, 2011; Translators without Borders, 2008). It has also been used for large scale collection of linguistic data for research purposes

or machine translation training (for example, in Ambati & Vogel, 2010; Bloodgood & Callison-Burch, 2010).

- **Post-editing by the crowd**: systems allowing a large crowd of mostly amateurs to correct the output of machine translations systems, often with the aim of improving the system's accuracy. Examples of this include Asia Online's Wikipedia translation project (Asia Online, 2011), as well as features which allow anonymous users to correct the outputs produced by systems like Google Translate (Google translate, 2007) and Microsoft's Bing Translator (Microsoft Collaborative Translation Framework, 2011).

It is worth noting that the above flavors of collaborative translation are not mutually exclusive. In fact, it is quite common for an organization to leverage more than one of those approaches at the same time. For example, some translation crowdsourcing initiatives and online marketplaces also include features for sharing and collaborating on resources like terminology databases and translation memories. Post-editing by the crowd can also be used as part of a translation crowdsourcing initiative, and so on.

Also, many of these "new" approaches are in fact very similar to more conventional technologies that have existed for years, such as translation workflow systems, terminology databases and translation memories. All of those earlier technologies were already collaborative in that they allowed groups of customers, managers and translators, to coordinate their activities. In a sense, one might say that the collaborative translation revolution is not so much about introducing new technologies, as it is about using existing groupware technologies with much larger groups of people, where members of these communities know less about each other and have fewer a priori reasons for trusting each other.

2.2. Common issues in Collaborative Translation

As can be seen from the above list, collaborative translation represents a rich and complex envelope of processes and technologies. Determining which approach can be used in which context and tweaking it to meet one's goals is still somewhat of black art, and currently, trial and error is often the only way to find out.

To complicate things further, there are many poorly understood issues and open questions regarding the best way to deploy collaborative translation in specific contexts, and this comes out clearly from the proceedings of a recent workshop on that topic held at the 2010 conference of the Association for Machine Translation in the Americas (AMTA) (AMTA, 2010). Here is a sample of the most common themes we have encountered in five years of advocating collaborative translation to translators, service providers and technology vendors.

2.2.1. Business goals

Collaborative translation is not an end in itself, and it is only relevant to the extent that it can support business goals of an organisation. Different flavors of these technologies have completely different kinds of benefits, and it is important for practitioners to understand what they are likely to get from deploying them.

For example, agile translation teamware may be used as a channel for more varied and horizontal communication inside a translation team (Beninatto & De Palma, 2008; Calvert, 2008; Yahaya, 2008), in order to provide feedback loops that allow customers to communicate more rapidly with the translators who carry out the actual work, and to do so earlier in the project life-cycle. Collaboratively built terminology resources and shared translation memories may allow an organization to collect linguistic data from a wider range of contributors (for example, domain experts), and at lower costs. However, this may come at the cost of having less control over quality of the data or its specificity to one's own context and domain.

Online translation marketplaces may allow customers to recruit the best and most qualified translators for a given project and cut down on the intermediary costs, and conversely, it may allow specialized freelancers to market their skills to a wider and larger group of customers.

In the case of translation crowdsourcing, the benefit that most readily comes to mind is cost reduction, but organizations that have used this approach are quick to point out that it may not be the most important one. Other benefits which are commonly mentioned include: community involvement, increased brand loyalty, faster turnaround time, supporting the long-tails of low-density languages and transient content (e.g., user-generated content), and production of translations that are more in tune with the particular linguistic idiosyncrasies of the actual users of the content (Baer, 2010; Meyer, 2011).

2.2.2. Quality control

All flavors of collaborative translation are more grassroots and less tightly controlled from the top than is typically found in professional translation contexts. This is true even for collaborative approaches that are aimed specifically at professionals (e.g. agile translation teamware). Therefore, a common question is how quality control can still be exercised in such decentralised environments. The answer of course depends on the context, and the level of quality that is needed to meet the customer's business goals ("fit for purpose" quality).

In some cases, customers may want in-house professional translators to revise and approve each and every translation produced by members of the group or crowd, before they are actually published (Facebook eventually opted for this approach after some embarrassing incidents). In other cases, it may be sufficient to ask translators to go through an initial screening test and then let them loose on the content. This approach is currently used by Translators without Borders (Translators without border, 2011; De Palma, 2011) and Kiva.org (Baer & Nagle, 2011). In other cases still, we may have the crowd or group itself carry out quality control, through mechanisms like voting, mutual revision and automated reputation management. This approach is used by Facebook (Ellis, 2009), as well as by research projects that are collecting parallel corpora (Ambati & Vogel, 2010; Bloodgood & Callison-Burch, 2010).

It is worth noting that by and large, there is an assumption in professional circles that decentralized, collaborative translation will lead to lesser quality output. While this may be true in some contexts, it is far from inevitable, and there may be situations where collaborative processes can in fact lead to higher quality, through appropriate leveraging of the so-called wisdom of crowds effect (Surowiecki, 2004). Unfortunately, although there are known principles for increasing the chances that a group will collectively act smarter than its individuals (namely, diversity, independence, and aggregation), the specifics of how they can be applied in given translation contexts is still somewhat of an open question.

2.2.3. Crowd motivation

A key ingredient in any collaborative translation initiative is the presence of a compelling incentive for members of the group or crowd to participate. Even with agile translation teamware where use of the system by employees or subcontractors is mandated from above, the approach still cannot be successful without minimum buy-in from translators.

Motivation issues are most critical in crowdsourcing scenarios, and this is possibly the main reason why it has yet to become widespread. The most successful cases have been in contexts where members of the crowd are emotionally invested in the content being translated. In the case of Facebook, this emotional bond came from the social nature of the application which people use to connect with friends, relatives and acquaintances. In the case of the Haiti earthquake relief initiative (Munro, 2010), it came from the diaspora's attachment to their native country, while for Kiva and Translators without Border it may come from a perception that the organization is pursuing worthy humanitarian goals. Finally, in a case like TEDTalks (TED Open Translation Project, 2011), it comes from the compelling, high profile nature of the talks and speakers that people are translating. Although this has not been documented in writing, some of the practitioners who participated in the TAUS roundtable and the AMTA Collaborative Translation workshop (AMTA, 2010) mentioned that for some of the volunteer translators, pride in their native tongue was also an important motivating factor. Surprisingly enough, even for-profit companies like Adobe and Symantec have found that some of their end-users are passionate enough about their products to volunteer time for translation of content (Meyer, 2011).

All of the motivators mentioned so far are, to a certain extent, altruistic and disinterested. But that is not always the case. Researchers involved in collection of linguistic data have also reported (although not in writing) that some of the volunteers were actually second language learners who saw translation as a good way to practice a language and get feedback about their production, while being of service to the research community. In a different context where Adobe was able to co-opt third party vendors into translating highly technical content, the motivation came from the fact that this particular content was critical to that third party's niche business (Meyer, 2011). Baer and Nagle also report that, in the context of Kiva.org, some of the amateur volunteer translators from third world countries were contributing in order to establish a good track record in translation, in the hope that it would eventually allow them to make a career of it.

Finally, there will be cases where money is the only realistic incentive, and an open question is the extent to which this type of situation will predominate or not in collaborative contexts (especially crowdsourcing). Another open question which is relevant in that type of situation, is how to determine a level of compensation that is high enough to motivate members of the crowd to participate and do a good job, but not so high that it interferes with intrinsic motivators (Mason & Watts, 2009; Rogstadius et al., 2011) or attracts people who are out to game the system (for example, by entering random text, or raw machine translation taken from free systems like Google or Bing).

2.2.4. Role of professionals

Not surprisingly, a pressing question with collaborative translation is the role of professionals in this brave new world. While some forms of collaborative translation (agile teamware and online marketplaces in particular) are designed for professionals, there are many flavors of translation crowdsourcing that seem to de-emphasize their role. But that need not be the case. For example, one might use a small "crowd" of paid professionals working in parallel on a large project, as a way to dramatically decrease lead time, while ensuring professional level quality (Beninatto & De Palma, 2008). Even in cases where the crowd consists mainly of unpaid (or low-paid) non-professional translators, professionals could still be used to revise and vet the final result. In that sense, crowdsourcing might allow professionals to delegate simple routine parts of the translation to the crowd, and focus their talent on more challenging aspects such as terminology, style and fluidity (Orr Priebe, 2009).

Crowdsourcing may also open new types of jobs for professionals, for example, community management and coaching. Finally, given that a frequent goal of crowdsourcing is to allow the translation of content that otherwise would not have been translated at all, and that some part of this work will have to be revised or facilitated by professionals, it may be that crowdsourcing will not so much decrease demand for professionals, as it will change the nature of their interventions.

2.2.5. Parallelism and de-contextualization

Most implementations of collaborative translation involve some level of parallelism, in other words, splitting the work into smaller chunks, and dispatching them to different members of a community. Parallelism can help by dramatically decreasing lead time, or by making it possible to recruit volunteers who might otherwise not be willing to commit to the translation of complete documents. The granularity of chunks may vary widely across applications, ranging from complete sections or documents, down to single sentences.

In spite of its advantages, parallelism presents some dangers in that it de-contextualizes translation, which in turn can affect quality and consistency of the end result. It can also decrease job satisfaction, by making it harder for the translator to see how his work is contributing to a meaningful complete picture. Fortunately, there are ways to offset these drawbacks, for example, revising documents in a more global, document wide fashion, or implementing back channels like chat rooms and discussion forums to allow translators to socialize and get a sense of the big picture (Munro, 2011). However, such measures can probably never completely resolve the tension between parallelism and de-contextualization.

3. Using design patterns to capture collaborative translation best practices

As can be seen from the previous section, collaborative translation is a complex space of possibilities, and it can be challenging to choose and fine-tune appropriate processes and tools to meet specific needs. While there are several case studies that describe how specific collaborative translation approaches have been successfully implemented in the context of specific organizations, sifting through those can be time consuming for a practitioner wanting to emulate the success of others. There is a clear need for a more compact, well-validated and easy to consult compendium of best practices in that area.

In this section, we argue that such a compendium could be written in the form of a collection of design patterns.

3.1. About design patterns

A design pattern is a formal way of documenting a common solution to a common problem in a particular field of expertise. The idea was introduced by Christopher Alexander in the field of architecture ("Pattern (architecture)", 2011) and was subsequently adopted by other disciplines, including computer science ("Design pattern (computer science)", 2011), user interface design ("Interaction design pattern", 2011) and education ("Pedagogical patterns", 2010). Patterns do not exist in isolation, and they are typically organized into collections of interlinked patterns for a given field. Such collections are referred to as pattern languages.

Pattern languages are a very flexible way of describing the solution space for complex domains. Instead of having to subscribe to all-encompassing, one-size fits all solution, practitioners can cherry pick the patterns that best represent their particular context, then adapt and re-combine them in original ways to fit a given situation. Another advantage of patterns is that they provide practitioners with a common vocabulary for sharing and talking about solutions to problems in their domain. In software design for example, it is quite common for developers to refer to complex designs using standard pattern names like *Singleton, Observer* or *Adapter* ("Design pattern (computer science)", 2011), without having to explain them from scratch.

Another advantage of design patterns is that they can evolve with time, as we learn more and more about their respective applicability in different contexts. Indeed, it is quite common for design patterns to be stored on wiki sites which are open to modification by the public. In fact, the world's very first wiki site was deployed by Ward Cunningham for the very purpose of creating a collection of design patterns in the field of software engineering ("WikiWikiWeb", 2011). Given that collaborative translation is still in its infancy, this ability for patterns to evolve seems like a highly desirable attribute.

Although the format and structure of a pattern is open-ended and can be tailored to the needs of particular domains, there are a number of characteristics which have been found useful across disciplines. These are described below.

Clear Name: Each pattern has a short name (2-5 words) which clearly communicates the pattern's essence to the reader. Good names are important, because they provide the basic vocabulary that practitioners can use to discuss the solution space for problems in their domain. Coming up with a good name is often the most challenging part of pattern writing, and the inability to do so is often a symptom that the author hasn't yet grasped the actual core of the solution he is trying to describe.

Context: Each pattern must describe the context in which it applies. For example, is this pattern applicable to collaborative translation at large, or is it only relevant in volunteer-based translation crowdsourcing situations? Without proper context, the reader cannot easily determine the applicability of the pattern to his current situation.

Problem Description: The pattern must describe the exact nature of the problem that it solves. A common approach is to describe the problem in terms of tensions between opposing forces. Something along the lines of: *"On the one hand, one would want X, but on the other hand, one would also want Y, and the two are partly incompatible for reasons A, B and C".*

Solution: The pattern must describe the solution to the problem. Again, this is often framed in terms of a way to balance the opposing forces mentioned in the *Problem Description* section, so as to reach a sustainable equilibrium. The solution should be general enough to be applied in very different situations within its context, but still specific enough to give constructive guidance to the practitioner.

Links to related patterns: Patterns generally do not exist in isolation, and relate to other patterns in a given domain. These links can be made explicit through inline references in different sections of the pattern, but also in a separate *Related Patterns* section.

Real-life examples: Good patterns provide references to real-life examples where it has been shown to work. Such examples are important because they provide a sense of how well-tried the pattern actually is.

Figure 1 provides an example of a pattern for the domain of collaborative translation.

4. The Collaborative Translation Patterns Repository

In order to kick-start the creation of a collection of patterns for collaborative translation, TAUS organized a one-day workshop which was held at Localization World 2011 in Santa Clara, on October 10th, 2011. The workshop brought together 12 practitioners, which included seasoned users of collaborative translation from organizations like Adobe, Symantec, Kiva and Worldwide Lexicon. The list of participants also included practitioners who did not have hands-on experience with these approaches, but were seriously considering them. After short presentations by the experienced users, participants brainstormed a list of best-practices that were mentioned in one or more of them. Each best-practice was given a clear, communicative name, as well as a short description of what it entails. We then collaboratively tried to organize those practices into groups of related themes.

Publish Contributions Rapidly

Context   *Motivation :*

This pattern is useful for motivating contributors in any collaborative translation context, but it is particularly useful in translation crowdsourcing scenarios.

Problem description

Contributors are often motivated by a desire to have a positive impact on the community they are participating in. However, they cannot achieve this sense of being useful, if their contributions do not become available to the rest of the community in a reasonable amount of time.

Solution

Therefore, minimize the delay between the moment when a member of the community contributes to the site, and the moment where it becomes publicly available to the rest of the community.

Ideally, the contribution should become visible to the rest of the community as soon as the user clicks on the *Save* button. This "ideal" may not always be achievable, for example in situations where some level of quality control must be done before publication. But even in those situations, you may want to consider a Publish then Revise approach rather than the more conventional revise then publish.

Links to related patterns
- Point System is another way for a contributor to get a sense of how useful he has been to the community.
- Campaign Progress Gauge is another practice which allows members of the community to see the positive impact of their actions. The main difference is that it operates more at a community/project level rather than at a individual/contribution level.

Real-life examples
- At Facebook, translations become available in a matter of hours.
- In the context of software localization by the crowd, Adobe makes a conscious effort to wrap the community's translations into every new releases of the product.

Figure 1: Example of a design pattern for collaborative translation. Words that are underlined are references to other patterns in the same domain.

4.1. Initial set of best practices

This exercise resulted in an initial set of 53 best-practices, organized into 6 themes. They are listed below. We do not have sufficient room in this paper to discuss each practice in detail, but the name is usually sufficient to provide the gist of what it pertains to. Interested readers can get more detail about specific practices at www.collaborative-translation-patterns.com.

4.1.1. Planning and scoping

This theme contains practices that come to play before a collaborative translation community or project is actually started. It currently includes the following practices:

- Align Stakeholder Expectations
- Early Clarification of Translator Expectations
- Backup Plan
- Project Check Points
- Appoint Initial Community Manager

Design Pattern theme.

4.1.2. Community motivation

This theme contains practices that help with the recruitment, retention, and motivation of members of the translator community. It currently includes the following practices:

- Publish Contributions Rapidly
- Campaign Progress Gauge
- Contributor Recognition
- Leader Board
- Official Certificate
- Point System
- Offer Double Points
- Give Unique Branded Products
- Contribution Loop
- Contributor of the Month
- Grant Special Access Rights
- Rewards for Contribution
- Campaign

4.1.3. Quality

This theme contains practices which help ensure that translations produced by the community are of an appropriate level of quality. It currently includes the following practices:

- Publish then Revise
- Content-Specific Testing
- Entry Exam
- Peer Review
- Automatic Reputation Management
- Random Spot-Checking
- Revision Crowdsourcing
- Users as Translators
- Voting
- Transparent Quality Level

4.1.4. Contributor career path

This theme contains practices which allow people in the community to grow into different roles and participate meaningfully and to the best of their ability and availability. It currently includes the following practices:

- Flexible Contributor Career Path
- Lurker to Contributor Transition
- Anonymous Translation
- Find the Leaders
- Support Variable Levels of Involvement
- Community Manager
- Content Prioritizer

4.1.5. Right-sizing

This theme contains practices which are used for splitting large communities or big chunks of work into smaller and more manageable ones. It currently includes the following practices:

- Contributor-Appropriate Chunk Size
- Community-Appropriate Project Size
- Break Up Crowd Into Teams
- Require Minimal Involvement Level
- Keep the Crowd Small
- Volunteer Team Leaders

4.1.6. Tools and processes

This theme contains practices that specify important characteristics of the online tools used by the community, as well as the processes and workflows that they implement. It currently includes the following practices:

- Hint at Content Priority
- First In, First Out
- Task Self Selection
- Layered Fallbacks
- Official Linguistic Resources
- Automatic Equivalents Suggestions
- Provide Context
- In-Place Translation
- On-the-Side Translation
- Community Forum
- Analytics for Content Priorization
- Simplicity First

4.2. Interesting trends

Looking at the set of initial best-practices mentioned in Section 4.1, we can see a number of interesting trends.

Firstly, it is worth noting that most of the practices relate to the context of translation crowdsourcing. This is not surprising, given that this is the flavor of collaborative translation that seems to have captured the imagination of more people in the field. However, it does point to the need for more exploration of other collaborative modalities in translation.

Secondly, most of the practices are not specific to translation per se. To be sure, some practices like *Users as Translators* (the idea that end users of a particular piece of software or web site may be uniquely qualified to translate its user interface) are only applicable in a translation context. But other practices, like *Voting* (inviting members of the crowd to vote on the quality of content produced by other members of the crowd), are useful for any kind of crowdsourcing effort, and the majority of the patterns we list above seem to fall in that category. This raises the following question: *"Are the best practices for translation crowdsourcing essentially the same as those for crowdsourcing in general, or are there some unique problems in translation that call for unique solutions?"*. The same question could be asked for other flavors of collaborative translation. For example, are the best-practices needed in the context of building collaborative terminology resources different from the ones which have been used for some years to build collaborative knowledge sources like Wikipedia and Wiktionary?

One point which is not apparent from the list of best-practices, but which came out clearly in the discussion at the roundtable, is that _Community Motivation_ issues seem the most difficult ones to resolve in a translation crowdsourcing context. In contrast, there was a sense that _Quality Control_ issues tend to resolve themselves, provided that enough of the "right" people can be enticed to participate and that you provide them with lightweight tools and processes by which they can spot and fix errors.

Another interesting point which is not directly apparent from the above list is that different kinds of organizations seem to use different best-practices. For example, when it comes to vetting translators, Adobe and Symantec (two software vendors who use crowdsourcing for translating material related to their products) employ similar, fairly open practices. In contrast, Kiva and Translators without Borders (two not-for-profit humanitarian organizations) use a more closed approach that requires contributors to pass an _Entry Exam_. Liz Nagle of Kiva explains this difference by the fact that translation is core to their operation. Indeed, without translation, Kiva cannot achieve its mission of facilitating microloans, because loan applications are usually written in the native tongue of the applicant (often small density languages) which usually differs from the language of their donor population (mostly English).

The fact that different types of organizations need different kinds of practices is a strong argument in favor of a patterns-based approach, because it allows practitioners to cherry-pick and adapt those practices that seem most applicable to their situation.

5. Conclusion

Collaborative translation has the potential for significantly changing how we translate content. However, it presents potential adopters with a complex envelope of possible approaches which can be hard to navigate. There is a clear need for a concise body of knowledge that summarises current best practices in that domain.

We believe that a collection of design patterns is a good way to achieve that, and we have presented a first attempt at generating such a repository. The result of this effort now resides on a wiki site which is open for editing and commenting by people in the community (collaborative-translation-patterns.com).

While this site is a good start, it raises some interesting questions. For one thing, most of the practices that have been documented so far in this repository are not that different from best-practices which are being used for crowdsourcing in other domains. It is worth asking whether there is anything particular to translation which requires our field to come up with its own set of best-practices, or do we simply need to learn more about practices for crowdsourcing in general? Also, the repository as it currently stands, focuses mainly on translation crowdsourcing, which is only one of many possible flavors of collaborative translation. It would be interesting to try and better document practices for other flavors as well.

It is our hope that this site will continue to grow and be improved, as we learn more and more about good ways to implement collaborative translation applications that work and are acceptable to all parties involved, and we encourage the reader to contribute to it.

Acknowledgements

The authors are indebted to Rahzeb Choudhoury (TAUS) who helped organize the roundtable which served as the starting point for the collaborative-translation-patterns.com repository. Also, to the participants of the roundtable who shared their own experience and best-practices with us: Dirk Meyer(Adobe), Jason Rickard (Symantec), Liz Nagle (Kiva), Terena Bell (In Every Language), Renato Benninato, David Canek (MemSource), Christopher Klapp (Firma8), Brian McConnell (Worldwide Lexicon) and Laura van Nigtevegt (Spil Games).

References

Ambati, V., Vogel, S. (2010). Can crowds build parallel corpora for machine translation systems? *Proceedings of the NAACL HLT 2010 workshop on creating speech and language data with Amazon's Mechanical Turk*, Los Angeles, California, June 2010.

AMTA (2010). *Collaborative translation: technology, crowdsourcing, and the translator perspective*. AMTA 2010, Oct 31, 2010, Denver, Colorado, USA. Retrieved from http://www.wiki-translation.com/AMTA+2010+Workshop.

Asia Online. (2011, October 17). *In Wikipedia, The Free Encyclopedia*. Retrieved from http://en.wikipedia.org/w/index.php?title=Asia_Online&oldid=456007085#Port al_Initiatives

ATA (2011). Press release, Head of largest professional translators' organization blasts LinkedIn CEO for "thoroughly unprofessional practices". June 30, 2009. Retrieved from http://www.atanet.org/pressroom/linkedIn_2009.pdf

Baer, N. (2010). Crowdsourcing: Outrage or opportunity? *Translorial, Journal of the Northern California Translators Association*, February 2010.

Baer, N. (2010). *Trends in crowdsourcing: Case studies from not-for-profit and for-profit organisations*. ATA 2010, Oct 27-30, 2010, Denver, Colorado, USA. Retrieved from http://www.wiki-translation.com/tiki-download_wiki_ attachment.php?attId=62.

Baer, N., & Nagle, L. (2011). *Scaling and strengthening a closed crowd: Lessons from Kiva's evolving model*. TAUS Roundtable on Collaborative Translation, Santa

Clara, Oct 10, 2011. Retrieved from http://collaborative-translation-patterns.com/tiki-download_file.php?fileId=2

Beninatto, R., & De Palma, D. (2008). Collaborative translation. *Multilingual*, 2008 Resource directory & index 2008. Retrieved from http://www.scribd.com/ doc/4069269/Structuring-Collaborative-Translation-20-Less-Delivery-Time-Better-Quality)

Bloodgood, M., & Callison-Burch, C. (2010). Using Mechanical Turk to build machine translation evaluation set. *Proceedings of the NAACL HLT 2010 workshop on creating speech and language data with Amazon's Mechanical Turk*, Los Angeles, California, June 2010.

Calvert, D. (2008). Wiki behind the firewall – Microscale online collaboration in a translation agency. *ASLIB Translating and the Computer 30*, Nov 27-28, 2008, London, UK.

De Palma, D. (2011). Translators without borders extends its reach. *Common Sense Advisory Blogs*. Retrieved from http://www.commonsenseadvisory.com/ Default.aspx?Contenttype=ArticleDetAD&tabID=63&Aid=691&moduleId=3 91

Design pattern (computer science). (2011, October 17). In *Wikipedia, The Free Encyclopedia*. Retrieved from http://en.wikipedia.org/w/index.php ?title=Design_pattern_(computer_science)&oldid=456093478

Ellis, D. (2009). A case study in community-driven translation of a fast-changing website. In *Internationalization, Design and Global Development Lecture Notes in Computer Science*, 2009, Volume 5623/2009, 236-244, DOI: 10.1007/978-3-642-02767-3_26.

Goddard, P. (2010). The power of ProZ. *ITI Bulletin*, JanFeb 2010.

Google translate. (2007, December 1). In *Wikipedia, The Free Encyclopedia*. Retrieved from http://en.wikipedia.org/w/index.php?title=Google_translate&oldid=175 043259#Features_and_limitations

Google Translator Toolkit. (2011, August 30). In *Wikipedia, The Free Encyclopedia*. Retrieved from http://en.wikipedia.org/w/index.php?title=Google_Translator_ Toolkit&oldid=447439495

Interaction design pattern. (2011, July 16). In *Wikipedia, The Free Encyclopedia*. Retrieved from http://en.wikipedia.org/w/index.php?title=Interaction_ design_pattern&oldid=439853212.

Kudoz, (2011, October 17). *Kudoz term questions – Translators helping translators*. Retrieved from http://www.proz.com/kudoz/.

Mason, W., & Watts, D. J. (2009). *Financial incentives and the "performance of crowds"*. KDD-HCOMP '09, Paris, France, June 28, 2009.

Meyer, D. (2011). *Community translation: Leveraging communities and crowds*. TAUS Roundtable on Collaborative Translation, Santa Clara, California, USA, Oct 10, 2011. Retrieved from http://collaborative-translation-patterns.com/tiki-download_file.php?fileId=2.

Microsoft Collaborative Translation Framework (2011, October 17). *Collaborative translations: Announcing the next version of Microsoft Translator technology – V2 APIs and widget*. Retrieved from http://blogs.msdn.com/b/

translation/archive/2010/03/15/collaborative-translations-announcing-the-next-version-of-microsoft-translator-technology-v2-apis-and-widget.aspx.

Munro, R. (2010). *Crowdsourced translation for emergency response in Haiti: the global collaboration of local knowledge.* In *Proceedings of Collaborative Translation: technology, crowdsourcing, and the translator perspective*, AMTA 2010, Oct 31, 2010, Denver, Colorado, USA. Retrieved from http://www.wiki-translation.com/tiki-download_wiki_attachment.php?attId=63)

MyMemory. (2011, June 19). In *Wikipedia, The Free Encyclopedia.* Retrieved from http://en.wikipedia.org/w/index.php?title=MyMemory&oldid=435180033.

Orr Priebe, S. (2009). *Tom Sawyer – A crowdsourcing pioneer?* TCWorld, November 2009. http://www.tcworld.info/tcworld/outsourcing/article/tom-sawyer-a-crowd sourcing-pioneer/

Pattern (architecture). (2011, May 21). In *Wikipedia, The Free Encyclopedia.* Retrieved from http://en.wikipedia.org/w/index.php?title=Pattern_(architecture)&oldid =430249377.

Pedagogical patterns. (2010, December 16). In *Wikipedia, The Free Encyclopedia.* Retrieved from http://en.wikipedia.org/w/index.php?title=Pedagogical_patterns &oldid=402717235

ProZ.com. (2011, September 5). In *Wikipedia, The Free Encyclopedia.* Retrieved from http://en.wikipedia.org/w/index.php?title=ProZ.com&oldid=448648429.

Rogstadius, J., Kostakos, V., Kittur, A., Smus, B., Laredo, J., & Vukovic, M. (2011). An assessment of intrinsic and extrinsic motivation on task performance in crowdsourcing markets. *Proceedings Of the Fifth International AAAI Conference on Weblogs and Social Media*, Barcelona, July 17-21, 2011.

Stejskal, J. (2009). Ask not what the crowd can do for you, but what you can do for the crowd. *The ATA Chronicle*, August, 2009.

Surowiecki, J. (2004). *The wisdom of crowds: Why the many are smarter than the few and how collective wisdom shapes business, economies, societies and nations.* Random House, NYC, NY, USA.

Translated.net (2011, October 17). *Fast and easy professional translation services.* Retrieved from http://www.translated.net/.

TranslatorCafe (2011, October 17). *TranslatorCafe.com – A place for translators, interpreters and translation agencies.* Retrieved from http://www.translatorscafe.com/.

Translators without borders (2008, December 20). In *Wikipedia, The Free Encyclopedia.* Retrieved from http://en.wikipedia.org/w/index.php?title=Translators_without_ borders&oldid=259138738

Urban Dictionary (2011, October 17). *Urban dictionary.* Retrieved from http://www.urbandictionary.com/.

TAUS Data Association (2011, October 17). *TAUS Data Association.* Retrieved from http://www.tausdata.org/.

TED Open Translation Project (2011, October 17). *TED open translation project.* Retrieved from http://www.ted.com/index.php/OpenTranslationProject/.

Wiktionary (2011, October 17). *A multilingual free encyclopedia.* Retrieved from http://www.wiktionary.org/.

WikiWikiWeb. (2011, August 16). In *Wikipedia, The Free Encyclopedia*. Retrieved from http://en.wikipedia.org/w/index.php?title=WikiWikiWeb&oldid=4451266 72

Yahaya, F. (2008). Managing complex translation projects through virtual spaces: A case study. *ASLIB Translating and the Computer 30*, Nov 27-28, 2008, London, UK.

Has translation gone online and collaborative?: An experience from Minna no Hon'yaku

Kyo Kageura

University of Tokyo

Takeshi Abekawa

National Institute of Informatics

Masao Utiyama

National Institute of Information and Communication Technology, [1]Baobab, Inc.

Miori Sagara

National Institute of Information and Communication Technology, [1]Baobab, Inc.

Eiichiro Sumita

National Institute of Information and Communication Technology, [1]Baobab, Inc.

We have been running Minna no Hon'yaku (MNH: Translation of/by/for all), an open online translation hosting and translation-aid service, since April 2009, with use by NGOs specifically in mind. We subsequently started two sibling services, i.e. Ryugakusei Net @ MNH, a commercial "crowdtranslation" site, in March 2010, and Kotoba no Volunteer @ MNH, a project for collecting and making available expressions useful in disaster and post-disaster situations in different languages, in May 2011. This paper aims first to introduce basic features of these three systems and their state of usage, and second, to clarify the nature of activities being carried out using these systems and the relationships between the nature of activities and various factors that contribute to shaping the activities. While what is discussed is based mainly on the insights we have obtained from our experience designing, developing and running these systems, we attempt to situate the observation within a general framework discussion of online and/or collaborative translation.

1. Introduction

In accordance with the ongoing process of "globalisation", the new mode of or environment for translation has been under discussion for quite some time (Cronin, 2002), and online collaborative translation, "crowdtranslation" and user-generated translation (UGT) have become a hot topic (Désilet, 2010; Malcolm, 2010; OTT, 2009; Perrino, 2009; Prior, 2010).

In the practical arena, several successful cases of a new model of translation, such as Yeeyan[1] or the "crowdtranslation" of the Facebook interface,[2] have become widely known. Correlating at least partially with these trends, a number of open and/or online translation environments have become available, such as Google Translator Toolkit,[3] Traduwiki,[4] Wikitranslation,[5] TED,[6] Minna no Hon'yaku (MNH),[7] Lingotek,[8] and Omega-T.[9]

The multiplicity and diversity of online collaborative translation services, projects and systems indicate that the nature of the activities being carried out as well as the factors that lead to the success of these activities, and the system features useful for these activities, can be rather different from situation to situation (cf., DePalma & Kelly, 2008). This issue, however, has remained underaddressed, especially from the point of view of those who design, develop and manage systems and/or services.

Our team has been developing and running Minna no Hon'yaku (MNH: translation of/for/by all),[10] a translation hosting site with rich translation-aid functions that enable translators to efficiently manage the translation process, including reference lookup and intra-site communication tools such as message exchange and a bulletin board. MNH was made public on April 2009, shortly before the public launch of Google Translator Toolkit. Since then, we have made public two sibling sites: Ryugakusei Network @ MNH (MNH for the foreign student network: RNMNH) in March 2010, and Kotoba no Volunteer @ MNH (MNH for language volunteers: KVMNH) in May 2011.

Against this backdrop and on the basis of our own experiences, this paper first introduces basic features of the three systems we developed and their state of usage, and then examines and clarifies the nature of the activities being carried out using these systems and the relationship between the nature of these activities and the various factors that contribute to shaping them. The status of the systems and the activities being carried out on these systems are then examined in relation to the general concepts of online collaborative translation, "crowdtranslation" and UGT.

2. MNH and the two sibling MNH systems

We describe here the basic features of MNH, its two sibling systems, and their current status. Details of MNH and its technical components, which provide the common basis for all three systems, are described in Utiyama, et. al. (2009), Abekawa & Kageura (2007), Abekawa et al. (2010) and Takeuchi et al. (2007). Some data cannot be disclosed, so parts of the descriptions deliberately remain general.

2.1. The main MNH site

2.1.1. Basic characteristics and functions

The main MNH site was initially developed to assist NGOs whose work includes translating in-house or other documents and volunteer translators involved in translating online news and articles. Though we had a few specific Japanese NGOs in mind, MNH was and is intended to be used by a wide range of users all over the world.

Figure 1: The English Language Version of MNH Portal Toppage

MNH consists of three parts: (1) the MNH translation document portal (Figure 1); (2) the MNH translator platform (Figure 2); and (3) the translation-aid editor QRedit (Figure 3). Anybody can register at MNH anonymously, translate documents, and publish translations via the MNH portal, if copyright permits (translations that are not published are stored on the user's private page). In relation to the issue of copyright, MNH promotes the CreativeCommons license. Registered users can issue open translation requests to other users as well.

The translator platform provides a series of functions which enable users to carry out translation efficiently and work collaboratively, as well as improve their translation competence (Utiyama et al., 2009; Abekawa et al., 2010). These functions include, among others: (1) registration of user-defined reference resources such as terminologies and parallel texts; (2) definition of groups and projects, within which users can share documents, user-registered reference resources, translation tasks and communications; (3) communication by means of message exchange and a bulletin board; and (4) comparative display of different translation versions.

Figure 2: A user space on the MNH translator platform, showing the list of translated documents

Translation itself is carried out on and facilitated by the integrated translation-aid editor QRedit, which was specifically developed for and is provided on the MNH translator platform. It is a two-pane translation editor and has the following features (Abekawa & Kageura, 2007): (1) lookup of high-quality reference resources provided by MNH and of user defined resources, lookup of parallel texts of the user's choice, and seamless connection to online resources including Wikipedia and Google web and dictionary search; and (2) an easy-to-use and effective interface which enables translators to focus on translating. Users can choose synchronous or asynchronous scrolling of SL and TL texts; the basic unit of synchronisation is the paragraph.

2.1.2. Current status and usage

As of August 2011 (MNH was made public in April 2009), the status and usage of MNH is as follows:

(1) The system can deal with English-Japanese, Japanese-English, English-Chinese, Chinese-English, and English-Catalan language pairs. Japanese, Chinese, English and Catalan interfaces are available, the first three of which were provided by our team, and the last by the voluntary work of Dr. Bartolome Mesa of Universitat Autonoma de Barcelona. A Japanese-German dictionary (Apel, 2011) will be incorporated soon, together with a German interface.

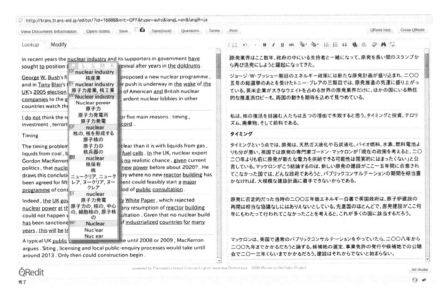

Figure 3: The translation-aid editor Qredit, with source language text in the left-hand pane, target language text in the right-hand pane, and dictionary lookup displayed in the small pulldown window in the left-hand pane.

(2)　Over 7,500 documents have been translated using the system, of which about 3,000 have been published via the MNH portal. Most translations are English-to-Japanese, with Japanese-to-English coming second.[11] News articles, reports, press releases, articles in online journals, and Wikipedia articles are among the most frequently translated materials. Translation requests are rarely made.

(3)　The number of registered users is over 1,700. Active users include some prominent NGOs, such as Amnesty International Japan, Democracy Now! Japan and the Japan Breastfeeding Support Network, while scores of personal users are translating a variety of texts on a regular basis.

(4)　Three book translation projects (one already published by a commercial publisher, two to be published)[12] have been completed, with two other projects ongoing, to the best of our knowledge.

(5)　A joint project by the Centre for Translation Studies, the University of Leeds and Kobe University of Foreign Studies used MNH (Clark, 2011); several Japanese universities are preparing to use MNH in their translation education programmes.

The typical patterns of usage of MNH are personal use and group- or project-based use. Figures 4(a) and 4(b) illustrate the basic configuration of these two usage patterns, respectively.

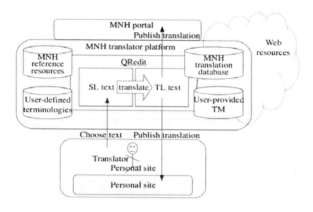

Figure 4(a): Basic configuration of the personal use of MNH

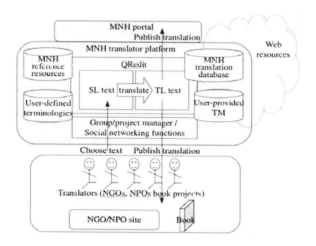

Figure 4(b): Basic configuration of the group-based or project-based use of MNH

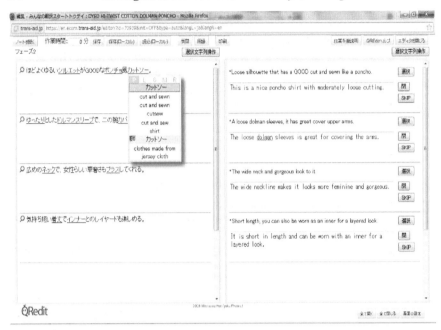

Figure 5: The extended version of QRedit used in RNMNH

2.2. Ryugakusei Network @ MNH (RNMNH)

2.2.1. Basic characteristics and functions

Ryugakusei Network @ MNH (henceforth RNMNH) is a spin-off from
MNH, run by a venture firm, Baobab, Inc. It is a commercial site aimed at
collectively translating documents provided by clients, focusing mainly on
Japanese as the source language and English, Chinese and Korean as the
target languages. RNMNH charges clients a minimum of 3.5 yen per
Japanese character, depending on the type of the text, while the average
Japanese translation company charges 15 to 20 yen per character.

Translations are done by foreign students in Japan; in order to
register at RNMNH, they must pass a proficiency test which is evaluated by
professional translators. Students are paid 1.1 to 1.6 yen per character,
depending on the level of quality.

RNMNH consists of a translator platform and QRedit. The core
functions of the RNMNH translator platform and QRedit are the same as
those of MNH. The differences are: (1) RNMNH has a translation text
delivery function, as the system provides translators with texts to be
translated; (2) it provides richer social networking and community-making
functions including connection to Facebook and Twitter; (3) the unit of

syncronisation in scrolling the source language and target language text is set to the sentence by QRedit; and (4) "draft translations" made by a high-quality phrase-based statistical machine translation (SMT) developed by NICT (Finch & Sumita, 2008) are provided on QRedit, which translators can use as a base translation (Figure 5).

2.2.2. Current status and usage

As of August 2011, the status and usage of RNMNH is as follows:

(1)   10,740,000 Japanese characters have been translated from Japanese to English, 3,900,000 from Japanese to Chinese, 2,760,000 from Japanese to Korean, and 1,000,000 from Chinese to Japanese using the system. 400 Japanese characters roughly correspond to 200 English words (JTF, 2005). RNMNH took only three months from the start of service to achieve translation of a million Japanese characters per month for Japanese-to-English translation, while the well-known Japanese social translation site myGengo took 16 months to achieve the same level.[13]

(2)   A total of 489 translators are registered at RNMNH (221 Japanese-to-English, 98 Japanese-to-Chinese, 162 Japanese-to-Korean, and 8 Chinese-to-Japanese).

(3)   Over 80 percent of the applicants passed the proficiency test for Japanese-to-Chinese and Japanese-to-Korean, 55 percent for Japanese-to-English, and 30 percent for Chinese-to-Japanese translation.

(4)   Analysis of translators' log-in times indicates that on average they earn 1,200 yen per hour, with the lowerst earnings 600 yen per hour and the highest earnings 2,100 yen per hour.[14]

(5)   Among the most successful translation projects carried out so far are multilingualisation of online shopping sites for health products and clothing. The main texts consisted of descriptions of commercial items. These were characterised by a high rate of repetition of similar expressions, such as "keep away from children", which contributed not only to the efficiency of recycling translations but also to improving the performance of SMT through adaptation.

Figure 6 illustrates the basic pattern of use of RNMNH.

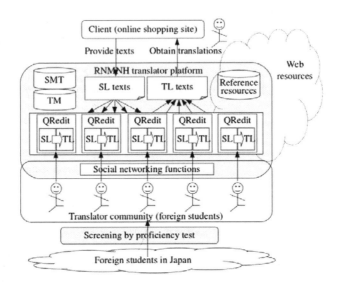

Figure 6: The basic pattern of use of RNMNH.

2.3. Kotobano Volunteer @ MNH (KVMNH)

2.3.1. Basic characteristics and functions

Kotoba no Volunteer @ MNH (KVMNH) is another spin-off project from MNH, started in May 2011. It is designed to accumulate and share expressions useful in disaster and post-disaster situations in multiple languages. The project was started following the Great East Japan Earthquake in March 2011based on the recognition that people were frustrated at not being able to provide useful information, due to the language barrier. While there are useful phrase books and pamphlets for that purpose, the range of expressions contained in them is limited. The objective of KVMNH is therefore to collect as many useful expressions as possible in a bottom-up manner from members of the public by means of crowdsourcing. Unlike the move reported by Munro (2010), which focuses on immediate response to the Haiti quake, KVMNH aims at preparing for future disasters.

KVMNH assumes, and aims for, the simultaneous collection of translations in many languages. The languages currently covered are Japanese, Korean, English, Simplified Chinese, Malay, Dutch, Brazilian Portuguese, Portuguese, Russian, Thai, Arabic, Tagalog, Danish, Vietnamese, German, Traditional Chinese, Spanish, French, Hindi, Bahasa Indonesia, and Italian.

Unlike MNH and RNMNH, KVMNH does not have a separate portal, translator platform or translation-aid editor. The characteristic features of KVMNH are: (1) it emphasises the translation request function to collect as many useful phrases as possible, because the consolidation of the range of expressions to be translated by users is an important aspect of the project; (2) it also gives importance to social networking functions, including connection to Facebook and Twitter; (3) the translation editor provides lookup of possible translation equivalents in many language pairs by connecting to external multilingual resources (Figure 7);[15] and (4) the expressions or texts on KVMNH are covered by a CreativeCommons Attribution licence.[16]

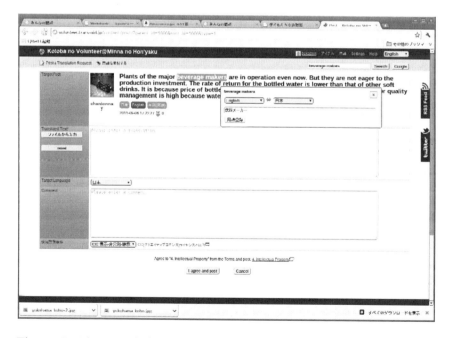

Figure 7: The translation editor embedded in KVMNH, with a popup showing the Japanese translation of the specified part of the English text.

2.3.2. Current status and usage

As of August 2011, the status and usage of KVMNH is as follows:

(1)   The number of translation requests to date is 197, all in Japanese, of which 146 have been translated into Korean, 127 into English, 100 into Simplified Chinese, and 60 into Malay, Dutch, Brazilian Portuguese, Portuguese, Russian, Thai, Arabic, Tagalog, Danish, Vietnamese, German, Traditional Chinese, Spanish, French, Hindi, Bahasa Indonesia, and Italian. The 60 translations in 17 languages are basic expressions provided by the system as an incentive to trigger contributions to KVMNH.

(2)   The number of registered users is 17.

This project is still in an embryonic stage. Figure 8 illustrates the basic usage pattern of KVMNH.

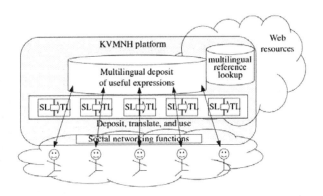

Figure 8: The basic pattern of use of KVMNH

3. The nature of "translation" activities and related elements

While these three systems are broadly referred to as online platforms for collaborative translation, the nature of activities being carried out using these systems as well as the role and status of the systems are very different. In this section, we will critically analyse these differences on the basis of observations of the typical usage patterns of these systems illustrated in Figures 4, 6 and 8. There is some intentional overlap between the descriptions in this section and those in the previous section for the sake of clarity. In the discussion below, the descriptions of MNH and RNMNH are based both on observations of actual use as well as on reflections about the strategic definitions of the systems, while the descriptions of KVMNH are based mostly on the strategic definition of the system, as a sufficient amount of data on actual use has not yet been accumulated at the time of writing.

3.1. Human elements and human factors

3.1.1. Players involved

Players taking part in these systems as well as their dispositions are different, as can be seen from Figures 4, 6 and 8. In MNH, the main players are those who translate, including both professional and non-professional translators. They may work individually, or they may work as volunteers for NGOs. In either case, it is translators who decide what to translate on MNH (recall that the use of the translation request function is negligible). MNH also has readers of the MNH portal site. The system itself (and the management team behind it) remain hidden behind the scenes, unless trouble occurs in the system.

In RNMNH, the main players are clients who provide texts and money. The system itself plays an active role in RNMNH: (1) the system management team chooses translators among applicants at the screening stage; and (2) the system decides and delivers a unit of texts to the translator upon the translator's request. The task of translators on RNMNH is limited to the translation of provided texts. There are no readers.

The configuration of players in KVMNH is very different from the other two systems. KVMNH does not consolidate translators as an independent player. Rather, it assumes a single type of player, who can be broadly labeled as participants in the KVMNH project. Participants are the ones who take the initiative in every respect, i.e., in contributing important expressions to KVMNH, in translating expressions, and in using them.

3.1.2. The nature and motivation of translators

In MNH, translators translate documents of their own choice; their goal is to disseminate information, and as part of this mission, they translate. This is typically the case with NGOs, whose mission in most cases is not translation itself. This does not necessarily mean that those involved in translation on MNH are not inherently "translators" as such; translators actively using MNH include professional translators or competent linguists working voluntarily for NGOs, though there are also people without translation training or experience. Typical translators on MNH can best be characterised as people who have already been translating, are translating and would be translating anyway, with or without MNH.

As translators working on RNMNH are foreign students whose main motivation is to gain income by working part-time, most have no experience of translation, although they are screened for language proficiency. Thus, the kind of people RNMNH mobilises are those who would not have been doing translation were it not for RNMNH.

KVMNH expects lay participants rather than translators, who are interested in multilingual communication and are committed to the stated aim of KVMNH. No control is imposed upon the qualification or background of participants.

3.1.3. Translator groups or communities

While there are groups of translators collaborating on MNH, using the group or project functions, they did not come together as a result of MNH, but already existed as groups before they started using MNH. The rounded rectangle surrounding a group of translators in Figure 4(b) illustrates this situation. Group use by NGOs is a typical case, in which the group members are limited to those already belonging to the NGOs, because the mission of most NGOs is not translation per se but other activities such as working for human rights or engaging in solidarity actions.

In contrast, translators who register at RNMNH basically have not known each other before joining RNMNH; thus, a new community is created via RNMNH. The rounded rectangle surrounding the community of translators that overlaps with the RNMNH platform in Figure 6 illustrates this situation.

The status of the community on KVMNH is similar to that of RNMNH, except that the community on KVMNH is intended to be open to everyone, and participants are expected to take part not only in translation but also in consolidating the range of expressions collectively.

Table 1 summarises the characteristics of the human elements examined so far.

Table 1: Players and characteristics of translators and translator community

	MNH	RNMNH	KVMNH
Players	translators, readers of MNH portal	clients, RNMNH, translators	participants as contributor, translator and user
Translators	volunteer, individual or working for NGOs, can be professional	foreign students	anybody
Motivation of translators	to disseminate information	part time job	for public good and common use
Groups or community	outside MNH	on RNMNH, closed	on KVMNH, open

3.2. Units of translation

Let us first introduce the following terms (note that they are defined here for the sake of the discussion in this section, and that the definitions do not necessarily reflect general usage):

- mission unit (MU): a set of documents to be translated in a mission. It can be finite and concrete, or open-ended.

- independent document unit (IDU): a block of text that constitutes a socio-physically independent unit. A book or an article is a typical example of an IDU. An IDU can be a mission unit, or can constitute a part of a mission unit; a mission unit can be a part of an IDU, though this is perhaps less common.

- coherent textual unit (CTU): a block of text that has a coherent unit of discourse. In the case of a book, chapters or sections or a shorter meaningful span of paragraphs can be a CTU. In the case of an article, the article itself as well as its sections, subsections, etc. can be a CTU.

- translation unit (TU): the minimum chunk of text that a translator bases his or her "rhythm" tackling translation. Most typically it is a paragraph, but it can be a sentence.

3.2.1. The nature of MUs

In MNH, a typical MU is a set of documents which NGOs deal with or which are relevant to individual translator's topic of interest. In the case of a book translation project, the mission unit is the book to be translated. In any case, it is the translators who define the MU. As different translators or groups of translators define their own MUs, multiple MUs coexist on MNH, over which MNH has no control.

In RNMNH, a typical MU is the texts contained in a particular shopping site or a meaningful subset of the site provided by a client. The MU consists of a finite amount of texts. When translation projects with more than one client are running in parallel, multiple MUs exist in parallel on RNMNH. Unlike MNH, it is RNMNH, not translators, which manages these MUs; translators are essentially indifferent to MUs.

KVMNH defines the nature of the MU as a range of expressions useful in disaster and post-disaster situations, but the actual set of texts that is to constitute the MU in concrete depends on participants. KVMNH has by definition only one mission and a corresponding MU, which it hopes to build up in a bottom-up manner by crowdsourcing.

Table 2: Characteristics related to the units of translation

	MNH	RNMNH	KVMNH
Mission Unit	a set of articles or a book	a set of texts on the site	a set of useful expressions
Who defines MU?	translators	clients	KVMNH and participants
Number of MU	many, uncontrolled	many, controlled	one
IDU	an article or a book	NA	NA
Who defines IDU?	translators	NA	NA
CTU	an article, a chapter, a section, etc.	a description a commercial item	NA
Who defines CTU?	translators	RNMNH	NA
Level of coherency	tight	loose	NA
TU	a paragraph	a sentence	any expressions
Who defines TU?	MNH	RNMNH	participants

3.2.2. The nature and disposition of IDUs, CTUs and TUs

On MNH, translators typically translate such texts as news or journal articles, press releases, NGO reports, and Wikipedia articles, which constitute both IDUs and CTUs simultaneously. In the case of a book translation, the book itself constitutes both an MU and an IDU, while chapters, sections, subsections and other coherent subsets of the book constitute CTUs. While MNH does not provide any mechanism to impose restrictions on the definition and management of these units, QRedit is optimised for texts consisting of a few to a score of paragraphs. So the de facto basic unit of manipulation by MNH is a CTU. As most translators we consulted, both professional and volunteer, regarded the paragraph as a basic TU, MNH QRedit sets paragraphs as TUs; it displays a ruler between paragraphs and synchronises the scrolling of SL and TL texts at the paragraph level.

On RNMNH, typical MUs dealt with by RNMNH, i.e., online shopping sites, are characterised by lack of units corresponding to IDUs. The CTU is the description of each commercial item on the site, though the textual coherency is in general looser than the kinds of documents typically translated on MNH. In the translation process, RNMNH automatically defines the unit of texts to be delivered for each translator. A typical unit of delivery consists of descriptions of one to five items, depending on the length of the descriptions.[17] The TU is set to a sentence by RNMNH QRedit. The imposition of TUs on QRedit is stricter in RNMNH than in MNH.

A standard unit registered to KVMNH are independent expressions or sentences, corresponding to the stated mission of KVMNH, i.e., accumulating useful multilingual expressions. Thus KVMNH does not deal with IDUs or CTUs. As the units to be registered are defined by participants, however, texts consisting of a paragraph or two are also registered to KVMNH. As a system mechanism, KVMNH treats any text in the same manner as individual sentences or short expressions.

Table 2 summarises the nature of textual units treated by translators using the three systems.

3.3. Quality control and support environments

3.3.1. Quality requirements and control

In MNH, it is translators or groups of translators who are in charge of setting quality requirements and controlling translation quality. Quality requirements may depend on the nature of texts. For instance, an in-depth report by a human rights NGO needs to be translated to a professional level of quality, while a press release prioritises timeliness, precision of essential information and impact. As a system, MNH does not provide any direct mechanism to control the quality of translations, although it does provide a series of support mechanisms that contribute to the improvement of translations and of translators' ability.

RNMNH is different from MNH in two respects. First, the quality requirement is set by clients. The quality requirement is not fixed and is still evolving, for several reasons: (1) RNMNH's main competitions are MT-based web-translation services from Japanese to English, Korean and Chinese, so the baseline requirement was from the beginning very low; (2) many clients, however, began to realise that low-quality translation harms their reputation; but (3) they still try to reduce cost. Currently, the minimum requirement among most clients is "not perfect but comfortable enough for readers". Second, RNMNH is in charge of quality control, as it is RNMNH which contracts with clients. RNMNH controls the quality of translations in two stages, i.e., by screening translators and by providing (monetary) incentives to translators.

As the expressions collected via KVMNH are intended for use in disaster and post-disaster situations, a lack of precision could have serious consequences. Quality requirements should thus be set tightly. Nevertheless, KVMNH relies upon participants as a whole for maintaining quality. This is based on the premise that the basic conditions for the wisdom of the crowd (Surowiecki, 2004) to work properly are satisfied in the case of KVMNH: the range of expressions to be dealt with are potentially necessary for anybody and in most cases participants can evaluate the quality of expressions for their own languages independently.

3.3.2. Support environments

Corresponding to the differences that we have discussed so far, the effective elements in support mechanisms and environments to promote translation activities and to control or improve translation quality also differ in the three systems.

For translators using MNH, the core and straightforward translation-aid functions including access to reference resources are the most important elements. In addition, two elements are worth noting. Firstly, especially for NGOs, translation memory (TM) consisting of past translations of their own documents is of utmost importance. Secondly, the contrastive display of different versions of translations which highlights differences has turned out to be useful especially for self-training of inexperienced translators (Abekawa et al., 2010). The types of support effective on MNH are those which enable translators to improve translation efficiency and quality as well as translators' competence.

As for RNMNH, although translation-aid functions including MT draft translation play an important role, indirect, environmental support features proved to be essential to maintain and improve the overall quality of translation. This corresponds to the fact that translators on RNMNH do not have a strong independent motivation for translation and are indifferent to MUs, so they have little loyalty to the cause. In relation to the textual units, these environmental supports consist of several small points: (1) to deliver units of text small enough for translators to feel comfortable dealing with in a short amount of time; (2) to enable translators to skip sentences that are considered as too difficult to translate; (3) to provide a link to the original page so that the translators can check the contextual background. In relation to human factors, environmental supports are designed: (1) to promote the identity of a member of the community through social networking functions; and (2) to nurture healthy rivalry by acknowledging the most productive translators every month. We would perhaps be able to say that the types of support useful in RNMNH are to improve collective efficiency and the overall quality of products, rather than to improve individual translations and the ability of individual translators.

We have not yet consolidated important elements of the support environment for KVMNH.

Table 3: Quality control and support environments

	MNH	RNMNH	KVMNH
Quality requirement	can be high	comfortable enough for readers	can be tight
Who decides the quality requirement?	translators	clients	participants (collectively)
Who is in charge of quality control?	translators	RNMNH	participants (collectively)
Effective support features	direct, TM and contrastive display of versions	indirect, choice of textual units and promoting community	NA
Translation quality	varies, professional/publishable on the high-end	comparable to existing Japanese TSP	NA
Effect on quality	reduction in translation time, general improvement of translations	help maintain the overall quality	NA

3.3.3. Translation efficiency and quality

The actual quality of translations made using MNH varies, and is hard to grasp. However, the quality on the high end is clear: It is comparable to the professional level, as is indicated by the fact that books translated using MNH have been published as paper-bound books as commercial products, and also by the fact that the system is used by Amnesty International Japan and Democracy Now! Japan, where professional translators are working voluntarily together with non-professional translators. In relative terms, an initial experiment showed that using MNH led to a reduction in translation time, which in turn resulted in a slight improvement in the quality of draft translations (Utiyama, et. al., 2009).

The preliminary evaluation by professional translators of the quality of translations made on RNMNH also showed that the overall quality is comparable to the translations provided by an established translation company, although the details of the methods of evaluation and detailed figures cannot be reported here for reasons of confidentiality. Unlike MNH, the relative improvement in the translation quality cannot be evaluated, as we cannot ask translators working on RNMNH to do translations in a different environment.

We have carried out no quality assessment of translations for KVMNH so far.

Table 3 summarises the differences related to quality control and requirements.

4. Different life with common technologies

Having described the basic features of the three systems and clarified the characteristics of activities being carried out on these systems, it is time to examine and evaluate the position of these systems within a broader and more general framework set by the concepts of online collaborative translation, crowdtranslation and UGT.

From the various features and characteristics of the activities and the status of systems summarised in Tables 1 to 3, the positions of the three systems in relation to translators are clear: MNH and KVMNH are translator- or participant-driven, while RNMNH is client- and system-driven.

4.1. MNH and online collaborative translation

The translation activities on MNH are carried out online, and, in the case of translations by NGOs, they are often collaborative, so they can be described as online collaborative translations. The collaborative aspect, however, is independent of translation being carried out online, as the collaboration existed prior to the introduction of MNH. As such, MNH did not work as a driving force for opening a new arena or mode of online collaborative translation. Rather, MNH is best described as an integrated online tool and environment for existing translators (the creation of such a system was in fact our original intention).

Due to the fact that major users of MNH are those continuously involved in translation activities, the diachronic dimension becomes important in MNH. This is reflected, for instance, in the support elements highly valued by translators; both TM and the self-training of translators are more effective over the long-term. While we can reasonably calculate that MNH has been a moderate success, the ultimate success or failure of MNH depends on the extent to which it can support the continuous activities of translators or groups of translators working on a voluntary basis.

4.2. RNMNH and crowdtranslation

RNMNH is better described as a framework for clients to fulfil their translation needs at lower cost. For that purpose, it relies on foreign students who are native speakers of the target language. The types of texts dealt with are those which have not been translated, except by MT. So RNMNH has opened a new opportunity for and area of translation from the business point of view. In terms of the mode of translation, it can be described as crowdtranslation, if the meaning of the term is stretched a little, as is quite often the case.[18] In a sense, while in MNH the system is a tool and translators are the major players, in RNMNH, the system is the main player and translators are dependent players. That the useful support features for RNMNH are concerned with the present activities and community is correlated with this characteristic of RNMNH.

Although we have not discussed this so far, an essential merit of RNMNH—which was also one of our original intentions—is that it has so far materialised a win-win model for clients and translators. Clients are happy with the cost-performance of RNMNH; foreign students, many of whom are living in rural areas, where opportunities to obtain part-time jobs are often scarce, are happy to be able to work online and earn more than they would working at shops or restaurants. In addition, the project has so far not encroached on the traditional area of translation covered by professional translators. What is yet to be seen in relation to this issue is to what extent this win-win situation is based on a particular social situation, and to what extent the win-win situation can be attributed to the RNMNH model. If RNMNH can suggest a general business model of translation which always results in a win-win situation for all the actors involved, it will make a real contribution to the practice of crowdtranslation in a wider sense.

4.3. KVMNH, crowdsourcing and UGT

While both MNH and KVMNH are translator- or participant-oriented, their status is completely different. KVMNH is first and foremost a mission oriented site, or a project, with translation-support tools. KVMNH can be described as an orthodox case of aiming at crowdsourcing, in the sense that both the problems and the solutions are to be consolidated collectively by participants, under an abstract mission statement provided by KVMNH.[19] It has an interesting status in relation to UGT. In standard cases of successful UGT such as Facebook translation, the users who contributed the translations are users of Facebook, i.e. users were already there prior to the translation project being carried out. On the other hand, if we look at the case of KVMNH from the UGT point of view, what is to be used is exactly that is to be contributed to KVMNH by users. Although the basic definition of KVMNH is rather simple, if the site takes off, perhaps we will be able to learn more about whether there can be something essentially new in crowdtranslation and UGT online.

5. Conclusions

This paper has examined the nature and status of online translation activities carried out on the three systems we developed and manage. In the process, we examined interrelated factors and elements, i.e., types of texts, players, the role of the system and how they depend on each other, consolidating the activities in these three systems in relation to the translation referred to under the broad banners of online collaborative translation, crowdtranslation, and/or UGT.

A few years ago, Alain Désilet stated that "Massive Online Collaboration is revolutionizing the way in which content is produced and consumed worldwide, and this is bound to also have a large impact on the way in which content is translated" (Désilet, 2007). But is this really the case? The observations above suggest that the reality on the ground is not quite as dramatic, although this may simply be a reflection of the modest achievements of the three systems discussed in this paper; a greater impact on the way in which content is translated may have been demonstrated if other systems had been the target of discussion.

Even so, it is our hope that the above discussion still provides useful information for those who are trying to understand the current state of play at the grassroots in the area of online collaborative translation, crowdtranslation, or UGT, as well as for those who are designing and developing a system or are planning to launch a translation enterprise or a translation project.

Acknowledgements

The work reported here is partly supported by the Japan Society for the Promotion of Sciences (JSPS) grant-in-aid (A) 21240021 "Developing an integrated translation-aid site which provides comprehensive reference sources for translators". The first author would like to thank Professor Anthony Hartley, Centre for Translation Studies, University of Leeds, for useful discussions about the topic reported here.

References

Abekawa, T., & Kageura, K. (2007). A translation aid system with a stratified lookup interface. *Proceedings of the 45th Association for Computational Linguistics Demos and Poster Session*, 5-8.

Abekawa, T., Utiyama, M., Sumita, E., & Kageura, K. (2010). Community-based construction of draft and final translation corpus through a translation hosting site Minna no Hon'yaku (MNH). *The Seventh International Conference on Language Resources and Evaluation* (LREC 2010).

Apel, U. (2011). *WaDoku Jiten*. Retrieved from http://www.wadoku.eu/

Clark, L. (2011). *Online Student Collaboration: English-Japanese Japanese-English Translation* (Master's thesis). Centre for Translation Studies, University of Leeds.

Cronin, M. (2003). *Translation and Globalisation*. London: Routledge.

DePalma, D. A., & Kelly, N. (2008) *Translation of, by, and for the People: How User-Translated Content Projects Work in Real Life*. Lowell, Mass: Common Sense Advisory.

Désilet, A. (2007). Translation Wikified: How will massive online collaboration impact the world of translation. *ASLIB Translating and the Computer 29*.

Désilet, A. (Ed.). (2010). *AMTA 2010 Workshop on Collaborative Translations: Technology, Crowdsourcing, and the Translator Perspective*.

Finch, A., & Sumita, E. (2008). Dynamic model interpretation for statistical machine translation. *Third Workshop on Statistical Machine Translation*, 208-215.

Howe, J. (2006). The rise of crowdsourcing. *Wired, 14*(6), Retrieved from http://www.wired.com/wired/archive/14.06/crowds.html

Huberdeau, L-P., Paquet, S., & Désilets, A. (2008). The cross-lingual Wiki engine: Enabling collaboration across language barriers. *Proceedings of Wikisym 2008*.

JTF (2005). *2005 White Papers of Translation: The Second Report of the Translation Industry Survey*. Tokyo: Japan Translation Federation [in Japanese].

Malcolm, R. (2010). Crowd control. *ITI Bulletin*, Jan-Feb, 6-9.

Munro, R. (2010). Crowdsourced translation for emergency response in Haiti: the global collaboration of local knowledge. *AMTA 2010 Workshop on Collaborative Translation: Technology, Crowdsourcing, and the Translator Perspective*.

NICT (2011). *Support page for translation applications*. http://mastar.jp/translation/index-en.html

OTT (2009). *Open Translation Tools 2009*. http://www.aspirationtech.org/events/opentranslation/2009

Perrino, S. (2009). User-generated translation: The future of translation in a Web 2.0 environment. *The Journal of Specialised Translation, 12*. Retrieved from http://www.jostrans.org/issue12/artperrino.php

Prior, M. (2010). The open-source model. *ITI Bulletin*, Jan-Feb, 10.

Surowiecki, J. (2004). *The Wisdom of Crowds*. New York: Doubleday.

Takeuchi, K., Kanehila, T., Hilao, K., Abekawa, T., & Kageura, K. (2007). Flexible automatic look-up of English idiom entries in dictionaries. *MT Summit XI*, 451-458.

Utiyama, M., Abekawa, T., Sumita, E., & Kageura, K. (2009). Hosting volunteer translators, *MT Summit XII*.

---

[1]   http://en.yeeyan.com/

[2]   http://blog.facebook.com/blog.php?post=20734392130

[3]   http://translate.google.com/toolkit/

[4]   http://traduwiki.org/

[5]   http://www.wikitranslation.org/

[6]   http://www.ted.com

[7]   http://trans-aid.jp

[8]   http://www.lingotek.com

[9]   http://www.omegat.org/

[10]   The team consists of the Library and Information Science Course, Graduate School of Education, University of Tokyo, Japan, the Language Translation Group, National Institute of Information and Communication Technology, Japan, and the Research and Development Center for Informatics of Association, National Institute of Informatics, Japan. Dr. Bartrome Mesa of the Autonomous University of Barcelona, Spain, and Dr. Ulrich Apel of the University of Tubingen, Germany, kindly assisted our team by extending the language pairs dealt with by the project.

[11]   Note that Yeeyan, widely held to be one of the most successful community translation sites, had nearly 30,000 translations published on the site at the end of 2009. Taking into account the difference between the Chinese-speaking and Japanese-speaking populations, it can be said that MNH is doing reasonably well.

[12]   The one already published is Caldicott, H. and Eisendrath, C. *War in Heaven*, NY: New Press, 2006. The other two books to be published are: Blum, W. *Killing Hope: US Military and CIA Interventions since World War II*, NY: Common Courage Press, 1995 and Scahill, J. *Blackwater: The Rise of the World's Most Powerful Mercenary Army*, NY: Nation Books.

[13]   http://mygengo.com/

[14]   Incidentally, this amounts to a maximum of about 1,300 (calculated at 1.6 yen per word, which is close to the reality for productive translators) to 1,900 (calculated at 1.1 yen)

Japanese characters being translated per hour and a minimum of about 375 (calculated at 1.6 yen per hour) to 545 (calculated at 1.1 yen per hour, which is close to the reality for non-productive translators) Japanese words per hour.

[15] At present, KVNMN uses Google Translate through api, but the choice of the resource is currently under review.

[16] Incidentally, NICT, the main body in charge of KVMNH, has a plan to use the data to improve its own speech and text MT services VoiceTra and TexTra, originally intended for facilitating travel conversations (NICT, 2011).

[17] At the early stage, RNMNH provided translators with randomly chosen sentences, based on the belief that preferentially providing frequently repeated sentences, such as "keep away from children", would greatly improve the efficiency of translation and MT as well which would optimise the translation of the mission unit. This turned out to be totally wrong, and we changed our system so that the provided texts maintain the unit of description of individual commercial items.

[18] If we stick to the original definition of crowdsourcing that was set out by Jeff Howe as "the application of open source principles to fields outside of software" (http://crowdsourcing.typepad.com/), crowds are supposed to contribute not only to the solutions but also to the definition of problems. This strict definition does not hold for RNMNH.

[19] http://volunteer.trans-aid.jp/content/help/first/

II. FINDINGS FROM COMMERCIAL MARKET RESEARCH PERSPECTIVES

From crawling to sprinting: Community translation goes mainstream

Nataly Kelly, Rebecca Ray & Donald A. DePalma

Common Sense Advisory

The notion that "two heads are better than one" is hardly new when applied to translation. The entire corpus of Buddhist sutras was translated into Chinese collaboratively by foreign and Chinese monks over a thousand-year period which began in the 1st century A.D. (Chueung, 2006). However, the dominant model used today for translation in the commercial sector depends on a process that largely inhibits collaboration. This article presents some of the latest findings from research on the state of community translation, based on multiple market research studies carried out over a five-year period, including a comparative analysis of 100 community translation environments and interviews with stakeholders. The research reveals that, over the course of the last several years, translation industry participants have been moving away from the traditional process toward a more dynamic and collaborative model. As community-based models have grown in popularity, distinct types of environments have emerged as well.

1. The TEP model as de facto industry standard

Over the last few decades, the majority of private-sector translation work has been carried out using the translate-edit-proofread (TEP) model (Kockaert & Makoushina, 2008). The translation step is typically performed by a single translator, followed by a review of the translation by a senior translator who is known as an editor. Finally, a third individual reviews the text to verify that numbers were rendered accurately and that no information appears to have been omitted. The TEP model emerged from the publishing field, and is based on Gutenberg's printing requirements, in which the author submitted the manuscript, another individual typeset the material, and then a third party reviewed the galley proofs as many times as necessary to prevent any errors from appearing in the final print run (DePalma & Beninatto, 2007).

The TEP model has various drawbacks related to translation quality and efficiency. Firstly, the individuals who are located downstream in the production chain usually have less information than those upstream. If the editor knows less about the topic or source text than the translator, he or she is likely to introduce errors instead of correcting them. Another common problem is that the reviewer may not have received the same set of instructions as the editor. The model also can be less than optimal from a timing perspective. Each individual works on a task before handing it off to the next person in the process, as in an assembly line. As a result, translators, editors, reviewers, and production staff often spend a great deal of time waiting for the person ahead of them to finish instead of advancing the translation project. The TEP model is the most widely used model in the commercial sector today because of the way most translation services are purchased or sold. The vast majority of organizations on the demand side of the market, that is to say, consumers of translation services, do not contract directly with freelance translators—rather, they hire translation companies, also known as language service providers (LSPs) to produce the translations (Kelly & Stewart, 2011). The LSPs manage the translation projects, including the translators, editors, and proofreaders who carry out the TEP steps.

However, some quality steps are not carried out by the LSP, but by the client. For example, the client often assigns an individual to review the translation for accuracy and provide feedback, a process known as "end client review" (Bass, 2006). Typically, this review takes place after the TEP steps have been carried out, and the review is usually conducted by the client's internal staff, usually located in the country where the target text will be used, or by a partner organization such as an in-country public relations firm or advertising agency. Perhaps the greatest drawback of the TEP model is that it only enables individuals to detect errors at certain checkpoints or at the end of a project. As Malcolm Williams writes in his book on translation quality assessment (TQA), "TQA has traditionally been based on intensive error detection and analysis and has therefore required a considerable investment in both human resources" (Williams, 2004, p. xv). While researchers find that TEP presents various challenges when it comes to quality control, they also highlight the fact that professional-level quality can be obtained through community translation models (Zaidan & Callison-Burch, 2011).

When errors are spotted at the end of a project, it can be extremely costly and time-consuming to fix them. With the TEP model, it is quite common for a client reviewer to spot a problem with a translation after it has already been delivered and the TEP process has been fully completed. Therefore, while the TEP model has been the prevailing model used in the industry, its disadvantages are sufficient in number and severity to cause the stakeholders on both the supply and the demand side—but especially the clients themselves—to consider other solutions.

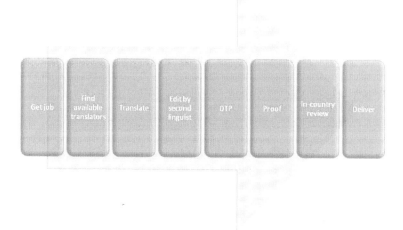

Figure 1: Timeline for Traditional Translation: Each Step Waits for a Hand-Off (DePalma et al., 2007).

2. Toward a Collaborative Translation Model

In response to the growing presence of online communities and the challenges associated with the TEP model, a collaborative translation model began to emerge in which translation could be performed entirely in a virtual, web-based or cloud-based environment (DePalma et al., 2007). Crowdsourcing is one example of such collaboration methods. In this model, collaborators can be either volunteers, employees, paid professional translators, or a mixture of all of these groups. Under this model, a project manager would first set up a project in the community, running the original document against translation memory files and optionally using machine translation to pre-translate the text. The project manager would then upload material to be translated, check a vendor database for the best resources and invite them to join the "project community," which is likely to include translators, consultants, client reviewers, and desktop publishing staff. A project community differs from the traditional notion of a "project team", primarily in that project teams for TEP processes are usually organized by language, whereas a project community would include many teams working on different languages but would also allow participants to interact across language groups. In other words, the teams would not be segregated by language in a community-based model. Finally, the project manager would monitor the performance of the community to ensure that questions were answered, files were available, and deadlines were met. While translation management system (TMS) tools facilitate much of the project management tasks with a traditional TEP process, in community translation environments, it is less typical for the project manager to rely on external software. Instead, the metrics and tracking tools are usually built directly into the environment itself. And, in some cases, specific tools are used to facilitate the community translation work.[1]

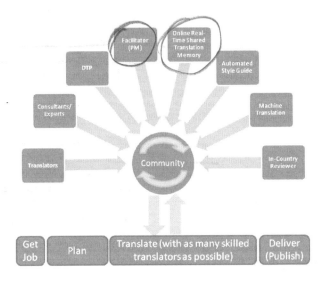

Figure 2: Timeline for Collaborative Translation: No Wait Time Between Activities (DePalma et al, 2007).

Under this model, translators would work asynchronously, for example, by putting 20 translators on a project for five days instead of having five translators work for 20 days. The project managers would rely on the other community members to proofread and improve each other's contributions to the translation. Also, individuals with subject-matter expertise would be invited to participate in the community to vet the translations, ask questions, and suggest improvements. The real-time interaction would enable errors to be corrected earlier in the process. In other words, reviewers would not be left downstream in the process, but could provide input during the process, which would also serve to help with translator training. Through this collaborative process, the editing stage would be eliminated, since quality improvement would take place at essentially the same time as translation. This enables organizations to produce translations much faster than they would by using traditional TEP methods.

2.1. The People: Optimizing Client-Vendor Relations and Staff Roles

Within the TEP model, companies adopt a sequential process where—in its simplest form—the work passes from the client to the LSP, who in turn hands it to the translator, who returns it to the LSP, who sends it to a separate editor who is also usually a freelancer, who returns it to the LSP, who conducts a final quality assurance check or "proof," most typically using internal staff, and then delivers it to the client. In a collaborative environment, these hand-offs become redundant, since tasks do not need to be completed before they are transferred to the next agent. Under the community translation model, the client becomes part of the project community.

The other participant roles also change significantly under this model. Individual translators face seismic changes. They cease to be individuals working alone in their pods, and become active members of a community environment. Suddenly, in order to do their jobs well, instead of resolving their queries by looking terms and phrases up in dictionaries, they can enter questions within an online group environment, where they can ask follow-up questions and submit queries on specific use cases, complete with contextual information, examples, and exceptions. They can also review other people's translation memory files, something that does not typically happen with the TEP model. Granted, even using the TEP model, translators can access terminology databases and their own translation memory files, along with any that are provided by the LSP for a given project. The major difference with the community-based model is that the translator's ability to access shared knowledge repositories increases, taking the translators out of the silo of working alone at home and bringing them into a virtual workspace where they can benefit from real-time consultation with peers.

The project manager role also shifts significantly with the collaborative model. Instead of just shepherding files between the various parties, the project manager becomes a facilitator, the person who builds the team, keeps it on task, and brings into the community the resources required for each phase of the project. Most project managers working with the TEP model already use TMS tools in order to carry out the standard project management tasks related to the TEP process. However, because those tasks change in a community-based model, so does the role of the project manager. Some project management tasks become automated through the environment or portal itself. For example, a translation job in an online collaborative setting might be automatically marked as "complete" once a certain number of segments are translated by the group. In a TEP process, a project manager would carry out a manual check before marking a project complete using a TMS tool, and at that point, automatic messages might be sent to different project participants. In a community environment, there might not be any need for messages to be sent to participants since they can access the same information in other ways—for example, via a dashboard or by hovering over a given project with their mouse.

The editor/reviewer function also morphs in a collaborative model. In this model, expertise is available not just toward the end of the process, but integrated throughout in the form of real-time shared translation memories and automated style guides. In the TEP process, a style guide is essentially a document with rules regarding grammar, usage, and style. In a collaborative model, many of these rules are built into the environment directly in order to prevent mistakes. For example, a TEP process for a company like Twitter might have a style guide that instructs a translator not to capitalize the word "tweet". If a translator overlooks this, it might be caught by an editor or proofreader, or perhaps by an end client reviewer, but there is always a chance that it might not be caught. In a collaborative portal, an automatic message would appear if the translator tries to capitalize the word "tweet" to instruct the translator not to do this the moment they type it into the environment. Other rules might prevent the translator from submitting an item with an error until it is corrected, thereby focusing on error prevention instead of error correction. In some cases, authoring or controlled language tools might be used to enforce such rules. In other cases, the rules are built directly into the online environment.

In a collaborative model, human subject matter experts coexist and contribute to high-quality translations in the first pass. In fact, in a collaborative model, subject matter experts do not just do a final review at the end, but rather, are relied upon throughout the process to answer questions in a timely manner so that translators are not left waiting. Translators, thus, no longer rely on the editor's eyes to catch their mistakes at the end, and must be trained to ask questions to help them translate correctly from the start. Typically, these subject matter experts are the same individuals who would be performing end client review in a TEP process. The difference is that their input is provided at the start of the project and throughout instead of afterward. Thus, the focus shifts from fixing translations that are potentially full of errors to creating a correct translation from the start, with the feedback and guidance of the subject matter experts at an earlier point in the process. It is important to note that subject matter experts and client reviewers are not present for every single project, regardless of which model is used. In other words, there are many translation projects following a TEP process that do not involve any client reviewers. Likewise, there are plenty of community translation projects that do not benefit from client reviewers either. However, for those projects that do require subject matter expertise, a community-based model ensures that said expertise is shared at an earlier point, at the time the translation is actually performed as opposed to after the fact.

Perhaps surprisingly, this model is not necessarily more expensive. Giving translators the ability to collaborate enables them to share their

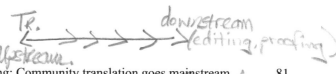

expertise easily and quickly. The heart of the difference is in the collaboration itself. In online environments, translators can talk with each other and prevent errors from being made in the first place. In a traditional process, a translator working in isolation might make his or her best guess at a given translation. The only possibility for a colleague to catch the error comes further downstream in the process, at the editing stage or perhaps even at the client review stage. In a collaborative model, the mere fact that the translator has access to other human beings with knowledge means that the translator does not have to wait until the editing process to obtain feedback. The translator can simply post a question in an online forum and check the responses. The translator may gain additional insight from people who actually use the product or service for which the material is being translated. This enables the translator to produce the correct translation from the start, as opposed to waiting for someone to spot the error—which might never happen.

The role of the vendor manager becomes extremely important in a collaborative model. Vendor managers that work at most LSPs today tend to manage a large database of translators, editors, and other linguistic workers. Today, most vendor management that takes place is rather simple – resources are organized by language pair and sometimes by location and tool expertise. However, to segment the database and manage it in real time, organizing vendors by more specific criteria, such as gender, subject matter expertise, or national origin. In the case of gender, this might be important for certain types of projects—for example, where the content requires an audio component and a female voice has been requested by the client. Vendors must also be sorted using other criteria, such as past quality scores and client feedback regarding project performance. The real-time nature of the collaborative model makes the role of the vendor manager more important than in the TEP model. The key difference is that in a collaborative model, the work happens in real time, and thus the vendor manager's role becomes more prominent.

The nature of teams is also different in a collaborative model from the way teams work in the TEP model. With the TEP model, translation teams usually consist of translators working within the same language combinations. With a collaborative model, the ability to collaborate and learn from each other can cross language pairs. For example, Spanish translators can leverage solutions found for Portuguese or Italian translations. Japanese translators can be warned up-front about bugs and poorly written or ambiguous source language that the German team finds while localizing and translating. Chinese client-side reviewers can communicate with the project consultants to clarify terminology issues in real-time. For example, a Chinese end client reviewer might warn project consultants that an image or term in Chinese is acceptable in mainland China but has negative connotations or would not be appropriate for Chinese communities in other countries. This finding could affect not only the Chinese language content but also content written in other languages or problems that could exist in both Simplified and Traditional Chinese.

2.2. Process: Improving project management through communities

Is there are issue with product delivery?

Speed is a critical issue for most clients of translation services (Kelly, 2011). Timelines are often tight, which means that project managers often resort to individual heroics in order to get work done. In the TEP model, cramming a lot of work into a short timeframe is typical for the delivery of most projects. In contrast, collaborative translation requires more advance preparation and organization before a project starts: recruiting and setting up communities, sourcing and training the best talent, configuring automated style and terminology tools, pre-translating material, and populating translation memory files that can be used for the project. This is most typically done not using the traditional commercial off-the-shelf tools that are common for TEP processes, but rather, by creating environments in which these rules and resources are available directly within the system itself. Nearly all collaborative translation environments that exist today have been developed in-house.

Benefit for End-client

As Table 1 shows, several core elements related to project management are different with a collaborative model. The traditional TEP model focuses on *error correction*, whereas the collaborative model focuses on *error prevention*. A community that is optimized for collaborative work has automated systems in place, in addition to a larger number of eyes that can catch errors at the time they are introduced, instead of at a later phase, which is the case with the TEP model. The community serves to "self-correct" as the translation process unfolds. This is a very different process from the one used under the TEP model, which involves catching errors after the translations have been produced. For example, in a typical TEP process, let us assume that a translator uses an incorrect term for a translation, and let us also assume that this term is not available in any of the terminology databases, style guides, or translation memory files. The translator might do this accidentally, simply because the translator cannot locate the term in any existing resources and does not have the ability to submit a query about the term, in the rush to get the translation off to the next phase, in which the editor will review it. The translator will submit the translation with the error, and it is possible that the editor and proofreader will not detect the error either. When the translation reaches the end client reviewer, the end client reviewer spots the error and requests a correction. At this stage, the error may already have been recorded in the translator's translation memory file and terminology database. So, to purge the error, the translator will make the correction, re-submit the file to the editor, and the process essentially starts over once again. In many cases, more errors and problems are introduced at the time the corrections are made. For example, an editor might replace a single word but inadvertently include a typo. With a collaborative model, the error would much more likely be caught at the time the translation was actually created, because the translator would have had the ability to ask for help from the other members of the community, including other translators who might have already found acceptable ways of translating a tricky term in a similar language, as well as the same end client reviewers and subject matter experts who would sit at the end of a TEP process instead of being available at the start.

Table 1: Process-related issues for collaborative translation

Process Issue	TEP Model	Collaborative Model
Reliance on planning and advanced preparation	Low	High
How translation activities are performed	Sequential process	Parallel / Simultaneous activities
Quality control focus	Error correction	Error prevention
Information availability	Limited by language pair or project team	Shared across the entire community
Decisionmaking	Select participants make subjective choices based on their individual knowledge and expertise	Large community of translators and experts arrive at group consensus
Feedback provision	Comments flow from all parties back to the project manager (single point of failure)	Real-time tagging allows information to be shared openly by all project participants
Compensation	Price per word model; more words equates to more money regardless of actual effort	Compensation reflects contributions to the process that are not necessarily tied to translated words (contextual insight, clarifications, edits, etc.)

Instead of reporting issues to the project manager as happens in the TEP model, translators in the collaborative model tag and insert comments in real time in the original document, thus helping translators in other languages who might otherwise face the same difficulties. Collaboration

Nataly Kelly, Rebecca Ray & Donald A. DePalma

Volunteer Profile: Why comm. translation is so prevalent + Afterthought/caveat to definition

Benefit of comm. translation.

Basis for part of Questionnaire.

facilitates the elimination of silos of knowledge and makes the whole system or community smarter and more efficient.

The per word/per line/per page pricing model that characterizes the TEP model is not well-suited to the collaborative model, which rewards more than just translating individual words. The collaborative model prizes contributions to the process that include contextual support, answers to questions from the community, clarifications, and edits. This model of rewarding supra-translation activities provides an incentive for community members to contribute beyond just the language transfer. The vast majority of work that is performed through collaborative translation is carried out by volunteers. More often than not, these individuals are not professional translators, but rather, fans or members of existing online communities that exist to support the discussion of a given product, service, or cause. It is important to understand that community translation is not emerging as a "replacement" for the TEP model, at least, not right now, but rather, as a natural consequence of the increased presence of global online environments in which people gather online. Typically, these individuals participate in community translation projects not because they are paid to do so, but because of some other reason. For example, perhaps they are motivated, to see a software product released in their native language, and they realize that by contributing to the translation, they will receive it faster. In other examples, such as the 2010 earthquake in Haiti, they volunteer to help fellow human beings and/or loved ones in emergency situations through community translation. In many cases, the volunteer translators themselves are subject matter experts, with knowledge of the product or topic that is highly specialized. Whereas a professional translator would typically study product documentation and terminology in order to familiarize himself or herself with a product, the individuals who already use these products on a daily basis already understand what different terms mean, and are therefore in some ways more qualified to translate the terminology than professional translators might be.

Domain Experts.

Included in volunteer definition/ translation introduction.

This definition also serves to support some of the hypothesised motivations of the ↑

2.3. Technology: Leveraging automation

→ Anticipated benefit(s) for Clients

In the collaborative translation world, translations are done more efficiently because of technologies that enable these communities to work together seamlessly. In this model, translation happens on the web, all the time, by linguists, subject matter experts, and individuals who are passionate about a particular product, issue, or cause, who can be available regardless of location or ownership of desktop translation tools. One could argue that collaboration is possible even in a TEP model. However, the technology infrastructure available through Web 2.0 allows more extensive and continual collaboration through asynchronous workflow and remote

Add to def. of comm. translation—Online (Link to characteristics of other online communities benefiting from more extensive research).

Part of comm.T (Web 2.0)

operations that are much more flexible and reliable than the typical technologies used with a TEP model (Hartley, 2009).

In a collaborative model, translation communities rely on commonly used technology like instant messaging (including via social media platforms), SMS, discussion groups, RSS feeds, social tagging, content categorization, and voting. Since 2005, language software developers have been working on a wide range of translation memory and automated translation innovations to enable translation assets and workflow to reside comfortably and natively in the cloud (Sargent, 2010). In other words, technology developers are working to make it easier for translators and other collaborators to interact in a web-based environment and work on projects without the need to install any desktop software (see Table 2).

Table 2: Technology-Related Issues for Collaborative Translation

Technology Area	TEP Model	Collaborative Model
Communication with other group members	E-mail / Telephone	Discussion group, chat, social and professional network, Skype, Wiki, Groove
Translation memory	Desktop translation memory applications like Trados and Déjà Vu	Next-generation translation memory tools from companies like Alchemy, Elanex, Kilgray, Lingotek, Lionbridge, and XML-Intl
Style compliance	Style guides	Authoring tools such as acrocheck and AuthorAssistant
Content creation	Standalone desktop content creation tools such as Word and FrameMaker	Open documents; XML everywhere; DITA

3. Facebook's Early Adoption of the Collaborative Translation Model

Several companies—including Facebook, Sun, Microsoft, and Plaxo—were early adopters of collaborative translation models and participated in detailed interviews with the authors about their models, including their reasons for adopting community translation processes, their challenges, lessons learned, and their recommendations for others. The findings from all four of these early adopters were documented extensively in a more comprehensive report, which includes the case study presented below

(DePalma & Kelly, 2008). Of these community translation pioneers, perhaps no company's model has received as much attention as that of Facebook. The firm even went on to apply for a patent for the specific community translation platform that it developed (Wong et al., 2008). For this reason, we have elected to describe Facebook's experience in more detail in the section that follows, focusing on the elements of its adoption of a collaborative model that serve to highlight the differences between this model and the traditional TEP model.

Facebook blended its initial reliance on translation agencies with the linguistic skills of an enthusiastic community whose members wanted to use Facebook in their languages. The company's translation process evolved into a four-step process:

(1)   **Translation.** Facebook users translate strings and sentences in the interface and help files. The site has many members, so there can be multiple translations for the same English text;

(2)   **Voting.** Members of the community vote on the translation alternatives. Popular translations rise to the top of the selection pool. Facebook maintains a leader board that shows who's who among the volunteer translators. Facebook members can override the most popular translation, but only with a compelling justification, given that these end users are considered to be the de facto experts;

(3)   **Collaboration.** Facebook's user-translators review and solve trickier or more difficult translations on discussion boards;

(4)   **Review.** Professional translators review all translations. They review which community members generate the most popular translations and the scores they receive.

Facebook provides a platform for developing applications that site members can install and run. The company used this same capability to deliver the Translation App, the application that underlies its collaborative translation process. The application works as a home page and staging point for the translation community. It highlights Facebook's three major localization steps—glossary creation, content translation, and testing and verification—and clearly indicates the progress the translation community is making toward the completion of each step, using a dashboard-type display.

Facebook built various quality control mechanisms directly into the Translation App. It automatically presents glossary entries with definitions and approved translations for the technical terms found in each translated element. And, it puts automatic checks in place to verify that capitalization and punctuation conform to style specifications for different element types. For example, if a common term such as "Like" must be capitalized in order to be considered correct, the tool would not allow a translator to submit a translation of this term without the term being capitalized. It would flag it as unacceptable and prompt the translator to fix it before it would be considered an acceptable submission. Professional reviewers use the same application as the community translators.

Determining what content to translate and into which languages can be one of the most daunting tasks for any company. To focus its planning efforts, Facebook added two triage steps to its decision-making process. Facebook began by determining which content assets had to be offered in other languages. Its analysis found 300,000 words destined for other languages, comprised of 125,000 words in user interface elements, another 125,000 in legal and help content, and 50,000 words of miscellaneous content (DePalma & Kelly, 2008). These categories reflected top translation priorities, with user interface text as the first—and in some cases, the only—content to be translated. When it comes to language selection at Facebook, not all languages are created equal. Each receives a level of support based on its strategic importance, determined largely by the number of local internet users. Supported languages get full internal support. Unsupported languages get lower levels of support or no support at all.

Facebook wished to accomplish three specific goals with its community translation initiative. First, the company wished to deliver localized sites in a fraction of the time required with conventional methods such as TEP. Notably, cost reduction was not among the factors. Second, the company wanted to ensure high quality, and to use the most appropriate terminology for the audience in question. Third, the company was motivated to bring the social networking tool (i.e., Facebook website) to more communities around the world (DePalma & Kelly, 2008).

Facebook found that collaborative translation delivered dramatic improvements in speed. Initial discussions with language service providers revealed that using traditional processes would enable the first translation to be delivered in a matter of months. Facebook believed that the size of the community would allow it to deliver the translations in days or weeks instead. Using collaborative translation, volunteers completed the Spanish and German localizations in just one week, while the French team took just 24 hours to produce its language variant (DePalma & Kelly, 2008).

The Facebook translation system brought together a unique combination of people, processes, and technology. The company needed translators with linguistic skills and subject-matter expertise, both of which could be found in its user community. Facebook confirmed that collaborative translation offered significant quality benefits because its community provided it with expert reviewers. The resulting translations met the company's requirements—they were clear and unambiguous and conveyed the meaning of the original, but they did not sound unnatural or forced.

Facebook devised a system with many conventional translation steps, such as style specification, glossary development, and linguistic quality assurance. The organizers added two important elements—immediate feedback and correction. Facebook also wanted to simplify the job for its voluntary translators, so its software platform eliminated the need for manual processing beyond translation. Due to its use of collaborative translation, Facebook was able to extend the benefits of localization to a larger international community. More Facebook users were able to interact with the service in their own languages; the process itself was conducive to creating greater brand awareness through social networking and word-of-mouth marketing. For example, a U.S.-based member working on a translation project for Colombian Spanish could easily invite friends in other countries to join the network and participate in the translation project for other national varieties of Spanish.

Application developers also benefited from Facebook's foray into international markets. The company gave Facebook members who are interested in localizing their own applications access to the same technology, language assets, and processes that it used for its own localization efforts. Facebook applied its vision and expertise in social networking to mobilize communities of user-translators. Several facets of its program stand out. One of the noteworthy features of its model is that the translation takes place fully within the community itself. While a language version is "under construction", only those members working as user-translators on that translation project can actually see what's going on with the target language.

Another unique element is that Facebook offers multiple variants of Latin American Spanish. This approach not only customizes the content for the distinct user groups, but reduces the chances of community infighting due to one nationality dictating the fate of the terminology and idioms that other members would have to live with. Facebook also uses real-time tracking to stay on top of progress. The company monitors the translation process closely, keeping this information in front of translators as a way of marking progress and keeping participants focused on the tasks at hand. The company also gives great visibility to the volunteers who do the most to make translation happen. Each language has a leader board that monitors progress and recognizes the leading contributors. It logs the total number of winning words and phrases they have submitted and the number of votes they have received.

However, in spite of its many benefits, the Facebook project also had its share of problems. First, the company found that it had to actively pursue contributions and engagement in order to keep contributors active. Second, the maintenance of the platform itself was a large chore, involving access control, scalability, and security issues. And, of course, the company struggled with some of the same quality assurance concerns that all companies deal with. Facebook also faced criticism of its user-based translation effort, primarily from observers who viewed the initiatives as a form of doing translation on the cheap. However, it is important to consider the fact that Facebook realized minimal or no cost savings from its community efforts. Its large investment in technology offset most of what it saved from getting translations from its members. It did benefit financially from translating unsupported languages, automating the localization process, and prioritizing text segments to be translated, so that localized sites can be operational sooner. In fact, commercial language service providers for supported languages translate more than half of Facebook's content, and they are paid for it. The company also engages these providers to evaluate the work of its volunteer translators (DePalma & Kelly, 2008).

4. Community translation enters the mainstream

Although community translation, also commonly referred to as crowdsourced translation due to its use of a "crowd" or a "community" to perform translation tasks, is still in its infancy from some perspectives, it is definitely spreading and becoming integrated into more traditional translation workflows. A recent study of 104 community translation platforms reveals a typology with three different environments (Ray & Kelly, 2011). The first is driven by a cause (often charitable), the second is geared toward a for-profit product or service, and the third is centered around outsourcing.

In the widely-used *cause-driven* type of collaborative translation environment, people choose content that interests them, and they translate it at their convenience. The material may relate to the latest world disaster, non-profit activities, newspaper content, videos, or anything else that attracts their attention. Volunteers are generally not remunerated in any way, but they are often recognized in some public fashion on the organization's website.

Media content is a popular cause-driven source of crowdsourced translation in many parts of the world. It covers printed content (newspapers, magazines, books), as well as audio and video. Also known as "fansubbing" or "fandubbing" when applied most typically to animation films, these sites are common in markets where there is a great demand for foreign language content that creators either don't have the resources to localize or haven't yet found what they believe to be the appropriate business model to do so.

Implementations in the *product-driven* category of collaborative translation are generally projects in which for-profit companies recruit and manage a crowd. The members of the crowd must often match a specific profile to be chosen to translate websites, software, documentation, or other content. Companies such as Adobe have adopted this model (Ray & Kelly, 2011). The volunteers are often remunerated through free products, services, or promotional merchandise from the company. As in other forms of the collaborative model, they are recognized in some fashion through leader boards, the company website, or credited on the piece of content they have helped to translate.

③. There are also outsourcing portals that offer crowdsourced translation as either their principal revenue driver or as one of their service offerings.[2] Anyone can purchase crowdsourced translation from such firms. The people who perform the language-related services are generally remunerated with actual money, not just in giveaways, praise or recognition within the community.

The actual working environment for translators, editors, and reviewers depends somewhat on the model under which they are working, as well as the type of content to be delivered. Our review of 104 community translation environments showed that there are currently three basic environments: wiki- or forum-based, database-driven, and full-blown collaborative translation platforms. The wiki-based model tends to be the simplest, but is very difficult to scale beyond just a few languages and one or two products or services. It requires no other investment than some type of wiki software or a forum, plus a part-time community moderator. It also makes it fairly easy to gauge how committed a user community might be if a larger crowdsourced initiative were launched. The database type was by far the most common environment of the sites we reviewed. These environments give users either a simple interface or a full-fledged dashboard to carry out the translation work.

The full-fledged collaborative translation platforms are the least common, but offer the most benefits, since they are built with crowdsourced translation in mind. This means that there is an underlying translation platform that provides some type of terminology management, the possibility of translation memory re-use, access to machine translation, or application programming interfaces to allow for fairly easy integration. These platforms are also usually more flexible and feature-rich when it comes to integration with existing content management systems. The downside is that this model may require more upfront and ongoing investment in maintenance or fees for cloud services. However, it pays off in the medium to long term by allowing for scalability that the other models cannot allow. Best practices for all of these environments are starting to emerge in the areas of workflow, tool design, personnel requirements, community engagement and support, remuneration, recognition, and governance.

5. Conclusions regarding the future of crowdsourced translation

In spite of growing adoption rates on the demand side of the market, crowdsourced translation is not yet very popular among language service providers and groups that represent professional translators—in other words, the supply side of the market feels that this model is a threat to the status quo (Kelly, 2009; Zetzsche, 2009). However, on the demand side of the market, research carried out on early and recent adopters of

Introductory Remarks:

LSPs are not yet convinced by the community-translation model.

[handwritten: ④ See below H address / the issues of Speed, scale and / scope, which often pose problems. / Anticipated benefit enjoyed by / the client, thanks to / Volunteer Translators]

crowdsourced translation shows that these firms are realizing its many benefits (Ray et al., 2011). In particular, crowdsourced translation allows them to engage meaningfully with potential customers and constituencies on a long-term basis.

One important element of crowdsourced translation is that it empowers the actual end users by allowing them not only to determine which terms and phrases are most accurate for their content, but to decide which content to translate in the first place. Adobe, for example, has already gone a step further with its collaborative translation in China by encouraging its users to choose the content that they think should be translated, rather than mandating what they should do. Sometimes, not all levels of content must be translated—for example, certain sub-menus that are buried deep within a software program might rarely be accessed by users, and so perhaps might not merit translation. Norton has integrated a *[handwritten: Symantec.]* terminology component to encourage its community to suggest, discuss, and validate terms. This ensures that the terms that will appear in its products are not merely terms selected by whichever individual translator happened to work on a project, as would usually be the case in a TEP process, but rather, terms that have been suggested by actual consumers of their products and services and are more likely to be understood by other prospective customers. HootSuite allows its communities to determine which languages should be implemented next. Once it reaches a certain number of community members that use a given language, they use this feedback to initiate a community or collaborative translation process (Ray et al., 2011).

[handwritten in left margin: Who are the "main players" in collaborative translation?]

In general, smaller high-tech companies (such as HootSuite) and non-profit organizations (such as Kiva.org) make up the majority of early and current adopters for collaborative translation. However, the pressure to provide more local products, services, and content at a faster rate is forcing many organizations to consider more innovative solutions, such as collaborative translation. Of course, collaborative translation is not the only solution that clients are evaluating, but rather, one of many potential options that they are exploring. Other solutions to address the challenges of speed, scale, and scope include increased usage of automated or machine translation, centralized procurement of translation services, and enhanced investment in technologies, such as global content management systems, terminology databases, translation memory tools, authoring software, and TMS products. Some organizations are also employing more in-house translation staff in order to meet the demand for quick turn-around translation within their own time zones. In other words, collaborative translation should be viewed, not as a dangerous development that threatens the profession of translation, but rather, for what it is—the market's response to specific challenges that are not being satisfactorily addressed through traditional TEP models. *[handwritten: Why collaborative translation has come about?]*

It should also be noted that it is still quite rare, on a project by project basis, for community translation to "displace" work that could

[handwritten at bottom: However, it is not the right solution for every instance of translation]

Where is community translation used?

otherwise be handled via a TEP model by professional LSPs. The fact is that community translation processes are used within online communities and lends themselves to work that can readily be handled in such spaces. In other words, these projects are handled within communities that already exist—it would not be possible for organizations to simply round up volunteers and convince them to join communities for their causes or products, nor would it be cost-effective to do so for the majority of projects. Community translation is emerging for very specific purposes and in very narrowly defined contexts. However, more and more communities are being created each day—not only on product- and cause-specific websites that are managed directly by the client organizations, but also on social networks that are external to the organizations themselves. As the world becomes increasingly connected, and as internet users for more languages become accustomed to having the ability to access content in their own languages, the willingness to sit back and wait for organizations to go through a traditional TEP process will continue to fade. If individuals already know a product and speak multiple languages, they will be tempted to go ahead and suggest terms and translations themselves in order to get the product into their language(s) faster.

Take, for example, a bilingual Latino in the United States who uses an ancestry tracking website and wants to capture family history data from a Mexican grandparent who only speaks Spanish. This person is motivated to get the interface translated into the grandparent's language and will likely be happy to spend some of his free time in order to capture his own family history data more easily. Or, consider the Chinese- and English-speaking user of a mobile phone application who would love to have her children play the game, but her children have not yet achieved full proficiency in English. Would she be willing to translate 50 phrases into Chinese, her native language, so that she can share this game with her children? Or, take the case of the mobile health worker in India who treats patients who only speak Tamil, but the simple preventive steps that she needs to share with them are available only in Hindi. Would she be willing to translate this information into her native tongue in order to save the lives of more of her patients, versus repeating this information to them verbally over and over? There are many reasons why people volunteer to translate information in community translation environments. In some cases, it gives them access to content they wish to access, enjoy, or share in other languages. For many languages, the content would not actually be translated without community translation, because the market demand does not exist in some cases.

In conclusion, the differences between the TEP model that is the status quo in the market today and the emerging community translation model are vast. However, to understand these differences, it is important to also highlight the market drivers that are causing community translation to gain popularity, as well as to acknowledge that the scenarios in which

Market driven?

community translation is used, while somewhat limited at the present time, will become increasingly common as time goes on.

References

Bass, S. (2006). Quality in the real world. In K. J., Dunne (Ed.), *Perspectives on localization* (pp. 69-84). Amsterdam: John Benjamins.

Bauer, W. (1964). *Western literature and translation work in communist China.* Hamburg: Institute für Asien Kunde, Alfred Metzner Verlag.

Cheung, M. P. Y. (Ed.). (2006). *An anthology of Chinese discourse on translation.* (Volume 1: From Earliest Times to the Buddhist Project). Manchester: St. Jerome.

DePalma, D. A., & Beninatto, R. S. (2007, December). *Collaborative translation.* Retrieved from http://www.commonsenseadvisory.com/AbstractView.aspx?ArticleID=934

DePalma, D. A., & Kelly, N. (2008, August). *Translation of, by, and for the People.* Retrieved from http://www.commonsenseadvisory.com/AbstractView.aspx?ArticleID=889

Hartley, T. (2009). Technology in translation. In J. Munday (Ed.), *The Routledge companion to translation studies.* New York: Routledge.

Kelly, N. (2011, January). *Pick up the pace: Speed as a differentiator for LSPs.* Retrieved from http://www.commonsenseadvisory.com/AbstractView.aspx?ArticleID=1310

Kelly, N., & Stewart, R. G. (2011, April). *Translation vendor management: What clients really think about language service providers.* Retrieved from http://www.commonsenseadvisory.com/AbstractView.aspx?ArticleID=1407

Kelly, N. (2009). *Freelance translators clash with LinkedIn over crowdsourced translation.* Retrieved from http://www.commonsenseadvisory.com/Default.aspx?Contenttype=ArticleDetAD&tabID=63&Aid=591&moduleId=391

Kockaert, H., & Makoushina. J. (2008). Zen and the art of quality assurance: quality assurance automation. In *Proceedings of the thirtieth international conference on translating and the computer Conference Information: Translating and the Computer* (30th ed), ASLIB, London.

Munro, R (2010). *Crowdsourced translation for emergency response in Haiti: the global collaboration of local knowledge.* Paper presented at the Association of Machine Translation for the Americas Conference, AMTA, 2010. Retrieved from http://amta2010.amtaweb.org/AMTA/papers/7-01-01-Munro.pdf

Ray, R., & Kelly, N. (2011, February). *Trends in crowdsourced translation.* Retrieved from http://www.commonsenseadvisory.com/AbstractView.aspx?ArticleID=1316

Sargent, B. B. (2010, February). *The new vortex around TMS-In-the-Cloud.* Retrieved from http://www.commonsenseadvisory.com/AbstractView.aspx?ArticleID=834

Williams, M. (2004). *Translation quality assessment: an argumentation-centred approach.* Toronto: University of Ottawa Press.

Wong, Y., Grimm, S. M., Vera, N., Laverdet, M., Kwan, T. Y., Putnam, C. W., Olivan-Lopez, J., Losse, K. P., Cox, R., & Little, C. (2008). *Community translation on a social network*, U.S. Patent Application Serial No. 329288. Washington, DC: U.S. Patent and Trademark Office.

Zaidan, O. F and Callison-Burch, C (2011). Crowdsourcing translation: Professional quality from non-professionals. In Association for Computational Linguistics (Ed.), *Proceedings of the 49th Annual Meeting of the Association for*

Computational Linguistics, (pp. 1220-1229). Portland, Oregon, June 19-24, 2011.

Zetzsche, J. (2009, November/December). About missed opportunities. *ATA Chronicle.* Retrieved http://www.internationalwriters.com/toolkit/09_Nov_Dec_Missed Opps.pdf.

---

[1] Examples of community translation tools include but are not limited to: CrowdIn (http://crowdin.net/), CrowdSight (http://www.welocalize.com), GetLocalization (http://www.getlocalization.com), GlotPress (http://trac.glotpress.org/), LingoTek (http://www.lingotek.com), Transifex (http://ww.transifex.net/). Inclusion in this list does not constitute an endorsement by the authors.

[2] Examples of outsourced community translation providers include but are not limited to: Crowdflower (http://crowdflower.com/), Microtask (http://www.microtask.com), MyGengo (http://ww.mygengo.com), OneHourTranslation (http://www.onehourtranslation.com), ServioTranslate (http://www.serv.io/translation), SpeakLike (http://www.speaklike.com), and Zhubajie (http://ww.zhubajie.com). Inclusion in this list does not constitute an endorsement by the authors.

III. ETHICAL IMPLICATIONS

The ethics of crowdsourcing

Julie McDonough Dolmaya

School of Translation, York University

Because crowdsourced translation initiatives rely on volunteer labour to support both for-profit and not-for-profit activities, they lead to questions about how participants are remunerated, how the perception of translation is affected, and how minority languages are impacted. Using examples of crowdsourced translation initiatives at non-profit and for-profit organizations, this paper explores various ethical questions that apply to translation performed by people who are not necessarily trained as translators or financially remunerated for their work. It argues that the ethics of a crowd-sourced translation initiative depend not just on whether the initiative is part of a not-for profit or a for-profit effort, but also on how the project is organized and described to the public. While some initiatives do enhance the visibility of translation, showcase its value to society, and help minor languages become more visible online, others devalue the work involved in the translation process, which in turn lowers the occupational status of professional translators.

1. Introduction

In June 2009, LinkedIn, the online professional networking platform, invited its members to complete a survey about their interest in translating the LinkedIn website. However, when respondents were asked what kinds of incentives they would expect, only non-monetary options were offered. These ranged from nothing ("because it's fun") to recognition on translation leaderboards/user profiles (e.g., "You're the #1 translator of LinkedIn in French") or an upgraded LinkedIn account.[1] Many professional translators (who represented about 50% of the 12,000 survey respondents) took offence to being asked to volunteer to translate for a commercial organization like LinkedIn, particularly one promoting itself as a networking site for professionals.[2] LinkedIn, though, argued that it was simply exploring various translation options, that novice translators would likely be interested in volunteering to help build their reputations, that crowdsourcing would not, in fact, generate savings for LinkedIn given the cost to develop a translation interface system, that adopting such an approach would allow LinkedIn to translate quickly into many languages, and that professional translators would likely be hired to review the content and provide backup translations (Newman, 2009).[3] The conflicting views of LinkedIn and these professional translators aptly illustrates the ethical questions surrounding crowdsourced translation, which is "undertaken by unspecified self-selected individuals" in digital media spaces (O'Hagan, 2009, p. 97) and is also called user-generated (O'Hagan, 2009; Perrino, 2009), open (Cronin, 2010), community (Kelly, 2009; Ray & Kelly, 2011), and/or collaborative translation (Kelly, 2009; Ray & Kelly, 2011).

In the two years following the LinkedIn controversy, similar questions have been discussed in various sources, including translator blogs (cf., McDonough Dolmaya, 2011), professional journals (e.g., Baer, 2010; Guyon, 2010; Dodd, 2011), industry reports (e.g., DePalma & Kelly, 2008; Ray, 2009; Ray & Kelly, 2011) and academic journals (e.g., O'Hagan, 2009; Perrino, 2009; Cronin, 2010). As one might expect, some professional translators share the same concerns as those offended by LinkedIn; Dodd, for instance, considers crowdsourcing "the exploitation of Internet-based social networks to aggregate mass quantities of unpaid labor" and worries this practice could lead to "a new *apartheid* economics of socialism for the workers, capitalism for the bosses" (Dodd, 2011, n.p.). Others, though, have been quite positive about the role of crowdsourcing in the industry and the changes this process brings to translation practice. For example, Baer (2010) argues that when crowdsourcing projects are effectively and appropriately designed, they can turn "what has been considered a threat to the translation industry" into a more acceptable and even positive model that "seed[s] collaboration between amateur and paid professional translators, provid[es] a training ground for new translation graduates, [and] expand[s] the material that gets translated, broadening access to information, and exposing more people to the translation process in all its complexity" (n.p.). Guyon (2010) pans crowdsourced translation interfaces, which often "[bear] no resemblance to the tools normally used by translators" and the fact that "for-profit corporations do not hesitate to cloak themselves in humanitarianism to convince the masses to translate their Internet products for free" (n.p.). However, he does laud the "non-hierarchized collaborative environment that is Wikipedia, [where] there are almost as many control mechanisms as there can be in the workplace, but with far more freedom of expression" (Guyon, 2010, n.p.).

This paper will critically examine the questions raised by these translation professionals, seeking not to provide definitive answers, but rather to examine several views and to study professional codes of ethics for insight. For reasons of space, three aspects of crowdsourced translation will be examined: participant remuneration, translation visibility, and the effect on minority languages. Together, these aspects encompass both the points raised by LinkedIn to justify its intention to crowdsource its website and the arguments professional translators have raised for and against crowdsourcing.

2. The ethical dilemmas posed by crowdsourcing

2.1. Remuneration

When participant remuneration in crowdsourced translation initiatives is discussed, a distinction is usually made between initiatives launched by non-profit and for-profit organizations, with the latter often subject to criticism (e.g., Guyon, 2010; Dodd, 2011). Therefore, this paper will distinguish between three types of crowdsourcing models (proposed by Ray & Kelly, 2011): product-driven, cause-driven, and outsourcing-driven. For the purposes of this paper, product-driven crowdsourced translation initiatives focus on localizing software or translating related documentation for free or open-source software projects, such as the productivity suite Open Office or the CAT tool OmegaT. Cause-driven initiatives centre around a project with a non-profit, often humanitarian mission. For instance, Global Voices Online is "a community of more than 300 bloggers and translators around the world who work together to bring you reports from blogs and citizen media everywhere, with emphasis on voices that are not ordinarily heard in international mainstream media,"[4] while the TED Open Translation Project aims to subtitle talks from the TED website, which "offers free knowledge and inspiration from the world's most inspired thinkers."[5] Finally, outsourcing-driven initiatives are launched by a for-profit company or organization that does not have a specific social or humanitarian mission but which does want to turn to the general public (namely its users) for its translating needs. Facebook and Twitter are both examples of companies that have launched outsourcing-driven initiatives.

Remuneration is such a thorny issue because it is tied to notions of professionalism: after all, as Chesterman (2001) argues, some people may not consider translation a true profession "because it does not seem to have a monopoly on a value goal that is not shared by other groups" (unlike medicine, with the goal of health or law, with the goal of justice) (p. 145); however, it is clearly a practice that "involves technical skills, is increasingly institutionalized, and seeks its own improvement via quality control systems and the training and accrediting of recruits" (p. 146). If translation is a skilled practice, then one should reasonably assume that translators deserve to be paid professional rates. For this reason, codes of practice from professional translator associations often address rates: the codes of the Asociación Guatemalteca de Intérpretes y Traductores, the Asociación Argentina de Traductores e Intérpretes and the Colegio de Traductores Públicos del Uruguay all oblige members not to charge fees significantly below specified rates; one Canadian association (the Ordre des traducteurs, terminologues et interprètes agréés du Québec) advises members to charge "fair and reasonable" fees, based on their experience, the difficulty of the text, and the importance of the project; the Irish Translators and Interpreters Association and the Spanish Asociación

Española de Traductores, Correctores e Intérpretes (Asetrad) oblige members to avoid accepting work at rates of pay unreasonably below market norms; etc. (McDonough Dolmaya, 2011). But of course, as Chesterman (2001) acknowledges, such associations have little ability to restrict accreditation and thereby prevent amateurs or non-members from setting themselves up as translators; by extension, they also have little to no authority over whether and how amateurs or non-members choose to be remunerated for translation work.

Is it ethical, then, for an organization to seek volunteers to translate its website or products, and to offer non-monetary incentives for doing so? In the case of product- or cause-driven initiatives, many professional translators would likely say Yes. The Asetrad code of ethics, for instance, allows members to accept below-market rates when translating for non-profit initiatives: in such cases members are obliged to inform clients of the market value of the translation work. Moreover, the fact that various professional translator networks such as Translators without Borders (TWB) and The Rosetta Foundation provide *pro bono* or heavily discounted services to not-for-profit organizations demonstrates the willingness of translators to volunteer their skills to support a mission or a social cause. Of course, motivations behind not-for-profit initiatives need to be critically examined: Baker (2006) notes that as an "offshoot of a commercial translation agency", TWB has conflicting humanitarian and commercial agendas (p. 159), but for reasons explored below, product- and cause-driven initiatives are not as ethically ambiguous as those launched by for-profit outsourcing-driven initiatives.[6]

If we look at how outsourcing-driven translation initiatives are often described, we get a sense of how for-profit companies are appealing to volunteers. Here are examples from initiatives launched between 2008 and 2011 by three social networking platforms:

> The HootSuite Translation Project was launched in August, 2010 with a goal to unite HootSuite users all across the world and enable them to use their favorite social media tools in their native languages. [...] It's an easy to use, crowd-sourced project where a few hundred owls can work to help make thousands of international hoot-fans happy. (http://blog.hootsuite.com/translation/)

> The Translations application by Facebook allows translators all over the world to translate Facebook into different languages. Join our community of translators and make Facebook available to everyone, everywhere, in all languages. (http://www.facebook.com/translations/)

Twitter has become a valuable tool for folks to exchange timely bits of information, whether it be a momentous news event, a personal story, or a random thought. We want everyone in the world to have the opportunity to engage in this important exchange, so we're calling on the help of real Twitterers to translate our site into their own language. You've helped define what's important about the product, so you should define your local experience, too. (http://support.twitter.com/articles/434816-about-twitter-translate)

In such texts, two arguments encourage user participation. First, HootSuite, Facebook and Twitter appeal to users' sense of community. The "thousands of international hoot-fans" who will be made happy by the translated user interface are, just like the "few hundred" potential translators, existing HootSuite users. The international users are disadvantaged, however, since they cannot access HootSuite in their native language; HootSuite translators would therefore be helping out fellow community members. Facebook does not make this same argument, but it does depict the translators as a "community." Finally, Twitter clearly emphasizes the role users can play in shaping Twitter, telling them to "define [their] local experience." In this case, users are working together to create something from which they will all benefit: a local version of Twitter.

This appeal to a user's sense of community seems to support Howe's (2008) argument that:

What unites all successful crowdsourcing efforts is a deep commitment to the community. This entails much more than lip service and requires a drastic shift in the mind-set of a traditional corporation. The crowd wants to feel a sense of ownership over its creations, and is keenly aware when it is being exploited. The company, in this context, is just one more member of the community and you don't have to watch Survivor to know that people who act duplicitously are kicked off the island. (pp. 15-16)

Interestingly, in Howe's view, the people (i.e., the crowd) possess the power: they determine whether they are being exploited and refuse to contribute to the crowdsourcing effort if they feel this is the case. Yet, this argument is a little too simplistic: it places the onus almost entirely on the crowdsourcers rather than the companies behind the crowdsourced initiatives. If we follow Howe's argument to its logical conclusion, every crowdsourced translation initiative in which people are participating must be ethical, because if the participants felt they were being exploited, they wouldn't participate. But what if participants aren't seeing beyond the "community" argument when they decide to translate for companies like

HootSuite, Twitter and Facebook?

After all, underlying these community-centred narratives is often a second argument: translators will help make the user interface accessible around the world to people outside the community. Thus, Twitter wants "everyone in the world to have the opportunity to engage in this important exchange," and Facebook translators will help "make Facebook available to everyone, everywhere." This latter argument is more problematic, as the companies are indicating that their motivations for translating their websites are not just a seemingly altruistic desire to give existing users a better experience (as the "community" narrative implies). A translated user interface will help Facebook, Twitter (and even HootSuite, although this is not explicitly mentioned) reach more users and therefore generate more revenue. Existing users may benefit from the translation by getting access to a "local" or "native-language" version, but the company benefits as well by getting access to users outside the existing community.

As Van Dijck & Nieborg (2009) argue, though not about translation in particular:

> [There is a] significant distinction between users of commercially driven online communities and not-for-profit, community-based exchange sites. [...] Most people who visit usergenerated content sites are 'driven' there by (viral) forms of social media ('friends' networks) or by plain marketing mechanisms. [...] What is designated as 'collectivity' or 'mass creativity' is often the result of hype from networking activity—a type of activity heavily pushed by commercially driven social platforms and aggregator sites. Established companies as well as e-commerce firms are looking for ways to engage with their customers online, to harness their knowledge potential and to engage in a meaningful dialogue. [...] To align all kinds of user motives for online participation as community driven is a rhetorical ploy popular among advertisers, who like to present telephone companies as being in the business of 'connecting people' or who promote credit card companies as 'facilitators of love and affection.' (pp. 863-864)

For Van Dijck & Nieborg, then, participants might not even realize they're being exploited, because they're unable to see through the "marketing mechanisms", "hype", and "rhetorical ploys." Moreover, because networks such as Facebook and Twitter do not cost any money to join, users may forget these services are earning (considerable) advertising revenue precisely because they are free.[7] Users may thus feel obliged to "give back" to the (ostensibly) free communities, even though Facebook and Twitter are for-profit ventures. The entire crowdsourcing initiative becomes suspect, because its community-centred focus is a device used to generate interest, commitment and involvement with a brand or company, which ultimately helps attract more users and thereby generate more revenue for the company. Thus, it is difficult to say for sure whether participants who want to contribute are indeed willing or whether they have been driven to participate—at least in part—by various marketing mechanisms. This makes the ethics of these initiatives murky at best.

2.2 Translation visibility

Because participants in crowdsourced translation initiatives are typically not financially remunerated, their efforts are often recognized in other ways, including optional "translator" badges (e.g., Wikipedia, Twitter), links to the translator's website or profile page (e.g., TED Open Translation Project, Der Mundo, Facebook, HootSuite, Kiva), photos of translators (e.g., TED, Global Voices Online, Der Mundo, Facebook, Hootsuite),[8] and translator leaderboards or top contributors page (e.g., HootSuite, Facebook, Twitter).

This kind of recognition provides visibility for more than just participating translators: as Cronin (2010) argues, crowdsourcing makes the general public more aware of the "demands of translation for large groups of global users" (2010, p. 4). As Dam & Zethsen (2008) argue in their study of the perceived occupational status of in-house Danish translators, the visibility of a profession contributes to its status (pp. 74-75); thus, by publicizing the activities of volunteer translators, crowdsourcing initiatives are helping translation become a more visible practice.

Yet visibility alone will not make translation seen as a high-status profession. As Dam & Zethsen note, educational requirements, money, power, worthiness and value to society are generally parameters Westerners associate with job prestige (p. 74). Crowdsourced translation initiatives usually do try to prove the worth of translation, as the above quotes from Facebook, HootSuite and Twitter demonstrate (it will help make Facebook "available to everyone, everywhere, in all languages", "thousands of international hoot-fans happy", etc.)—after all, if participants could not be convinced translation was a worthwhile activity with value for the community, they would probably not volunteer for the task.

The problem lies with the other parameters, particularly educational requirements and money: in a crowdsourced translation initiative, the most visible work is done by unpaid volunteers who do not necessarily have any formal translation training. The consequences, though, are varied. Some initiatives stress the difficulty of translation (e.g., TED),[9] implement a barrier to participation (e.g., Kiva, which gives applicants a translation test), and review submissions prior to publication (e.g., TED). Here, the status of translation is markedly higher, since the practice is depicted as beyond the skill of some people. Moreover, when the initiative is cause- or product-driven (as with TED and Kiva), the fact that participants are not financially remunerated is not as important, given the additional value of volunteering for a worthy cause, and the fact that translation is not the only unpaid activity. For instance, open-source software is created by volunteer developers, so it is not inappropriate for the translating to also be done by volunteers. Likewise, the TED Open Translation Project indicates that while translators are not paid, neither were the TED speakers whose videos are being subtitled.[10] Such projects highlight the difficulty and value of translation and therefore help enhance its visibility in society. They also provide a platform for the general public to gain more exposure to translation, and for novice translators to gain more practical experience. O'Hagan (2009, p.110), for instance, has suggested that fan translation networks can provide training environments for novices, so crowdsourced initiatives such as TED or Kiva could act in a similar way, though more research in this area, such as surveys of volunteers to determine how many obtained paid opportunities due to their participation, is needed.

Other initiatives, though, stress the "fun" and "easy" aspects of translation (e.g., Flock Localization Program,[11] Twitter),[12] point out that anyone—regardless of their second-language skills—can participate (e.g., Traduwiki)[13] and make the community responsible for quality control (e.g., Facebook), regardless of whether these users have any formal training in translation. Virtually all professional translator associations would object to this approach: seventeen codes of ethics studied by McDonough Dolmaya (2011) prohibit translators from accepting work for which they do not have the required competence, and six include restrictions on whether members should translate into a language they do not master like a native speaker. Moreover, when initiatives do not emphasize the difficulty of the translation process, the (generally amateur) bilinguals who participate are the visible face of translation, even if professional translators are hired to approve the final submissions, as sometimes happens (Baer, 2010).[14] The public perception of translation may therefore be lowered: it is portrayed as a task easily accomplished by anyone who speaks more than one language, however competently. When such initiatives are also outsourcing-driven, participants are helping a for-profit company reach new markets rather than helping a not-for-profit organization advance a social or political cause, which reduces the "worthiness" parameter that would help raise translation's status. This, in turn, helps depict translation as a task requiring little formal training (since virtually any bilingual Internet user can contribute), more suitable for a hobby than a profession (since companies like Twitter, Facebook and HootSuite do not appear to be paying for such fun and easy work).[15]

2.3 Translation and "minor" languages

While crowdsourcing does not always enhance the visibility and status of translation, its user-generated (O'Hagan, 2009; Perrino, 2009) nature could help reduce the uneven way language versions of software and websites have traditionally been made available. As Esselink (2000) argues: "Historically, the largest markets for localized products have been France, Germany and Japan. Medium-sized markets include Brazil, Italy, Spain, Sweden, Norway, and the Netherlands. Software publishers typically localize their products into FIGS (French, Italian, German and Spanish) and Japanese first. Swedish, Norwegian, Danish, Dutch or Brazilian Portuguese often follow as second tier languages" (p. 8). Similarly, Pym has noted that the extent to which a product will be localized depends not only on the current or potential target market size, but also on the extent of diversity within the market (2004). Thus, when companies are deciding whether to localize their websites for a Spanish-speaking market, they base their decision not on just the number of potential users in Mexico, for instance, but also on how many users in other regions also speak Spanish, since relatively minor changes could make the Mexican version suitable for other Spanish-speaking markets. Spanish would therefore be a more lucrative language than Finnish, for instance, which is not spoken in many regions outside Finland. When languages are considered in this way, markets with a small number of potential customers will get less (if any) translated content than areas where users speak languages used in several other markets.

On the surface, the user-generated nature of crowdsourcing could change this trend: after all, if users would like a Finnish translation, they simply have to prepare it themselves, once the translation interface is made available. In fact, various crowdsourced translation initiatives allow users to suggest or add languages (e.g., anobii.com; TED; Wikipedia; Flock;[16] OpenOffice;[17] Global Voices Online;[18] Twitter;[19] Facebook).[20] Accordingly, in some projects, "minor" languages are given the same attention as typical Tier 1 languages such as French, Italian, German and Spanish.[21] Thus, by March 2011, TED Talks had been subtitled for more than 80 languages, and while the three languages with the most translated talks were Spanish, French and Brazilian Portuguese (with more than 800 talks each), Bulgarian was a close fourth. In fact, more talks were available in Romanian (700+), Polish (600+), Turkish (600+) and Hebrew (600+), than German (500+), Japanese (400+), Dutch (400+), Swedish (100+) or Danish (50+).[22] Global Voices Online, another cause-driven translation initiative has similar results: although only seventeen languages are listed as "regularly updated," several would be considered minor, including Malagasy, Serbian, Swahili, Macedonian, Bangla, and Indonesian. As the Global Voices Lingua page notes, "the languages chosen reflect the momentum in their community of speakers," meaning site users largely determine the languages chosen for translation, the frequency at which the translated sites are updated, and the amount of information available in a given language.

And yet, target languages will inevitably be prioritized, even if user demand drives the initiative. Languages with more speakers online will have a larger community from which to draw volunteers, and so Spanish, French and Portuguese speakers, for instance, are likely to complete their localized versions before Swahili speakers, even if an interface is made available to all four communities at the same time. This fact is exemplified by the HootSuite Translation Project page (http://translate.hootsuite.com/), where bar graphs indicate that languages such as Japanese, French, Spanish, and Italian are almost completed and have recent activity, while versions like Romanian, Polish, Persian, Welsh, Czech, Chinese and Ukrainian remain virtually untouched, with the last activity over a year earlier. Even Facebook, available in 64 languages within three years of the 2008 launch of its first translated version, began with Spanish and then added French and German several weeks later (Arrington, 2008) instead of opening up the application to dozens of languages at once. And project-driven initiatives such as Thunderbird or OpenSolaris often have two or more language tiers with varying priority levels.[23]

Crowdsourced translation initiatives may appear to break down limitations on language availability (and in some cases, such as TED's Open Translation Project, they actually do result in major and minor languages receiving similar attention), but in some initiatives, they allow an organization to demonstrate its willingness to make a language version available, while making the community responsible for actually completing the translation. The fact that users request a target language does not mean it will ever be completed, nor does it automatically mean a minor language will be accessible before languages such as Spanish, French and German, the likely priorities of a non-crowdsourced project.

3. Conclusions

Clearly, the ethical implications of crowdsourced translation depend not just on whether the initiative supports an open-source project, a non-profit cause, or a for-profit service, but also on how the project is organized and described to the public. Although participants are generally not financially remunerated, crowdsourcing initiatives can still enhance the visibility of translation, showcase its value to society, and help minor languages become more visible online. Moreover, participants can still enjoy non-financial benefits: the satisfaction of supporting a cause, more exposure to the translation process, greater visibility for themselves as translators, etc.

On the other hand, it is difficult for outsourcing-driven translation initiatives to enhance the public perception of translation, particularly if such initiatives do not emphasize the skill and training involved in the process. This devalues the work involved in the translation process and contributes to lowering the occupational status of professional translators. This in turn challenges the idea that translation is a skilled practice requiring training, accreditation and quality control systems. Further, it affects the future of translation: by pushing professional translators into the shadows as the unseen and unknown revisers of the publicly visible (and often novice) volunteers, many crowdsourcing models are likely to leave only revision and consulting as areas of paid translation-related work, which may lead to this kind of work being seen as higher status activities than translation.

Finally, outsourcing-driven initiatives may appear to empower crowds, allowing them to determine what languages will be made available and how content will sound in the target language, but through marketing mechanisms, they also exploit participants' commitment to friends and family within the TL community, helping to make them feel they ought to help these TL speakers access website content in their own language. Moreover, these initiatives shift the responsibility for translation onto users, perhaps foreshadowing both a greater blurring of the distinction between translation consumers and producers, and a shift in the way translation is viewed, produced and received by Internet users, corporations, and translators themselves.

References

Arrington, M. (2008, January 21). Facebook taps users to create translated versions of site. Spanish, French and German available now. *TechCrunch*. Retrieved from http://techcrunch.com/2008/01/21/facebook-taps-users-to-create-translated-versions-of-site/

Baer, N. (2010, February 1). Crowdsourcing: Outrage or opportunity? *Translorial: Journal of the Northern California Translators Association*. Retrieved from http://translorial.com/2010/02/01/crowdsourcing-outrage-or-opportunity/

Baker, M. (2006). *Translation and conflict: A narrative account*. London: Routledge.

Boéri, J. (2008). A narrative account of the Babels vs. Naumann controversy: Competing perspectives on activism in conference interpreting. *The Translator, 14*(1), 21-50.

Chesterman, A. (2001). Proposal for a hieronymic oath. *The Translator, 7*(2), 139-154.

Cronin, M. (2010). The translation crowd. *Revista tradumàtica, 8*. Retrieved from http://www.fti.uab.cat/tradumatica/revista/num8/articles/04/04.pdf

Dam, H. V., & Zethsen, K. K. (2008). Translator status: A study of Danish company translators. *The Translator, 14*(1), 71-96.

Depalma, D. A., & Kelly, N. (2008). *Translation of, for and by the people: How user-translated content projects work in real-life*. Lowell, Ma: Common Sense Advisory.

Dodd, S. M. (2011, January 1). Crowdsourcing: Social[ism] Media 2.0, *Translorial: Journal of the Northern California Translators Association*. Retrieved from http://translorial.com/2011/01/01/crowdsourcing-socialism-media-2-0/

Esselink, B. (2000). *A practical guide to localization*. Amsterdam: John Benjamins.

Guyon, A. (2010). The ups and downs of online collaborative translation. P. Beaudry (Translated into English. French original 'Grandeurs et misères de la traduction collaborative en ligne'). *L'Actualité langagière, 7*(1). Retrieved from http://www.btb.gc.ca/btb.php?lang=eng&cont=1536

Howe, J. (2008). *Crowdsourcing: Why the power of the crowd is driving the future of business*. New York: Random House.

McDonough Dolmaya, J. (2011). A window into the profession: What translation blogs have to offer Translation Studies. *The Translator, 17*(1), 77-104.

McDonough Dolmaya, J. (2011). Moral ambiguity: Some shortcomings of professional codes of ethics for translators. *Journal of Specialised Translation, 15*, 28-49.

Newman, A. A. (2009, June 29). Translators wanted at LinkedIn. The pay? $0 an hour. *The New York Times, B2*. Retrieved from http://www.nytimes.com/2009/06/29/technology/start-ups/29linkedin.html

O'Hagan, M. (2009). Evolution of user-generated translation: Fansubs, translation hacking and crowdsourcing. *Journal Of Internationalisation and Localisation, 1*(1), 94-121.

Perrino, S. (2009). User-generated translation: The future of translation in a Web 2.0 environment. *Journal of Specialised Translation, 12, 55-78*.

Pym, A. (2004). *The moving text: Localization, translation and distribution*. Amsterdam: John Benjamins.

Ray, R. (2009). *Crowdsourcing: The crowd wants to help you reach new markets*. Romainmôtier, Switzerland: Localization Industry Standards Association.

Ray, R., & Kelly, N. (2011). *Crowdsourced translation: Best practices for implementation*. Lowell, Ma: Common Sense Advisory.

Sargent, Benjamin B. (2008, August 14). Community translation lifts Facebook to top of social networking world. *Common Sense Advisory Blogs*. Retrieved from http://www.commonsenseadvisory.com/Default.aspx?Contenttype=ArticleDetAD&tabID=63&Aid=525&moduleId=391

Van Dijck, J., & Nieborg, D. (2009). Wikinomics and its discontents: A critical analysis of Web 2.0 business manifestos. *New Media & Society, 11*(5), 855-874.

---

[1] The survey question is reproduced in the blog post Spanish/English translator Matthew Bennett wrote on the topic: http://www.matthewbennett.es/1094/crowdsourcing-translations-and-linkedin-a-response-to-the-global-watchtower-opinion/. The results of this survey question, along with a discussion between blog readers and LinkedIn representative Nico Posner, are published on LinkedIn's blog at: http://blog.linkedin.com/2009/06/19/nico-posner-translating-linkedin-into-many-languages/

[2] By March 2011, the Translators against Crowdsourcing by Commercial Businesses Group at LinkedIn had over 450 members. See its profile page at: http://www.linkedin.com/groups?about=&gid=2032092&trk=anet_ug_grppro

[3] LinkedIn's response to Matthew Bennett's first blog post about the survey is available on Bennett's blog at: http://www.matthewbennett.es/1084/linkedin-infuriates-professional-translators-10-big-questions/

[4] From the Global Voices Online About page at: http://globalvoicesonline.org/about/

[5] From the TED About page at: http://www.ted.com/pages/about

[6] Not all professional translators agree that having volunteers translate for non-profit causes or social movements is appropriate. Boéri (2008), for instance, analyzes the letter professional interpreter Peter Naumann published in AIIC's online journal *Communicate* regarding the World Social Forum's reliance on volunteer network Babels for its interpreting needs. In this letter, Boéri argues, Naumann paralleled "the glorious past of the profession" and "the dark ages brought about by capitalism and commodification, featuring a decline in quality and standards, superficial education and ignorant interpreters, and projected as a permanent threat to the profession" (2008: 39). Similar arguments are often used by professional translators

against crowdsourced translation (e.g., many of the bloggers discussed in McDonough Dolmaya 2011).

[7] This is because sites with a larger community of users will attract more advertisers. According to a March 19, 2011 article in Canadian newspaper *The Financial Post*, Facebook earned $0.74 billion US from advertising revenue in 2009, and $1.86 billion in 2010. Twitter earned $45 million US from advertising revenue in 2010 and was expected to earn $151 million in 2011. See http://ht.ly/4hOu6

[8] Kiva, TED and Global Voices Online, for instance, credit all translated texts, providing (optional) photos of translators and links to profile pages with whatever personal or professional details translators would like to share. See, for instance, http://www.kiva.org/lend/232136, http://www.kiva.org/lend/232195 and http://www.kiva.org/lend/229118 and these translations from the Global Voices Online Spanish and French sites: http://es.globalvoicesonline.org/2010/11/12/india-obamamania/, http://es.globalvoicesonline.org/2010/11/12/blogueando-desde-la-infancia-plan-ceibal-es-una-historia-de-exito/ and http://fr.globalvoicesonline.org/2010/11/11/48730/.

[9] The Style Guidelines page notes that "TED doesn't require translators to have any formal training, but we do ask that you be fluently bilingual, and that you take seriously the role of translating another person's ideas." It asks potential translators to consider how often they read, speak and write in the target language, adding that "If you find your skills are a bit rusty, you don't necessarily have to disqualify yourself. But you should commit to the research and time it will take to achieve an accurate translation. (It helps to have a pool of fluent friends and family on-hand.)" see: http://www.ted.com/pages/view/id/295

[10] See http://www.ted.com/pages/view/id/293

[11] See the Flock L10n website: https://sites.google.com/a/flock.com/flock-l10n/home

[12] According to the About Twitter Translate page: "Using the Translation Center is a fun and easy way for you to help make Twitter accessible to more people around the world" (see: http://support.twitter.com/articles/434816-about-twitter-translate)

[13] As Traduwiki explains: "By saying anybody can translate, we really mean it. Traduwiki hashes each text into smaller chunks. They're limited to 2 phrases maximum. Each text contains lots of short, easy to understand phrases. Usually, those phrases are grouped together. Even though you think you don't know master [sic] a language enough to use it, you can get the meaning of those phrases and thus, are able to translate them." See: http://traduwiki.org/About/About

[14] Twitter, for instance, indicates that "Once we've collected a good number of translations for every phrase across the site, we will review them and pick the most accurate one." (see: http://support.twitter.com/articles/434816-about-twitter-translate)

[15] Sargeant (2008) argues that because for-profit companies such as Facebook had to pay to develop the translation interface, they are not saving money by adopting the crowdsourced translation model. However, the money they have invested in the translation interface has not gone to the participants, who are the publicly visible translators. This helps lower the status of translation, since it does not appear to be worth paying for, while IT is.

[16] See the Localization Community Site at: https://sites.google.com/a/flock.com/flock-l10n/home/how-to-translate-flock

[17] See the OpenOffice Languages page at: http://wiki.services.openoffice.org/wiki/Languages. Users are able to add languages to the list and contact a mailing list if the language they would like to work with is not on the list.

[18] The Global Voices Lingua page notes: "Any additional languages for which there is momentum will be added to Lingua." See: http://globalvoicesonline.org/lingua/#get-involved

[19] The Twitter Translation Center page (http://translate.twttr.com/welcome) tells users: "Don't see your language? We're continually reviewing the list of languages we support, and would love your feedback."

[20] A 2008 blog post by Facebook designer Chad Little indicated that 55 additional languages had been added to the Facebook Translation Application based on user demand. http://blog.facebook.com/blog.php?post=20734392130

[21] Here, "minor" is used to refer to languages that, due to the size of the market, are not typically considered "Tier 1" or "Tier 2." These are languages that, compared to English, Spanish or French (spoken by many people in several large markets), are less lucrative investments, and are therefore usually given a lower priority in localization efforts.

[22] Indeed, as the TED Open Translation Project webpage indicates, TED's approach "allows speakers of less-dominant languages an equal opportunity to spread ideas within their communities." See http://www.ted.com/pages/287

[23] The OpenSolaris supports three languages tiers: Tier 1 (English, French, German, Japanese, Simplified Chinese, Spanish) and Tier 2 (Brazilian Portuguese, Italian, Korean, Russian, Traditional Chinese) languages receive full localization support, while dozens of others are internationalized but not fully localized. See http://hub.opensolaris.org/bin/view/Community+Group+int_localization/OpenSolaris201003TestPlan The Thunderbird localization page designates 10 languages (German, French, Japanese, British English, Spanish, Italian, Polish, Russian, Dutch, and Brazilian Portuguese) as Tier 1, meaning that the US English version of Thunderbird will not be released unless all Tier 1 language versions are also ready. All others languages are Tier 2 and will not delay Thunderbird's release. See https://developer.mozilla.org/en/Thunderbird_Localization

Translation ethics wikified: How far do professional codes of ethics and practice apply to non-professionally produced translation?

Joanna Drugan

University of Leeds

Translation involves ethical decision-making in challenging contexts. Codes of practice help professional translators identify ethical issues and formulate appropriate, justifiable responses. However, new and growing forms of community translation operate outside the professional realm, and substantial differences exist between the two approaches. How relevant, then, are professional codes in the new contexts? What alternative 'codes' (stated or implicit) have been developed by the new groups? The content of professional codes is compared here to a broad range of community approaches to identify themes common across both, and areas where the new community might be making an original contribution. This reveals different priorities in the professional and non-professional codes. Community translation initiatives have found novel solutions to some ethical problems and challenges, particularly in self-regulation and community policing, improved interpretation of code content, an emphasis on shared values rather than individual rights, and strong mentoring.

1. Codes in translation: confrontation, innovation

Professional codes of ethics have a long history, dating back to at least the 18th-19th centuries in the fields of law and medicine (Davis, 2003). In the late 20th century, as translation became professionalised or 'industrialised' in Gouadec's image (2009, p. 217), dozens of codes specific to translation and interpreting were developed in countries where these activities were practised by large numbers of linguists. Most professional translation associations with an online presence today post some version of a code of professional conduct or ethics.[1] Translation followed the classic pattern of the development of a profession leading on to its public codification (Brooks, 1989). Unsurprisingly, ethical codes were collectively identified as necessary: issues raised by translation are often 'profoundly ethical, and not merely technical' (Goodwin, 2010, p. 20). (Consider, for example, such daily ethical decisions as whether to accept work for clients in sensitive medical domains like abortion; or how extreme situations of conflict and war affect the translator's role.) Codes of ethics and conduct have been developed precisely to support professionals in considering such issues and to equip them to formulate appropriate and justifiable responses.

However, emerging forms of 'community' translation[2]—*pro bono*, political/activist, crowdsourced, fan translation, free/Open Source software (FOSS) localisation—operate outside this professional framework. Substantial differences exist between the two models: non-professional translations are usually not commissioned or assigned, but voluntary; unpaid or remunerated well below professional rates; lightly or un-regulated; subject to no contractual agreement or contracted on imposed terms with no negotiation; public, not confidential; continually evolving and editable, rather than finalised and protected. The translations are often collaborative and performed by self-selecting individuals from diverse backgrounds, whether in terms of training, experience, subject knowledge, competence or membership of professional associations. Community translation is thus not bound, or even directly addressed, by the existing professional codes.

Yet there is clearly a need for translators in non-professional contexts to be able to draw on such ethical support. One of the pioneers in crowdsourced translation, Wikipedia, found it such a bruising experience that those involved concluded 'Wikipedia is 10% translation and 90% confrontation' (http://meta.wikimedia.org/wiki/Meta:Babel). Most community translation initiatives exist online, and the potentially negative impact of this environment on aspects of ethical conduct has now been widely observed; see, for example, Bannerjee et al. (1998), Loch and Conger (1996), and Warner and Raiter (2005). As Floridi (1999) summarises:

> Because of the remoteness of the process, the immaterial nature of information and the virtual interaction with faceless individuals, the information environment (the infosphere) is easily conceived of as a magical, political, social, financial dream-like environment, and anything but a real world, so a person may wrongly infer that her actions are as unreal and insignificant as the killing of enemies in a virtual game. (p. 40)

The present article takes the leading professional codes as its starting point: how far are these appropriate or helpful in the new, challenging non-professional contexts? To illustrate the differences between the two models, themes common across the leading professional codes are identified, then a case study of one non-professional translation approach is outlined and mined for insights into how ethical issues are handled in the new community translation contexts. It is argued that the new translation communities are developing their own distinct, often tacit or implicit, 'codes' of ethics and practice.

Désilets (2007) first pointed to the emerging 'wikification' of translation, suggesting that the new model might have much to offer for established approaches to translation.

> Massive online collaboration might change the rules of the game for translation, by sometimes introducing new problems, sometimes enabling new and better solutions to existing problems, and sometimes introducing exciting new opportunities that simply were not on our minds before. (2007, n.p.)

Some such potential changes, solutions and opportunities lie in the important area of ethical behaviour. Certain community endeavours are breaking new ground in ethical translation activity - cf. initiatives such as high-speed MT and SMS/GPS addressing the translation needs of Haitians after the earthquake (Lewis, 2010; Munro, 2010). Professional translation might thus also be able to profit from the wisdom of non-professionals: the conclusion of this article summarises potential lessons from the new model and further questions raised by it Among an increasingly vocal chorus making bleak predictions for today's professional 'class' of translators (e.g., Gouadec, 2009), Garcia foresees 'an approaching future in which translation may once again be the realm of the gifted amateur or keen bilingual subject specialist', with professional translators working in 'low-paid, call-centre conditions' (2009, p. 199, p. 211). A final reason that these non-professional approaches to ethics matter, then, is that the context in which they were developed may one day prevail. Enlightened self-interest should lead professional translators to consider them carefully.

2. Methodology: Selection of ethical codes and community equivalents

There are many studies of ethical codes in one individual field (e.g., for accounting, information science or medicine), but thus far only one published study of codes particular to the translation profession (McDonough Dolmaya, 2011). There is no prior study comparing translation-specific codes with those of other professions, or with equivalents in non-professional contexts.

McDonough Dolmaya (2011) examined seventeen translation-specific ethical codes from fifteen countries, identifying common principles; she then compared these to professional translators' ethical concerns in online forums to identify gaps in the guidelines. The present study includes ten of the codes considered by McDonough Dolmaya and fourteen additional translation-specific codes, covering nineteen countries and three international organisations; all of these are available online in English or French, the languages available to the author (see Appendix 1). The selected codes were analysed (or re-analysed, in the case of those considered by McDonough Dolmaya) in order to categorise the ethical issues and principles they addressed—and those they did not. These broad categories for translation ethics were then compared to those identified in professional codes from other disciplines in the few cross-discipline studies available and in several discipline-specific studies from other fields.

For non-professional translation contexts, an online sample was again gathered, including some of the longest-running and largest community translation initiatives and again targeting those available in either English or French. See Appendix 2 for a list of the sixteen accessible sources analysed here; the corpus analysed for the present study also included four non-public 'codes' or agreements, provided to the author by community translation providers or organisations.[3] Two differences with the professional context were immediately apparent. First, community translation is more diverse and sometimes operates outside the law, e.g. bootleg fan translations. Second, non-professional ethical 'codes' were often not presented as such. Recognisable 'code-like' content was identified in files described as community guidelines, terms of service, user agreements, founding principles, charters, guiding principles, site rules, terms and conditions, cornerstones, manifestos, bylaws, policies and protocols. 'Code-type' content was also presented inside other material, e.g., FAQs and user-generated bulletin boards/chat rooms/threads dedicated to issues of ethics or conduct.

The two sets of translation 'code' content are compared in the next section, and a table presents these alongside typical code content from other professions. Following this, in Section 4, a brief discussion of a community translation case study focuses on how some gaps in the professional codes might be being addressed by emerging practice.

3. Comparing professional and non-professional codes

Comparative studies of codes of ethics across two or more *different* professions are scarce but point to a 'common base' for such codes,[4] in that they all 'address the problem of moral hazard, provide the norms of professional courtesy, and define the public interest' (Higgs-Kleyn & Kapelianis, 1999, 367). Codes in such analyses are often categorised by approach, as in Frankel's three types: 'aspirational' (those which focus on setting out ideals), 'educational' (those which provide commentary, improving understanding of issues) and 'regulatory' (those which lay down rules to govern professional conduct and adjudicate in cases of grievances); a code can contain elements of more than one type (1989, p. 109).Beyond this broad-brush common base, more specific shared concerns are found in the professional translation codes, as would be expected. Künzli's examination of ethical aspects of translation revision draws out 'commitment to the highest standards of performance, willingness to improve one's skills and knowledge, adaptability, discretion, professional appearance and loyalty' (2007, p. 24), for instance.

Table 1 allows comparison of translation-specific professional codes with the non-professional translation approaches sampled here and with those of some other professions. In the first column, it lists the ten most common principles or themes identified in translation-specific professional codes, in descending order, based on their frequency across the corpus considered for the present article. Next, the ten most common concerns in the community translation context, based on the sample considered here, are listed in descending order, based on their frequency across the corpus considered for the present article. Finally, in the third column, themes in other professions' codes are taken from the few comparative cross-profession studies available, including Brooks (1989), Davis (2003), Frankel (1989) and Koehler and Pemberton (2000); obvious caveats are that the lists for these cross-profession studies are now dated and generally restricted to North America. These themes are listed in alphabetical order rather than in order of frequency, as data were not always sufficiently precise or directly comparable, given the range of sources from which they were drawn. This table is not comprehensive, given the obvious problems of access to representative contemporary data for all professions. Nonetheless, the pattern of the main themes important in each context can be identified through this approach.

Joanna Drugan

Table 1: Comparison of professional translation codes with non-translation and community translation 'codes'

Professional Translation	Community Translation	Other Professions
Competence	General statement of philosophy (values, vision)	Competence
Confidentiality, trustworthiness	=2 Conduct of contributors	Conduct of personnel
Solidarity with other translators, professional loyalty	=2 Legal responsibilities	Confidentiality, trustworthiness
=4 General statement of philosophy	=4 'Client' right to block participation	Conflict of interest; impartiality
=4 Conflict of interest, impartiality	=4 Prohibitions (cheating, porn, spamming, trolling etc)	Customer needs and relations
Client needs and relations	=6 Competence	General statement of philosophy
=7 Quality of work	=6 Impersonation (use real identity, verifiable email address, confirm age)	Legal responsibilities
=7 Conduct of personnel, general behaviour	Confidentiality, trustworthiness	Product or service-related commentary
=9 Legal responsibilities	=9 Duty to report violations of code	Shareholders, stakeholders
=9 Commitment to ongoing professional development	=9 Ownership of translations	Social issues

Examining the themes in codes comparatively serves to highlight both similarities and some revealing differences between professional and non-professional approaches, which will now be summarised. First, there are evident conflicts, contradictions and gaps. Such problems are not unique to translation codes: they have previously been noted for other professional contexts (e.g., Savan, 1989). For instance, provisions around confidentiality are placed high in the concerns of most professional codes, but they also stress the duty of translators to report any suspected illegal activities or illicit content to the authorities (Wagner, 2005). How is the individual translator to resolve these conflicting duties with confidence? Künzli (2007) outlines a range of similar conflicts relating to loyalty and duties as outlined in professional codes: is the translator's primary allegiance then to the client, ST author, profession, or himself? Higgs-Kleyn and Kapelianis (1999) suggest that loyalty to the client usually trumps the other interests, as he is paying for the work; but as Künzli stresses, such issues can hardly be solved satisfactorily by individuals. There is a role here for translators' associations to address such dilemmas as the conflict between professional demands for speed and low cost, and the ethical commitment to 'thoroughness, reliability or quality' (2007, p. 53).

As well as conflicts within individual codes, there are contradictions and conflicts *across* different professional codes. This is important when we consider that translators are often bound by multiple codes simultaneously. For instance, a UK translator might well be a member of the Institute of Translation and Interpreting (ITI) and Chartered Institute of Linguists (CIoL), while carrying out work for a company which subscribes to the Association of Translation Companies (ATC) code and has also signed up to the Unesco Translator's Charter. Which code should have priority where there are conflicting provisions across a range of codes? Brooks sees a role for an ethical "ombudsman" in such scenarios (1989).

A final way in which professional codes fail translators is that there are gaps in their provisions, notably in interpreting the codes. If key terms such as accuracy are not defined clearly, translators 'may actually be endorsing slightly different values' without realising it (McDonough Dolmaya, 2011, p. 34). Similarly, gaps in enforcing ethical provisions are often raised in criticisms of professional codes. Professionals in different fields typically believe that 'their peers contravene their professional codes relatively often' (Higgs-Kleyn & Kapelianis, 1999, p. 363), yet there are few mechanisms to monitor non-compliance or reward the bravery of whistle-blowers (Higgs-Kleyn & Kapelianis, 1999, p. 365).

Despite their limitations, professionals surveyed for studies of other disciplines' codes overwhelmingly viewed their codes as necessary: an average of 81.8% saw them as 'very necessary' in one study of three professions (Higgs-Kleyn & Kapelianis, 1999, p. 369). If, despite their flaws, professionals view them so positively, they are clearly addressing a real need, at least in part. How then do community approaches address this need? Might their emerging strategies complement or complete existing professional codes?

As Table 1 makes clear, the non-professional codes (and equivalent documents) reveal different priorities. Most non-professional approaches emphasise two strategies in tandem. First, they typically place shared values and an explicit community vision much higher on the agenda than professional codes do. Over three-quarters of the codes from non-professional communities begin with a clear and often passionately expressed outline of the community's shared goals, frequently running into several hundreds of words, whereas this is very rare and significantly shorter where it is found in professional codes. The second common feature which can be observed far more strongly in the non-professional codes might seem initially contradictory. Whereas professional codes barely mention sanctions if members fail to respect their provisions, the non-professional equivalents almost invariably list very detailed potential infractions (from posting images of other users without their consent, to lying about one's age or stalking others) and the potential consequences. The most important issues in professional contexts, including confidentiality and competence, are still recognised, but much lower down the list of priorities; they are entirely absent from quite a few non-professional codes.

Instead, we see a new emphasis on community policing in the non-professional contexts. The professional codes rarely suggest members have a duty to monitor one another, but community codes make this explicit and frame it positively. There was another noticeable difference in emphasis here, with professional codes stressing members' duty of loyalty to one another, while the new communities seemed to have a different implicit concept of what being community-minded might mean. Loyalty here is to the community as a whole, rather than to potentially challenging individual *confrères*.

Interestingly, this different emphasis in the new codes addresses criticisms made by ethicists of many professional codes. The crucial importance of 'organizational culture' or 'climate' in fostering ethical behaviour has been repeatedly stressed as a significant gap in existing codes (Higgs-Kleyn & Kapelianis, 1999, p. 366). In summary, the standard non-professional approach (insofar as there is one) would be to emphasise the positive first (stress shared values, play to altruism), then make sure basic ground rules and monitoring are robustly in place to prevent the seemingly inevitable abuse.

A case study of a leading community translation approach can now help draw out how these strategies work in practice.

4. Case study: FOSS localisation

One of the most successful community translation endeavours has been the localisation of Free and Open Source Software (FOSS). Volunteers have collaborated online both to develop and localise software into a large number of the world's languages, particularly targeting those spoken by millions in developing countries with little access to standard ICT. FOSS is often presented by those involved in its development and use as ethical *per se* – challenging the monopolies of software developers, bridging the digital divide and bringing the communications revolution to millions who would otherwise be left behind. As Stallman summarises, "The term free software refers to the social and ethical importance of freedom, as well as to the practical benefits it brings" (Souphavanh & Karoonboonyanan, 2005, p. 7). It might be tempting to assume that the FOSS localisation community's shared goals and high ideals would lead naturally and unproblematically to shared ethical standards; but this assumption is disproved compellingly by this case study.

It is quickly apparent when reading FOSS user codes or home pages that abusive behaviour dogs the initiatives. The second point in the Sun Open Community Translation Interface Terms of Use relates to prohibitions including,

> unlawful, threatening, libelous, defamatory, obscene, pornographic, or profane material, any software virus, worm, or other material of a disruptive or destructive nature. [… Users] are further prohibited from using this Website to: (a) transmit spam, bulk or unsolicited communications; (b) pretend to be Sun or someone else, or spoof Sun's or someone else's identity; […] (e) disrupt the normal flow of dialogue or otherwise act in a manner that negatively affects Users' ability to use this Website. (n.p.)

All FOSS initiatives seem to face issues of spamming, trolling (deliberately posting inflammatory messages), angry reactions, impersonation, intentional harassment of other users and other disruptive behaviour – it is instructive to note how many new terms have been coined just for abusive behaviour in specific web contexts. Marshall (1999) has attributed this in part to Ogburn's "cultural lag" theory—that there is an inherent conflict between the rapid speed of modern technological advances and the slower speed by which ethical guidelines for their utilization are developed. Yet despite the barrage of unethical conduct (or perhaps, rather, precisely because they had to react to it), FOSS localisation initiatives have found novel solutions to ethical problems in non-professional translation.

In FOSS contexts, volunteers are involved in translation with no screening as to their competence or commitment. We might expect that any ethical commitment to professionalism, as stressed in professional translation codes, would be impossible. As Table 1 summarises, professional codes emphasise the need to address such issues as respecting deadlines, and only taking on work for which you are qualified and which you have the necessary resources to complete effectively. In FOSS contexts, these expectations are impossible. Instead of placing the onus on translators to ensure they are competent and ready to meet targets, systems are in place to support the volunteers so such issues are less problematic. Volunteers share the workload across large teams, with effective support through mentoring, specific discussion threads on technical (and other) themes, meaning that any potential lack of comprehension of the ST, for instance, is easily addressed by other motivated volunteers. Large online terminology databases with clear definitions have been drawn up by volunteers and amplified or amended as localisation took place. In contradiction of the professional aversion to admitting ignorance or "bothering" the client with queries, FOSS volunteers are actively encouraged to question ST sense and previous translators' (and developers') work. There are often "Report" features or voting mechanisms to signal issues with other participants' work.

Self-regulation by the community seems to work quite successfully on issues beyond professionalism too (banning nuisance members, reactions to trolling, the community coming together to shame abusers or denounce 'unnecessary complaining'), unlike many professionals who have a 'poor track record in this regard' (Frankel, 1989, p. 113), partly because there are 'too few rewards and too many risks' (Frankel, 1989, p. 114). It is difficult to see what rewards there might be in FOSS contexts either, and there are presumably risks there too (for instance, if you respond to the trolls, you are likely to be attacked more vehemently). Perhaps the community's strong commitment to a shared endeavour with noble aims, and knowledge that there will be support from peers, is the key to participants' willingness to react.

Among others, Frankel also recommends the institution of positive mechanisms to encourage "those who exhibit exemplary ethical behaviour" (Frankel, 1989, p.114) and this is a common feature in online community translation and FOSS, with features such as 'badges', kudos points and the possibility to become a (volunteer) 'leader' or mentor for others. An encouraging community atmosphere is also important to keep contributors coming back, normally through support and strong, inspiring leadership: the "Benevolent Dictatorship Principle" (Howe, 2008, p. 284). As the man who claims to have coined the term crowdsourcing stresses, 'communities need community leaders' (Howe, 2008, p. 285).

5. Conclusion: Solutions and further questions

Do the non-professional codes and case study offer any lessons for translation professionals and their codes? One encouraging example lies in the issue of interpretation of professional codes. As noted, a common criticism of professional codes in the past has been that there is a need for shared interpretation of the underlying meaning of key provisions. For Frankel (1989),

> The profession must institutionalize a process whereby its moral commitments are regularly discussed and assessed in the light of changing conditions both inside and outside the profession. The widespread participation of members in such an effort helps to reinvigorate and bring into sharp focus the underlying values and moral commitments of their profession. (p. 112)

To achieve this kind of ongoing reflection, Brooks has argued that professionals can find that 'discussion groups or case studies are helpful in fleshing out the meaning of their code' (1989, p. 124). Non-professional translation communities have benefited from having such discussions live, archiving their interactions and shared conclusions online; and recently, leading professional bodies seem to be following their example. The ATA now states in its Code of Ethics that it is preparing a "commentary" to the Code, "providing in-depth explanation and examples that reflect our common experiences […] to enable a deeper understanding of the effects of our behavior on ourselves, each other, and the industry as a whole'" (n.p.).

Another potentially rich area which professional associations might explore is the strong non-professional emphasis on shared values and ideals, rather than the individual rights which codes have tended to stress. It could be argued that professional codes' privileging of translators' rights has been fairly pointless. The Unesco Translator's Charter (1963/1994), for instance, lists a covetable range of 'rights' including that of the translator to own the copyright to all his translations (Section II, 15) or to have his name 'mentioned clearly and unambiguously whenever his/her translation is used' (Section II, 17a), yet almost fifty years after its adoption, those rights are even less widespread than in 1963. The non-professional stress on clearly defined values offers an alternative model, one already noted by Künzli as a positive (2007). In other professions, Frankel (1989, p. 112) emphasises the benefits of highlighting 'dominant values' (e.g., improving health care for medics). Some such dominant values for translation might be enabling communication or spreading knowledge; these might inspire members more than desirable, but almost certainly unattainable, 'rights'.

The new communities' shared ethos and continual fostering of emerging leaders are final aspects from which professionals might learn. There are already a few mentoring schemes in professional translation. That these are hugely popular and always oversubscribed demonstrates the hunger for such support from new members of the profession. Embedding mentoring and support schemes in professional development, and seeing this as a normal feature of career progression, could be done relatively easily using the online methods of the non-professionals.

Of course, there are also gaps in non-professional approaches, notably the evident scope for exploitation, abuse and driving down quality standards in some sectors. Both professionals and non-professionals can learn from the other approach.

This will be important as the new communities become established and long-running, with huge databases of past resources and a complex history to master, making participation more intimidating for new members ("newbies"). Many questions merit further study in this area. Will the communities continue to attract volunteers in sufficient numbers and be able to continue to provide supportive mentoring and leadership? Do non-professional codes support the oft-mooted idea of a shared 'model code' or meta-code of ethics? Might volunteering lead to higher motivation and, hence, higher quality levels, at least in some contexts? On what topics do non-professionals seek ethical support and guidance? Are these concerns reflected or addressed in professional codes; and if not, would professionals appreciate such guidance too? How are professional translators who act as volunteers in community translation projects placed in terms of ethics: do they import their professional ethics to these contexts or bend to the community's approach?

During the weeks following the Haiti disaster, many hundreds of translators—professionals and non-professionals—volunteered to translate and relay messages to help the rescue effort, often working long hours in difficult conditions on harrowing material. Chat rooms and discussion boards functioned as their "community", and it seems 'it was the sense of community that kept many going', knowing that they were part of a larger ongoing effort (Munro, 2010, n.p.). A final ethical concern of relevance to the translation profession has been its traditional isolation, with freelance translators working alone, often many miles from their nearest colleague, albeit that this has been mitigated somewhat recently through increased online networking and support, e.g., through Proz.com or LinkedIn groups. The non-professional online translation community, with its openness, shared values and supportive colleagues, might offer an inspiring and positively ethical model here too.

Appendix 1. Professional codes of translation ethics consulted

American Translators' Association (ATA). *Code of Professional Conduct and Business Practices.* Retrieved from http://www.atanet.org/aboutus/code_of_professional_conduct.php

Association of Translation Companies (ATC). *Professional Conduct.* Retrieved from http://www.atc.org.uk/code_conduct_atc.html; *Ethics.* Retrieved from http://www.atc.org.uk/ethics_atc.html

Association suisse des traducteurs, terminologues et interprètes (ASTTI). *Code de déontologie.* Retrieved from http://www.fit-europe.org/vault/deontologie-astti.html

Australian Institute of Interpreters and Translators Incorporated (AUSIT). *Code of ethics.* Retrieved from http://server.dream-fusion.net/ausit2/pics/ethics.pdf

Belgian Chamber of Translators, Interpreters and Philologists (CBTIP-BKVTF). *Code de déontologie.* Retrieved from http://www.translators.be/index.php?option=com_content&task=view&id=85&Itemid=108&lang=fr

Chartered Institute of Linguists (UK) *Professional Code of Conduct.* Retrieved from http://www.iol.org.uk/Charter/CLS/CodeofProfConduct Council17Nov07.pdf

Danish Association of State-Authorised Translators and Interpreters. *Code of Ethics.* Retrieved from http://www.fit-europe.org/vault/deont/dk-auth-eth.html

Indian Translators' Association *Code of Conduct.* Retrieved from http://www.itaindia.org/membership_information.pdf

Institute of Translation and Interpreting (UK) *Code of Professional Conduct* (two separate codes, one for individual members and one for corporate members). Retrieved from links to publications at http://www.iti.org.uk/indexMain.html

Irish Translators' and Interpreters' Association (ITIA).*Code of Practice and Professional Ethics.* Retrieved from http://www.fit-europe.org/vault/ITIA_code_ethics.pdf

Israel Translators' Association (ITA). *Code of Professional Conduct and Business Practices.* Retrieved from http://www.fit-europe.org/vault/conduct-ita.pdf

Japan Association of Translators Working with Translators (combination of advice for clients and definition of good translation practice, including issues of ethics and professional conduct). Retrieved from http://jat.org/past/working-with-translators/

Jednota tlumočníkůa překladatelů (Czech Republic). *Ethical Code.* Retrieved from http:// www.fit-europe.org/vault/ethics-jtp.html

LinguaJuris, Belgium, *Code de déontologie des traducteurs, des interprètes et des traducteurs-interprètes jurés.* Retrieved from www.linguajuris.org/data/Codede_Forum_linguaJuris.doc

National Association of Judiciary Interpreters and Translators (USA). Retrieved from http://www.najit.org/publications/Transcript%20Translation.pdf

Nederlands Genootschap van Tolken en Vertalers (NGTV), Netherlands, *Code of Honour.* Retrieved from http://www.fit-europe.org/vault/Erecode-ngtv.html

New Zealand Society of Translators and Interpreters (NZSTI) *Code of ethics.* Retrieved from http://www.nzsti.org/assets/uploads/files/codeofethics. pdf

ProZ.com (largest group of freelance translators, with over 300,000 registered in 2011; their two relevant codes were therefore included). *Professional guidelines*. Retrieved from http://www.proz.com/professional-guidelines/ *Guiding principles*. Retrieved from   http://www.proz.com/?sp=info/cornerstones

Sindicato Nacional dos Tradutores (SINTRA), Brazil. *Translators' Code of Ethics – SINTRA Bylaws*. Retrieved from http://braziliantranslated.com/sintrape.pdf

South African guidelines. Retrieved from http://translators.org.za/sati_cms/downloads/dynamic/sati_ethics_individual_english.pdf

Swedish Association of Professional Translators. *Code of Professional Conduct*. Retrieved from http://www.fit-europe.org/vault/deont/SFO-ProfPractice-en.pdf

Syndicat national des traducteurs professionnels (SFT), France. *Code de déontologie*. Retrieved from http://sft.fr/code-de-deontologie-des-traducteurs-et-interpretes.html

UNESCO Nairobi. *Recommendation* (1976) and *Translators' Charter* (1994). Retrieved from http://www.fit-ift.org/download/referencebil.pdf

Vereniging Zelfstandige Vertalers (VZV), Netherlands. *Code of Ethics*. Retrieved from http://www.vzv.info/index.php?section=2&page=198

Appendix 2. Online non-professional 'codes' of translation ethics consulted

Adobe community translation
http://tv.adobe.com/translations/guidelines
http://tv.adobe.com/translations/terms

Apache project
http://www.apache.org/foundation/bylaws.html

D-Addicts fansubbing forum
http://www.d-addicts.com/forum/viewforum_43.htm
http://www.d-addicts.com/forum/viewtopic_38531.htm

Doctors Without Borders/Médecins sans frontières Charter
http://www.doctorswithoutborders.org/aboutus/charter.cfm

Facebook translation Terms of Service
http://www.facebook.com/translations/index.php?app=1&aloc=en_GB&hel
p

Global Voices Project Lingua
http://globalvoicesonline.org/lingua/
http://globalvoicesonline.org/about/gv-manifesto/

Joomla! Open Source project
General Volunteer Code of Conduct: http://www.joomla.org/about-
joomla/the-project/code-of-conduct.html
Translation and Localization Policy:
http://community.joomla.org/translations/translation-policy.html

OpenOffice
Terms of use: http://openoffice.org/terms_of_use
Community forum: http://user.services.openoffice.org/en/forum/

Second Life community and translation guidelines
http://wiki.secondlife.com/wiki/Linden_Lab_Official:Discussion_guideline
s
http://wiki.secondlife.com/wiki/Community_Translation_Project

Sun Open Community Translation Interface
https://translate.sun.com/opencti/resources/tou.html

TranslateWiki.net
http://translatewiki.net/wiki/Support
http://en.wikipedia.org/wiki/Wikipedia:Text_of_Creative_Commons_Attrib
ution-ShareAlike_3.0_Unported_License

Translation Cloud Terms and Conditions
https://docs.google.com/document/pub?id=1S8DGTPb-
WOXJlJl44ct3dbbL2u87lHIXH6wzyuvx6dw

Translations for Progress
http://www.translationsforprogress.org/ngoguide.php
http://www.translationsforprogress.org/translatorsguide.php

Twitter Translation Environment – not translation-specific but users are
bound by the Twitter Rules addressing some relevant issues
http://support.twitter.com/articles/18311-the-twitter-rules

Ubuntu
Code of Conduct: http://www.ubuntu.com/community/conduct

Broader definition of 'values':
http://www.ubuntu.com/community/ubuntuvalues

Wikipedia. Various codes of relevance here, including the general:
http://wikimediafoundation.org/wiki/Terms_of_Use
And two more specific to translation:
http://meta.wikimedia.org/wiki/Translation
http://meta.wikimedia.org/wiki/Wikimedia_principles

References

Banerjee, D., Cronan, T. P., & Jones, T. W. (1998). Modeling IT ethics: A study in situational ethics. *MIS Quarterly, 22*(1), 31-60.

Brooks, L. J. (1989). Corporate codes of ethics. *Journal of Business Ethics, 8*(2/3), 117-129.

Chesterman, A. (2009). Ethics of translation. In M. Baker (Ed.), *Translation Studies* (pp. 34-43). Abingdon: Routledge.

Davis, M. (2003). What can we learn by looking for the first code of professional ethics? *Theoretical Medicine and Bioethics, 24*(5), 433-454.

DePalma, D., & Kelly, N. (2008). *Translation of, for, and by the people*. Lowell, MA: Common Sense Advisory.

Désilets, A. (2007). Translation wikified: How will massive online collaboration impact the world of translation? *Proceedings of translating and the computer (29)*. London: Aslib.

Frankel, M. S. (1989). Professional codes: Why, how and with what impact? *Journal of Business Ethics, 8*(2/3), 109-115.

Floridi, L. (1999). Information ethics: On the philosophical foundation of computer ethics. *Ethics and Information Technology, 1*, 37-56

Garcia, I. (2009). Beyond Translation Memory: computers and the professional translator. *The Journal of Specialised Translation, 12*, 199-214.

Gaumnitz, B. R., & Lere, J. C. (2002). Contents of codes of ethics of professional business organizations in the United States. *Journal of Business Ethics, 35*(1), 35-49.

Gneezy, U., & Rustichini, A. (2000). Pay enough or don't pay at all. *The Quarterly Journal of Economics, 115*(3), 791-810.

Goodwin, P. (2010). Ethical problems in translation. Why we might need Steiner after all. *The Translator, 16*(1), 19-42.

Gouadec, D. (2009). *Profession traducteur*. Paris: La Maison du Dictionnaire.

Higgs-Kleyn, N., & Kapelianis, D. (1999). The role of professional codes in regulating ethical conduct. *Journal of Business Ethics, 19*(4), 363-374.

Howe, J. (2008). *Crowdsourcing. How the power of the crowd is driving the future of business*. New York: Random House.

Koehler, W. C., & Pemberton, J. M. (2000). A search for core values. Towards a model code of ethics for information professionals. *Journal of Information Ethics, 9*(1), 26-54.

Künzli, A. (2007). The ethical dimension of translation revision. An empirical study. *The Journal of Specialised Translation, 8*, 42-56.

Lewis, W. D. (2010). Haitian Creole: How to build and ship an MT engine from scratch in 4 days, 17 hours, & 30 minutes. In F. Yvon & V. Hansen (Eds.), *EAMT 2010*.

Proceedings of the 14th Annual Conference of the European Association for Machine Translation. Saint-Raphaël, France.

Loch, K. D., & Conger, S. (1996). Evaluating ethical decision making and computer use. *Communications of the ACM, 39*(7), 74-83.

Marshall, K. P. (1999). Has technology introduced new ethical problems? *Journal of Business Ethics, 19*(1), 81-90.

McDonough Dolmaya, J. (2011). Moral ambiguity: Some shortcomings of professional codes of ethics for translators. *The Journal of Specialised Translation, 15*, 28-49.

Munro, R. (2010). Crowdsourced translation for emergency response in Haiti: the global collaboration of local knowledge. *AMTA Workshop on Collaborative Crowdsourcing for Translation.* Denver, Colorado, USA.

Savan, B. (1989). Beyond professional ethics: Issues and agendas. *Journal of Business Ethics, 8*(2/3), 179-185.

Souphavanh, A. and Karoonboonyanan, T. (2005) *Free / Open Source Software: Localization.* UNDP-APDIP. Retrieved from http://www.apdip.net/publications/fosseprimers/foss-l10n.pdf

Wagner, E. (2005). Does ITI's Code of Conduct need a makeover? *ITI Bulletin,* (May-June), 20-23.

Warner, D. E., & Raiter, M. (2005). Social context in Massively-Multiplayer Online Games (MMOGs): Ethical questions in shared space. *International Review of Information Ethics, 4*(12), 46-52.

Wooten, A. (2011). Can companies obtain free professional services through crowdsourcing? *Deserets news.* Retrieved from http://www.deseretnews.com/.

---

[1] See *Appendix 1* for a representative sample of codes in English and French. The terms 'code of conduct/ethics' are not defined here for reasons of space and because they are used interchangeably in professional contexts. Among others, Marshall (1999: 82) and Wikipedia (http://meta.wikimedia.org/wiki/Simple_View_of_Ethics_and_Morals) give relevant outlines.

[2] DePalma and Kelly (2008) and TAUS, among others, favour this term; other terms refer to the same phenomenon. Garcia (2009: 210) suggests 'hive' translation. I use the range here but prefer 'non-professional' translation, as the latter avoids potential confusion with community translation/interpreting as previously widely understood, i.e. translation for minority languages or in public service contexts. I include here initiatives where low payment is available to participants, e.g., TranslationCloud.net.

[3] These are not listed in the Appendix as they were given to the author for research purposes on the condition of confidentiality.

[4] In this, McDonough Dolmaya's approach is typical, in that it considers only those codes specific to the translation industry. Other surveys of ethical code content also focus on one profession alone, such as IT (Floridi, 1999) or business (Gaumnitz and Lere, 2002).

IV. CHANGE IN NORMS OF TQA AND LANGUAGE USE IN SUBTITLES FOR INTERNET CONTENT

From many one: Novel approaches to translation quality in a social network era

Miguel A. Jiménez-Crespo

Rutgers University, The State University of New Jersey

For decades, the fuzzy notion of translation quality has evolved parallel to the theorizations of translation and localization. This paper focuses on a novel approach to quality evaluation in the localization industry: how Facebook crowdsourced quality evaluation to an active community of users that votes on proposed translations. This approach, unthinkable a decade ago, seems to combine and distill some of the best aspects of several previous Translation Studies evaluation proposals, such as user-based approaches (Nida, 1964), functionalist approaches (Nord, 1997; Reiss and Vermeer, 1984) or corpus-assisted approaches (Bowker, 2001). These models were largely criticized at the time because they did not explicitly indicate how they could be professionally implemented. The current paper critically reviews the emerging crowdsourcing model in light of these approaches to quality evaluation and describes how mechanisms suggested in these earlier theoretical proposals are actually implemented in the Facebook model.

1. Introduction

Over the past twenty years, the production of digital content such as websites, software or videogames has increased exponentially. This digital revolution has led to a demand for the localization of digital texts into an ever-increasing number of languages (Cronin, 2003). Parallel to the development of the digital society, a new industry emerged in the 90s, the so-called "localization industry". This sector developed in order to cope with an increasing demand for localized products globally and has been constantly changing and adapting to the new technological challenges. One of the latest and most exciting developments is the crowdsourcing of both translation and quality evaluation to an active community of users. Crowdsourcing has recently drawn the attention of translation scholars (e.g., O'Hagan, 2009), but to date, the evaluation of quality through an active community of users has not been discussed in Translation Studies (TS). And yet, the development could be of interest to TS scholars as, it is often argued that localization practices have been established without fully making use of the body of knowledge of TS (Dunne, 2006a; Jiménez-Crespo; 2011, 2010b; Pym, 2003). The implications for industry quality evaluation practices are that they might lack the necessary theoretical bases to provide objective, valid and reliable results (Angelelli, 2009). However, quality evaluation is still a much debated issue even within TS; and localization continues to prove that, as Larose mentioned, the evaluation of translations "entails problems that are of cosmic proportions" (1998, p. 163).

From the early discussions on linguistic equivalence approaches (Carroll, 1966; Nida and Taber, 1969) to the functionalist (Nord, 1991, 1997) or discourse-based proposals (House, 1997; Reiss, 1971), models to assess translations have been firmly grounded in scholars' theoretical backgrounds. Nevertheless, it is agreed that the complexity and time consuming nature of these models often mean that they have not been fully implemented in professional or didactic contexts (Wright, 2006). For their part, the translation and localization industries have developed and implemented their own models (e.g., Sical, LISA, CTIC, ATA).[1] These have been classified from a TS perspective as experience-based or anecdotal (Colina, 2008), and are thought to lack the necessary empirical and theoretical bases to separate the subjective component inevitably present in any translation evaluation process (Hönig, 1998).

These different approaches and goals have led to a wide gap between TS scholars and the Localization and Translation Industries (Dunne, 2006a; Pym, 2003). The divide can also be witnessed in the emergence of a revolutionizing approach in social networking sites: the crowdsourcing of quality evaluation to a non-professional community of active users who vote on proposed translations. The goal of this paper is to explore what Facebook, the first model using a crowdsourcing approach to translation quality evaluation, can add to current TS research approaches. One of the motivations for investigating this topic is that it contradicts the most repeated mantra in the discipline: only translation evaluation built around explicit TS theoretical models can provide reliable and objective results (Angelelli, 2009; Colina, 2009; House 2001, 1997; Williams 2003). However, some scholars (e.g., Williams, 2003) have pointed out that current evaluation models are developed with certain translation types in mind and that, therefore, many of their underlying principles might not necessarily apply to other types of translations than the ones for which they were developed. This is the case for web localization on networking sites, and it could be argued that this is why established QA models might, so far, be unable to guarantee that final products are accepted by users of such sites as non-translated natural texts in the target language. The development of the novel Facebook evaluation model could also be due to localization being a relatively recent activity, and therefore, "there is no such classic set of canonized criteria for evaluating localization" (Wright, 2006, p. 257). In this sense, the development of the crowdsourcing model clearly responds to the faster pace at which industry practices develop as compared to TS research.

This paper is organized in the following fashion; after a brief theoretical review of research into translation quality evaluation, the novel approach used by Facebook will be explored, focusing on how it is related to quality evaluation proposals in TS. Next, the implications of this model for the discipline will be analyzed, and the ways in which it seems to distill aspects from several proposals that were difficult to implement professionally before the Internet era. These include the reader-based approached advocated by Nida and Taber (1964), or the identification of the subconscious set of cultural, linguistic and pragmatic conventions expected by end-users discussed in functionalist approaches (Colina, 2008; Nobs, 2006; Nord, 1997; Reiss & Vermeer, 1984). Moreover, this model resembles corpus-assisted approaches to quality evaluation since both help bring to the surface the framework of expected collocations and colligations in the minds of a large number of users of a specific discourse community (Bowker, 2001), thereby producing more naturally sounding translations (Zanettin, 1999).

2. Quality evaluation in Translation Studies and Localization

Quality evaluation is a central issue in TS. Most research focuses on two distinctive but related evaluation perspectives: the professional (e. g., Nobs, 2006; Sager, 1989) and the didactic (e. g., Nord, 1991, 1997; Waddington, 2001). Recently, the evaluation of quality in localization has attracted the attention of an increasing number of scholars (Bass, 2006; Böejel, 2007; Dunne, 2009, 2006; Jiangbo & Jing, 2010; Jiménez-Crespo, forthcoming, 2010a, 2008; Pierini, 2007). These studies indicate the need for further research into localization quality evaluation, given that the same set of criteria cannot be applied uniformly to all translation activity (i.e., Larose, 1998; Martínez Mélis & Hurtado Albir, 2001).

In general, one of the most discussed issues is the need to adopt models in order to control the subjectivity of evaluators (Angelelli, 2009; Colina, 2009; House, 2001; Martínez Mélis & Hurtado Albir, 2001). In one of the first attempts to study translation evaluation, Nida already (1964) believed that no translator or evaluator can avoid some degree of subjectivity and personal involvement in the interpretation of the ST. It is therefore widely accepted that the subjective component of the evaluation process will remain and has to be admitted (Hönig, 1998). As such, there are no means to prevent professional or non-professional evaluators from assessing translations by comparing them to an ideal text that they would have produced themselves, thus projecting individual standards onto the actual text. In this sense, it is understood that a single evaluator might not provide an objective measure of quality in translation (Rothe-Neves, 2002).

Another pivotal issue is the relative nature of translation quality, that is, quality should be understood as a prototypical concept that varies from context to context depending on the project, modality, goals, etc. In professional situations, it also needs to be understood as an industrial activity subject to specific time and money constraints that need to be accounted for (Wright, 2006). In the industry's literature, most international standards define quality as the capacity to comply with a set of parameters pre-defined by the customer. For example, the ISO 9000 defines quality as: "the totality of features and characteristics of a product or service that bears on its ability to satisfy stated or implied needs" (Ørsted, 2001, p. 443). Along the same lines, the definition laid out by the translation ASTM International standard defines quality as "the degree of conformance to an agreed upon set of specifications" (ASTM, 2006). Nevertheless and as previously mentioned, it is theoretically and methodologically impossible to predefine the notion of "quality" in all translated texts: For this reason, common definitions of quality usually focus on procedural aspects, as opposed to establishing what could be considered a "quality" translated text. Basically, such definitions govern procedures for achieving quality, rather than providing normative statements about what constitutes quality (Martínez Mélis & Hurtado Albir, 2001). They are generically process-oriented instead of product-oriented (Corpas, 2006; Wright, 2006). As a result, the final decision about quality resides in a time-constrained evaluation process carried out by one or more evaluators that might lack the necessary theoretical framework in order to separate out their own subjective judgment (House, 2001).

However, despite the criticism leveled at industry approaches, some of the solutions proposed by TS scholars to overcome the subjective bias have yet to have an impact on industrial practices. The most common solution proposed is to promote the adoption of models based on sound theoretical bases (Colina, 2008; House, 2001; Williams, 2003). At the dawn of TS as a discipline, Julianne House indicated that: "Evaluating the quality of a translation presupposes a theory of translation. Thus different views of translation lead to different concepts of translational quality, and hence different ways of assessing it" (1977, p. 7). This implies that the notion of quality evaluation in localization or in crowdsourcing models will be somewhat different from the analogous notion in T S, even though a consensus has not yet been reached in the discipline. In TS, theory is widely viewed as a prerequisite, and in this sense, the development of the Facebook model definitely goes against a basic principle in the eyes of translation scholars. Another common solution in TS has been to advocate for an empirical approach to quality evaluation, given that it certainly provides a more valid and reliable foundation (Angelelli & Jacobson, 2009; Colina, 2009; Rothe & Neves, 2002). All the same, it is generally understood that industry and TS models still need to be "validated by means of empirical research" (Martínez Mélis & Hurtado Albir, 2001, p. 274), that is, a combination of qualitative and quantitative approaches based on clearly established theoretical principles. This is the focus of the recently edited volume by Angelelli and Jacobson (2009). Other scholars have advocated for a combination of corpus based quantitative analysis in order to assist evaluators with more objective data during their evaluation processes (Bowker, 2001; House, 2001; Jiménez-Crespo, 2010a).

Against this backdrop of TS research, the crowdsourced quality evaluation model implemented by Facebook relies on two basic components: (1) the votes of a community of users on translations proposed by the members of that same community, and (2) an overview of the entire cycle by professional translators. The latter focuses mainly on the global process and the general macrostructural coherence and cohesion of the translation. This model has not been empirically verified nor is it based on a TS theoretical model. Nevertheless, it is clearly in line with the goals set forth by the ISO 900 quality standard, as it seems to satisfy "stated or implied needs". In order to fully understand the implications of this industry driven development, a description of this model is required.

3. The Facebook approach to quality evaluation

Facebook implemented a crowdsourcing model in order to translate their website initially in 2007. The motivation was reportedly not economic but rather participatory. It was observed that due to the novel and changing nature of digital genres, users' knowledge of the social networking sites could somehow be utilized to produce localized websites that better fulfill user expectations than those produced by professional translators. In fact, an exploratory study discussed in O'Hagan (2009) reported that the user group outperformed professional translators in certain translation tasks due to the former's familiarity with the inner workings of Facebook. Spanish was the first language into which Facebook was successfully translated, and the strategy was later implemented for French and German as well. Initially, the crowdsourcing translation application was advertised to foreign students at Stanford University, but soon enough it was advertised in technology blogs and the word got out fast. The first site was translated in one week, with the French translation being completed in a single day. Meanwhile, as of October 20011 the model has been implemented in 75 languages. Some of the language versions were initiated at the request of language communities around the world, such as the case of Basque.

The approach taken can be described as crowdsourced translations in which a company or collective (such as a non-profit) requests users to translate certain content, producing "solicited translations" (O'Hagan, 2009). The other possible non-professional approach is fan translation in which a group of users organizes itself to make content available in whichever desired language(s). This would be the case of fansubs translations of American TV series in China (Wu, 2010) or the fansubbing and scanlation of Japanese anime and manga respectively (O´Hagan, 2006). However, it should also be mentioned that the Facebook approach is a hybrid one, with users producing and voting on translations, while professional translators are hired to supervise and address potential issues for supported languages. In this sense, it can be argued that this hybrid model intends to extract the subconscious framework of expectations of users, while at the same time maintaining a professional overview of the entire cycle. Therefore, despite its many novel components, it cannot be considered a fully crowdsourced model such as the Wikipedia one. Generally, the model operates at the segmental or microtextual level, while the macrotextual level is mostly controlled by experts. This is of great importance according to Translation Studies literature, given that errors or inadequacies at the macrotextual level, such as terminological inconsistencies in a text or website, are considered more important than errors at the microtextual level (Larose, 1998; Nord, 1997; Williams, 2003). An example of this would be a typographical error in a single segment. Thus, the potentially more serious errors or inadequacies are controlled by experts rather than the translation community.

The following stages typify the process of crowdsourcing translations and quality evaluation in Facebook:[2]

(1)   First of all, a novel translation application is created and programmers extract all translatable strings from the initial English version, such as "upload photo", "log in" or "XX is now friends with XX". This is an ongoing process as Facebook continues to add new textual material to their website. Figure 1 shows some of the new textual strings for Spanish-Spain in October 2011. The entire experience is organized around a translation community in which users can see how many of their translations get published or voted for, in order to motivate them. They have to be Facebook members and they have to actively enable and open the translation application within the website in order to participate.

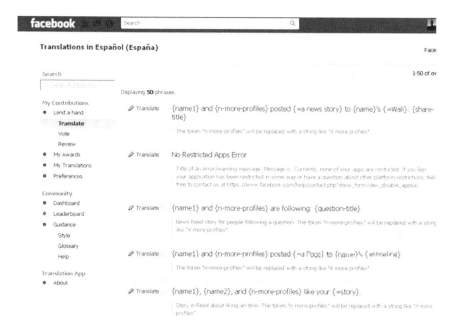

Figure 1: Extract of new textual strings in Facebook to be translated by users in October 2011.

(2)   The first actual translation step entails offering the Facebook glossary terms and the interface text strings to be translated by users. They are given an easy-to-use application, a brief style guide and a discussion forum where they can discuss terms, translation problems, etc. For example, in the Chilean Spanish forum, an entry discussed what type of Spanish users wanted for their Chilean site, mostly focused on what type of slang or idioms would be appropriate to appear on a website such as Facebook. In some cases, as with all localized textual strings, users are offered the context and the choice to annotate whether the gender or the prospective viewing user of the translation would pose a problem in the target language. For instance, the segment "memorize profile" includes the following contextual comment: "option for selecting a label on a contact form". An example of the case of gender problems in Spanish would be the case of the translation of the string "X is single", as the adjective "single" would need to agree with the gender of the person, either masculine "soltero" or femenine "soltera". During this stage, any translated term or string can be immediately voted positively or negatively by other users, and this approach is advertised to guarantee that the final published translations are those with the

highest quality. That is, translation quality is directly associated, at least in the eyes of the users, with the democratic will of the Facebook community.

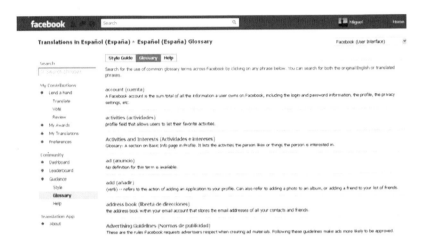

Figure 2: Facebook glossary for Peninsular Spanish that includes the source English term, its translation and a brief definition.

(3)   In the next stage, the translations proposed are voted on by the active community of users. In order to limit the potential choices, only three translations are normally presented with the source segment, although it is indicated how many total translations have been suggested. These are accompanied by up and down arrows representing the two possible options as seen in Figure 3: to like or dislike the translation. No option is offered to comment on the translation, although the forum offers the possibility of discussing any entry if users deem it appropriate. This voting stage would be the initial step in the quality evaluation process, followed by a complete evaluation by professional translators. During this stage, users are also encouraged to verify not just glossary items or strings, but also entire pages or messages in order to guarantee that they are consistent and accurate. However, it has been indicated by Facebook that the crowdsourcing model has been successful with small strings of text, but not with entire paragraphs or pages such as "Help" pages, etc. This sheds some light on the potential limitations of any crowdsourced quality evaluation model, with a microtextual or segmental focus, while the macrotextual aspects need to be dealt with by professionals.

Figure 3: Voting of proposed translations in the Facebook crowdsourced translation application.

(4)   During the last stage, a group of professional translators hired by Facebook checks and verifies all the translations, making sure that they are globally coherent and consistent. This allows the correction of any potential shortcomings: It has been indicated that the quality in fans translations is generally inconsistent (Diaz Cintas & Muñoz, 2006), even when, as previously mentioned, fans' apparent lack of formal translator training may be compensated for by their genre-knowledge (O'Hagan, 2009).

The translation application shown in Figures 1 and 3 includes eight options in its navigation menu: (1) Translate, (2) Vote, (3) Review, (4) My Awards, (5) My translations, (6) Preferences, (7) Dashboard (8) Leaderboard, (9) Guidance: style, glossary, help. Out of all the possible sections, one option involves guidelines for translation (9), five options (1, 2, 3, 5, 6) require the active involvement of the user, and two others (4, 8) focus on the translation community and on motivational issues, such as the option of viewing the translations proposed, voting on them, as well as the overall ranking of translators. Once users propose the translation for a segment or a glossary term, others can directly vote on these proposals through a thumbs up or thumbs down option. Options 2 and 3, voting and revision, are directly related to the quality evaluation process.

Now that the Facebook approach to quality evaluation has been briefly described, the next section turns to a review of the Facebook model in light of similarities and dissimilarities with proposals in TS since the 60s.

4. A critical review of the Facebook model in the light of Translation Studies

Even though there are several publications on the crowdsourcing of localization (Cronin, 2010; Muñoz Sánchez, 2009; O'Hagan, 2009), the outsourcing of translation quality to a community of users entails a brand new approach, and one that has not been discussed thus far in TS. Nevertheless and as previously indicated, it implicitly recognizes the role of the expectations of the end user or reader in the evaluation of quality, an idea that was first introduced by Nida and Taber (1964). This is also a central component in pragmatic and functionalist evaluation proposals (Colina, 2008, 2009; Nobs, 2006; Nord, 1997; Reiss, 1977; Reiss & Vermeer, 1984), and departs from much criticized models that focus exclusively on error detection (Nord, 1997). In general, this paper supports the functionalist view according to which it is "the text as a whole whose function(s) and effect(s) must be regarded as the crucial criteria for translation criticism" (Nord, 1991, p. 166). It also represents a combination of a mostly quantitative rather than qualitative processes, an approach advocated by House (2001), and also by Bowker (2001) in her proposal for a corpus-assisted approach to translation evaluation.

It should be mentioned that most TS proposals have been criticized at one point or another because they contain insufficient information about how one should proceed with the actual evaluation process (Angelelli & Jacobson, 2009). The Facebook model, despite not being grounded in TS theory, seems to represent an actual implementation of the reader-response approach advocated by Nida, and a novel, exciting gateway into the subconscious set of norms, conventions and expectations of users in fast evolving digital genres. The following section reviews the reader response approach and whether the Facebook model might represent an actual implementation of Nida and Taber's proposal.

4.1. The Facebook model and reader-response approaches to translation quality

The works of Nida (1964) and Nida and Taber (1969) are recognized as the first approach to translation quality that included reader responses as a basic component.[3] This can be described as a response-oriented or behavioral approach to translation evaluation and is based on Nida´s notion of "dynamic equivalence", that is, that the manner in which the receptors of the translated texts respond to the translation must be equivalent to the manner in which the receptors of the source text respond to the source text (Nida, 1964). In general, the overall criteria suggested by Nida and Taber (1969, p. 173) in order to evaluate translations are (1) the correctness with which the receivers understand the message, (2) the ease of comprehension and (3) the involvement a person experiences as a result of the adequacy of the form of the translation. In order to achieve this goal, the authors suggest so-called "practical tests" to measure this apparently similar response: (1) the cloze technique, related to the degree of predictability of the translation, which is achieved by providing a translated text with certain blank spaces and asking that these be filled in with the word that would best fit. (2) The elicitation of the receiver reaction to several translation alternatives. (3) Reading the translation aloud to another person and asking them to explain the contents of the text to other people who are not present during the original reading of the text. And finally, (4) reading aloud the translation to several individuals before an audience. The second "practical test", even when the author's proposal does not implicitly include the source texts, would be the one closest to current Facebook practices.

These reader-response approaches to translation quality have been extensively criticized, mainly for the lack of an explicit theoretical model of quality that might guide readers in their criticism, for not using the source text in the evaluation process (House, 1997), or for not controlling the inherent speculative and subjective component. However, Nida and Taber (1969) already indicated that the subjective bias can be overcome by sampling techniques, such as the ones used in Facebook. This proposal has also been criticized because it is normally assumed that translation evaluation is carried out only by experts such as professional translators, researchers, as well as translation or language teachers (Rothe-Neves, 2002), but not by non-professionals. Another point that has been criticized is that the method is based on the assumption that greater ease of comprehension might equal a better translation, or that reader response might not be equally important in all types of translation, such as in legal texts (Colina, 2008).

It is interesting to note that in the review of Nida's approach by Colina (2008), all of the objections against this model are, in fact, beneficial for the crowdsourced Facebook model in the specific contexts of web localization. First of all, web localization is a clear case of instrumental (Nord, 1997) or covert (House, 2001) translations, and therefore, the ease with which readers can interact with the translated material is of utmost importance (Jiménez-Crespo, 2009). In fact, localized websites are not called on to represent any previous source text, but rather a functional text in the target language (Pym, 2004). Secondly, Colina argues that "[t]he evaluation of the quality of a translation on the basis of reader response is time consuming and difficult to apply" (2008, p. 101). This might be the case in most QA settings, but the novel approach taken by Facebook might precisely prove that quality and translation evaluation is context-dependent and, in some cases, the inherent difficulty in crowdsourcing quality evaluation might be overcome by an active community of users. Additionally, Colina argues that "careful selection of readers is also necessary to make sure that they belong to the intended audience of translation" (2008, p. 101). Again, fans' knowledge of these newly emerging digital genres can definitely match the exact profile of the target user. Finally, it has also been suggested that the intended users of a translation might be different from the original ones, both culturally and temporally, and that the purpose of the translation might be different, so therefore, measuring an "equivalent response" might be impossible. Again, the readers or users recruited to participate in the Facebook quality model are basically those to whom the translation is addressed. Despite the fact that the Facebook model is not necessarily grounded in TS theory, research using Facebook data could provide data that is valuable in empirically revisiting reader response approaches, not from a linguistic equivalence paradigm (Nida, 1964), but rather from a functionalist approach such as in the empirical work of Nobs (2006). Additionally, Hönig mentioned, while discussing the subjective bias in evaluation, that: "the speculative element will remain – at least as long as there are no hard and fast empirical data which serve to prove what a 'typical' reader's responses are like" (1998, p. 32). Given that Facebook evaluators are typical readers of the site, empirical research using Facebook data could help move the quality evaluation in translation within the discipline further along. It therefore seems, at least in principle, that all the potential shortcomings of reader-response approaches in most evaluation settings are in fact beneficial to a crowdsourced model.

This review has shown that, even when QA crowdsourcing seems like a completely novel process, at the dawn of TS some proposals had already pointed to a few of the novel aspects of the Facebook model that could not be implemented prior to the unexpected explosion of Internet users around the world. In the evolution of quality evaluation research in the discipline, the next revolutionary development was the application of functionalism to quality assessment. The next section reviews how the shift towards the target context and the repudiation of any type of equivalence between source and target texts in the evaluation process (Nord, 1997) can find a parallel in the Facebook approach.

4.2. The Facebook model and functionalist approaches to translation quality

The development of functionalist theoretical approaches to translation in the '70s and '80s was instrumental in moving the focus of the evaluation process away from the highlighting of some sort of equivalence with the source text (Reiss, 1971) and towards the purpose or "skopos" of each translation assignment (Nord, 1997; Reiss & Vermeer, 1984). This entailed a shift in the definition of a quality translation from one that was somewhat "equivalent" to a source text to one that had the ability to fulfill the communicative purpose for which it was intended. This also introduced in mainstream TS the notion of "adequacy" in the evaluation process. In this switch, the receivers, together with their sociocultural context, play an essential role. Their frameworks of expectations also become essential during the translation and evaluation processes. Within this context, functionalists highlighted the importance that conventions play both in the production and reception of translations, since they can potentially differ between the same genres in different cultures (Nord, 1997, p. 54). During localization, and more importantly, during quality evaluation processes, it is key to guarantee that target texts contain whichever conventions users expect in whichever genre is translated or localized, as non-compliance with different genre conventions might have a detrimental effect on the reception of the text (Jiménez-Crespo, 2009; Vaughan and Dillon, 2006). Within the functionalist paradigm, conventions are defined as: "Implicit or tacit non-binding regulation of behavior, based on common knowledge and the expectations of what others expect you to expect from them (etc.) to do in a certain situation" (Nord, 1991, p. 96). These regulations of behavior are normally associated with different levels, such as "genre conventions" (Reiss & Vermeer, 1984), "style conventions", "conventions of non-verbal conduct" or "translation conventions" (Nord, 1997). Genre conventions play an important role in the identification and translation of most localized genres (Nord, 1997, p. 53). First of all, they function as signs that facilitate the recognition of a given genre. Secondly, they activate the expectations of the reader. And finally, they are signs that coordinate the text comprehension process (Reiss & Vermeer, 1984). Therefore, given that translation entails both a textual comprehension and a textual production process, conventions also play a crucial role in it (Göpferich, 1995; Nord, 1997).

However, it has been shown that localized websites tend not to comply with the conventions found in similar genres in target cultures (Jiménez-Crespo, 2010b, 2009). Normally, these websites show direct transfer of many source text conventions. As an example, Jiménez-Crespo (2009) demonstrated that US websites localized into Spanish show source-culture conventions such as the more prominent use of direct imperative forms of the verbs in navigation menus, while Spanish websites prefer infinitives or other non-personal forms. As previously mentioned, fans' knowledge of certain genres can lead to texts with higher levels of quality than those produced by professional translators (O'Hagan, 2009) and in part, this can be due to the fact that intensive users might possess what is known as "active competence" (Gläser, 1990, p. 72) in the knowledge of genre conventions. Normally, users and translators can possess active or passive knowledge of digital genre conventions (Jiménez-Crespo, 2009). Active competence can be defined as the ability of speakers of a language to recognize and produce the conventional features of textual genres, such as writing a résumé or an email. Nevertheless, most speakers might not be able to produce certain textual genres, such as a patent, a purchase contract or a privacy policy on a website, even though they might recognize prototypical instances of the genres and be able to identify the possible range of variation. This is referred to as passive competence (Gamero, 2001). In the ever-changing nature of digital genres, it is possible that translators and quality evaluators might not possess an active competence in any given textual genre, a problem that is referred to as "genre deficit" or "text type deficit" (Hatim & Mason, 1997, p. 133). This text type deficit might lead to the production of digital genres that to some extent lack the conventions expected by users. Thus, enlisting large numbers of users in the quality evaluation process is not only adequate, but also essential in order to identify by consensus what the specific conventions expected by the discourse community of users might be in each locale.

It should be mentioned at this point that for a convention to exist, alternative variants need to exist that fulfill the same communicative purpose (Göpferich, 1995). In the case where no alternative exists, conventions cannot exist, but rather we would be talking about norms. The Facebook evaluation model therefore, allows us to identify, within the range of possible variants that fulfill any communicative purpose, which alternatives are more frequent than others. This can naturally lead to websites that better match the framework of expectations of the community of users, and therefore, this can be associated with higher levels of quality in the eyes of the end users. All these issues should be framed within the context of rapidly evolving "imported" genres into most cultures, and therefore, enlisting the community of users in order to gauge the evolution or establishment of the features expected in these genres represents a positive addition to the process.

4.3. The Facebook model and corpus-assisted approaches to translation quality

The last evaluation proposal that has some parallels with the Facebook evaluation process is the corpus-assisted approach to quality evaluation (Bowker, 2001). For over two decades, the use of corpora during translation and evaluation has been widely promoted mostly from within TS for both didactic (i.e. Beebe et al., 2009; Bowker, 2001; Zanettin, 1998, 2001) and professional practices (i.e., Bowker & Barlow, 2008). Lynn Bowker pioneered the use of corpora during translation evaluation because this process "entails making judgments about appropriate language use, [and] it should not rely on intuition, anecdotal evidence or small samples" (2001, p. 346). In translation, the researcher also indicated that "corpus-assisted translations are of a higher quality with respect to subject field understanding, correct term choice, and idiomatic expressions" (Bowker, 1998, p. 631). Additionally, the researcher indicates that the quantitative approach provided by evaluation corpora can be better than using conventional resources such as dictionaries because these "are not always highly conducive to providing the conceptual and linguistic knowledge necessary to objectively evaluate a translation" (Bowker, 2001, p. 346).

An electronic corpus can be defined as a large principled collection of machine-readable texts that has been compiled according to a specific set of criteria in order to be representative of the targeted textual population. Among different corpus types (Laviosa, 2002), a carefully constructed evaluation corpus constitutes a source of conceptual and linguistic information that can objectively support evaluation decisions and judgments. Very few studies have focused on the use of corpora in localization (Jiménez-Crespo, forthcoming, 2010a; Shreve, 2006), and the only existing proposal for an evaluation corpus in TS is that of Bowker (2001). This evaluation corpus is intended for a didactic setting and it was presented as assistance to evaluators while making evaluation judgments. It comprises four different components: a comparable corpus, a quality corpus, a quantity corpus and an inappropriate corpus.

First of all, the comparable corpus includes both a translated and non-translated collection of texts. This corpus allows us to observe patterns in non-translated texts in the same genre and text type in order to produce more naturally sounding translations. The second component is a quality corpus, a small handpicked corpus consisting of texts that have been selected primarily for their conceptual content. The next component is a quantity corpus, an extensive collection of carefully selected texts in the same domain, genre, text type, etc. Finally, the researcher proposes a section called inappropriate corpus, a corpus that contains "inappropriate" parallel texts, that is, texts that are very similar to the original text but that include different web genres or subgenres. The combination of the large amount of data in these corpora would "make it possible to spot patterns more easily, to make generalizations, and to provide concrete evidence to support decisions" (Bowker, 2001, p. 353). It should be mentioned that the combination of corpora suggested by Bowker does not represent a corpus-based approach, but rather a corpus-assisted approach, as these corpora merely provide the necessary information to support evaluators' judgments. This use of corpora during evaluation has been criticized mostly because the proposal for evaluation does not include a fully-fledged evaluation method, but rather, a way to support the evaluator's intuition (Colina, 2009). The use of corpora is also reduced to the microcontext, that is, it is mostly geared towards finding the most common lexical or syntactic combinations, or, collocations and colligations.[4]

The basic premise behind the use of large computerized textual corpora in translation is that it can help produce more naturally sounding translations (Zanettin, 2001), as well as minimizing to some extent the amount of "shining through" (Teich, 2003) of the source text, or in other words, that it prevents lexical, syntactic or pragmatic features of the source texts ending up in the translation. In a sense, corpora provide a tool for translators to identify attested "units of meaning", that is, conventional ways of expressing specific meanings and performing specific functions in the relevant text-type variety within the target language (Tognini-Bonelli, 2001). This is due to the premise that a large body of texts that belong to the same text type and genre that have been naturally produced by speakers of any specific discourse community represents, to some extent, the subconscious set of expected features in any specific genre. This shared knowledge about specific genres and text types is accumulated by the repeated exposure of members of any discourse community to these genres and text types. From a cognitive perspective, the experience of being exposed to any common textual genre is guided by "schemata" (Rumelhart, 1980) or "frames" (Fillmore, 1976). A frame can be defined as a network of concepts related in such a way that one concept evokes an entire system. This notion underlies the idea of the "structure of expectations", or in other words, that each member of a discourse community organizes knowledge on the basis of their own experiences, and then uses this knowledge to predict interpretations regarding new information or experiences.

The novel nature of social networking sites means that in most languages, in a so-called "imported genre", international users might still lack the set of expected features when they interact with a localized social networking site in their own languages. They might possess a subconscious framework of what the most natural sounding site would be, and then compare it to what they would like to see in these sites. The same can be said of translators and evaluators trying to produce the best possible localized site. Therefore, even when one or a group of evaluators might eliminate any language or cultural errors in the localization, and the sites might appear lexically and syntactically correct, the combination of lexical or syntactic items might not appear totally natural to end users. To a certain extent, this is due to the fact that the localized text does not show the collocations and colligations that users are primed to expect in specific communicative situations (Hoey, 2005). In order to adjust translated texts to the expected primed features in the user's mind, one of the current approaches in TS is to resort to comparable corpora (Bowker & Barlow, 2009; Bowker, 2001; Jiménez-Crespo, forthcoming, 2010b, 2009; Shreve, 2006). Nevertheless, the compilation of a corpus of similar texts naturally produced in the target language is nearly impossible for emerging and imported genres. The Facebook approach to evaluation bridges this gap as it extracts from a large group of active users a snapshot of what would be more "natural" or "adequate", a notion related to their lexical and syntactic primings (Hoey, 2005). The goal of the Facebook model, despite a totally different approach, is therefore to identify what a community of users is primed to expect in this social networking genre. Thus, if discourse communities around the world would produce from scratch social networking sites that could be compiled in a corpus, the results of analyzing them would be similar to what they are already expressing by voting on Facebook proposed translations.

To sum up, I have argued in this section that the Facebook evaluation model, in which a large number of users votes positively or negatively on proposed translations, can help guarantee that the resulting website complies to the expected features in a digital genre that any discourse community might have. This is quite similar to the goals of corpus-assisted approaches: To explore the most common linguistic and pragmatic features in any genre, features that are extracted through the analysis of textual corpora of texts naturally produced by the target discourse community.

5.   Conclusions

The Facebook approach to quality evaluation seems to go against many of the theoretical principles and guidelines laid out by TS scholars. Nevertheless, this paper has tried to shed some light on how it actually distills and implements some of the most revolutionary ideas in TS since the 60s. The questions that the Facebook model poses to TS scholars are: Is translation theory a prerequisite for the evaluation of translation quality, or can professional QA continue to rely on other methods in order to satisfy "intended or implied needs" (ISO 900) given the time and economic constraints (Wright, 2006)? If the objective of localization is to produce websites that look like "they have been produced in-country" (LISA, 2004,

p. 11), is it more productive to enlist large numbers of non-professional users who have a deep knowledge of the digital genre, rather than professional translators-evaluators who might not yet possess the necessary "active competence" (Gläser, 1990) in the knowledge of the specific newly established genre conventions?

One of the most interesting aspects in the review of this model, in light of previous TS research, is that approaches that were previously criticized mainly due to the difficulty of their implementation can now be carried out thanks to the emergence of the wired digital world. As previously described, reader-based, functionalist and corpus assisted approaches to evaluation quality have been harshly criticized due to the impracticality of their implementation (Colina, 2008). However, to a great extent, the Facebook model represents an actual implementation of components of these models. This case proves that the impact of technology is not only going to radically change the practice of translation in ways never before imagined, but also has the potential to change the theorizations of translations. In the words of Jeremy Munday (2008): "The emergence of new technologies has transformed translation practice and is now exerting an impact on research and, as a consequence, on the theorization of translation" (p. 179). This paper has shown that the impact does not necessarily imply transformation in the future of theorizations of translation. By contrast, it may even allow translation scholars to revisit many existing ideas and theorizations that were forgotten due to difficulties in their implementation at the time. Today new technologies can enable us to research quality evaluation in novel ways, and the amount of data which can be gathered by companies that implement crowdsourcing represents an invaluable resource for further (translation) research.

It is hoped that this paper will help spark additional theoretical and empirical research into the fast evolving intersection of translation and technology. TS research has mostly been following in the tracks of industry developments, and only the determination and ingenuity of companies such as Facebook will put TS research into the leading role that, for example, applied sciences have in their respective industries.

References

Angelelli, C. (2009). Using a rubric to assess translation ability: defining the construct. In C. Angelelli & H. Jacobson (Eds.), *Testing and assessment in translation and interpreting studies.* ATA Scholarly Monographs Series. (pp. 13-47). Amsterdam: John Benjamins.

Angelelli, C., & Jacobson, H. (Eds.). (2009). *Testing and assessment in translation and interpreting studies.* ATA Scholarly Monograph Series. Amsterdam: John Benjamins.

ASTM (2006). *F2575-06 Standard guide for quality assurance in translation.*

Bass, S. (2006). Quality in the real world. In K. Dunne (Ed.), *Perspectives on localization* (pp. 69-84). Amsterdam: John Benjamins.

Beeby, A., Rodríguez Inés, P., & Sánchez-Gijón, P. (Eds.). (2009). *Corpus use and translating: Corpus use for learning to translate and learning corpus use to translate.* Amsterdam: John Benjamins

Börjel, J. (2007). *Language-specific quality issues in a real world localization process* (Master's thesis). Linköpings Universitet, Sweden.

Bowker, L. (2001). A corpus-based approach to translation evaluation. *Meta, 46* (2), 345-363.

Bowker, L., & Barlow, M. (2008). A comparative evaluation of bilingual concordancers and translation memory systems. In E., Yuste Trigo (Ed.), *Topics in language resources for translation and localization* (pp. 1-22). Amsterdam-Philadelphia: John Benjamins.

Carroll, J. B. (1966). An experiment in evaluating the quality of translations. *Mechanical Translation, 9*(34), 55-66.

Colina, S. (2009). Further evidence for a functionalist approach to translation quality evaluation. *Target, 21*(2), 235-264.

Colina, S. (2008). Translation quality evaluation: empirical evidence from a functionalist approach. *The Translator, 14*(1), 97-134.

Corpas Pastor, G. (2006). Translation quality standards in Europe: An overview. In E. Miyares Bermúdez &L. Ruiz Miyares (Eds.), *Linguistics in the twenty first century* (pp. 47-57). Cambridge: Cambridge Scholars Press/Santiago de Cuba: Centro de Lingüística Aplicada.

Cronin, M. (2010). The translation crowd. *Tradumática, 8.* Retrieved from http://www.fti.uab.es/tradumatica/revista/num8/articles/04/04central.htm

Cronin, M. (2003). *Translation and globalization.* London: Routledge.

Díaz-Cintas, J., & Muñoz Sánchez, P (2006). Fansubs: Audiovisual translation in an amateur environment. *The Journal of Specialised Translation, 6,* 37-52.

DIN 2345 (1998). *Übersetzungsaufträge.* Berlin: Beuth.

Dunne, K. (2009). Assessing software localization: For a valid approach. In C. Angelelli & H. Jacobson (Eds.), *Testing and assessment in translation and interpreting studies* (pp. 185-222). Amsterdam: John Benjamins

Dunne, K. (2006a). A Copernican revolution. In K. Dunne (Ed.) *Perspectives on localization* (pp. 1-11). Amsterdam: John Benjamins.

Dunne, K. (2006b). Putting the cart behind the horse: rethinking localization quality management. In K. Dunne (Ed.) *Perspectives on localization* (pp. 95-117). Amsterdam: John Benjamins.

Fillmore, C. J. (1976). Frame semantics and the nature of language. *Annals of the New York Academy of Sciences: Conference on the Origin and Development of Language and Speech, 280,* 20-32.

Gamero Pérez, S. (2001). *La traducción de textos técnicos.* Barcelona: Ariel.

Gläser, R. (1990). *Fachtextsorten im Englischen.*Tübingen: Narr.

Göpferich, S. (1995). *Textsorten in Naturwissenschaften und Technik. Pragmatische Typologie- Kontrastierung-Translation.* Tübingen: Gunter Narr.

Hatim, B., & Mason, I. (1997). *The translator as communicator.* London: Routledge.

Hoey, M. (2005). *Lexical priming. A new theory of words and language.* London: Routledge.

Holz-Mänttäri, J. (1984). *Translatorisches Handeln. Theorie und Methode.* Helsinki: Suomalainen Tiedeakatemia.

Hönig, H. G. (1998). Positions, power and practice: Functionalist approaches and translation quality assessment. In C. Schäffner (Ed.), *Translation and quality* (pp. 634). Clevedon: Multilingual Matters.

House, J. (2001). Translation quality assessment: Linguistic description versus social evaluation. *Meta 46* (2), 243-257.

House, J. (1977). *A model for translation quality assessment.* Tübingen: TBL Verlag Gunter Narr.

House, J. (1997). *Translation quality assessment: A model revisited.* Tübingen: Gunter Narr.

Jiangbo, H., & T. Ying (2010). Study of the translation errors in the light of the Skopostheorie. Samples from the websites of some tourist attractions in China. *Babel 56* (1), 35-46.

Jiménez-Crespo, M. A. (forthcoming). A corpus-based error typology: towards a more objective approach to measuring quality in localization. *Perspectives: Studies in Translatology.*

Jiménez-Crespo, M. A. (2011). To adapt or not to adapt in web localization: a contrastive genre-based study of original and localized legal sections in corporate websites. *Jostrans: The Journal of Specialized Translation*, 15, 2-27.

Jiménez-Crespo, M.A. (2010a). Localization and writing for a new medium: a review of digital style guides. *Tradumática, 8.* Retrieved from http://www.fti.uab.es/tradumatica/revista/num8/articles/08/08art.htm.

Jiménez-Crespo, M. A. (2010b). The intersection of localization and translation: A corpus study of Spanish original and localized web forms. *Translation and Interpreting Studies, 5*(2), 186-207.

Jiménez-Crespo, M. A. (2009). Conventions in localisation: a corpus study of original vs. translated web texts. *Jostrans: The Journal of Specialized Translation 12*, 79-102.

Jiménez-Crespo, M. A. (2008). *El proceso de localización web: estudio contrastivo de un corpus comparable del género sitio web corporativo.* Doctoral dissertation. University of Granada: Spain.

Larose, R. (1998). Méthodologie de l'évaluation des traductions. *Meta, 43* (2), 163186.

Laviosa, S. (2002). *Corpus-based translation studies.* Amsterdam: Rodopi.

LISA (2004). *Localisation Industry Primer*, 2nd Edition. Geneva: The Localisation Industry Standards Association (LISA).

Martínez Melis, N., & Hurtado Albir, A. (2001). Assessment in translation studies: Research needs. *Meta, 47*(2), 272-287.

Munday, J. (2008). *Introducing translation studies: Theories and applications.* 2nd edition. New York: Routledge.

Muñoz Sánchez, P. (2009). Video game localisation for fans by fans: The case of Romhacking. *Journal of Internationalization and Localization, 1*, 168-185.

Nida, E. (1964). *Towards a science of translation*. Leiden: Brill.

Nida, E., & Taber, C. (1969). *The theory and practice of translation*. Leiden: Brill.

Nielsen, J., & Loranger, H. (2006). *Prioritizing web usability*. Indianapolis: News Riders.

Nobs, M. L. (2006). *La traducción de folletos turísticos: ¿Qué calidad demandan los turistas?*. Granada: Comares.

Nord, C. (1997). *Translating as a purposeful activity. Functionalist approaches explained*. Manchester: St. Jerome.

Nord, C. (1991). *Text analysis in translation: Theory, methodology and didactic application of a model for translation-oriented text analysis*. Amsterdam-Atlanta: Rodopi.

O'Hagan, M. (2009). Evolution of user-generated translation: fansubs, translation hacking and crowdsourcing. *The Journal of Internationalization and Localization 1*, 94121.

O'Hagan, M. (2006). Manga, anime and video games: Globalizing Japanese cultural production. *Perspectives - Studies In Translatology 14* (4), 243-247.

Ørsted, J. (2001). Quality and efficiency: Incompatible elements in Translation Practice? *Meta, 46*, 438-447.

Pierini, P. (2006). Quality in web translation: An investigation into UK and Italian tourism web sites. *Jostrans, The Journal of Specialized Translation, 8*, 85-103.

Pym, A. (2004). *The Moving Text: Localization, Translation and Distribution*. Amsterdam-Philadelphia: John Benjamins.

Pym, A. (2003). What localization models can learn from Translation Theory. *The LISA Newsletter: Globalization Insider, 12* (2).

Reiss, K. (1971). *Möglichkeiten und Grenzen der übersetungskritik*. München: Hüber.

Reiss, K., & Vermeer, H. J. (1984). *Grundlegung einer allgemeinen Translationstheorie*. Tubinga: Niemeyer.

Rumelhart, D. E. (1980). Schemata: the building blocks of cognition. In R. J. Spiro, B. C. Bruce & W. E. Brewer (Eds.), *Theoretical issues in Reading Comprehension* (pp. 33-58). Hillsdale, NJ: Lawrence Erlbaum Associates.

Rothe-Neves, R. (2002). Translation quality assessment for research purposes: An empirical approach. *Cadernos de Tradução: O processo de Tradução 2* (10), 113-131.

Sager, J. (1989). Quality and standards: The evaluation of translations. In C. Picken (Ed.), *The translator's handbook* (pp. 91-102). London: ASLIB.

Shreve, G. M. (2006). Corpus enhancement and localization. In K. Dunne (Ed.), *Perspectives on localization* (pp. 309-331). Amsterdam-Philadelphia: John Benjamins.

Teich, E. (2003). *Cross-linguistic variation in system and text: A methodology for the investigation of translations and comparable texts*. Berlin: Mouton de Gruyter.

Tognini Bonelli, E. (1996). *Corpus theory and practice*. Pescia: Tuscan Word Centre.

Vaughan, M., & Dillon, A. (2006). Why structure and genre matter for users of digital information: a longitudinal experiment with readers of a web-based newspaper. *International Journal of Human Computer Studies, 64*, 502-525.

Waddington, C. (2001). Different methods of evaluating student translation: The question of validity. *Meta 46*, 312-325.

Williams, M. (2003). *Translation quality assessment*. Ottawa: Ottawa University Press.

Wright, S. E. (2006). Language industry standards. In K. Dunne (Ed.), *Perspectives on localization* (pp. 241-278). Amsterdam-Philadelphia: John Benjamins.

Wu, X. (2010). *Recreation through translation: Examining China's online volunteer translators*. Paper presented at Translation and the Humanities Conference, University of Illinois, Urbana-Champaing, October 14-16, 2010.

Zanettin, F. (2001). Swimming in words: Corpora, translation, and language learning. In G. Aston (Ed.), *Learning with corpora* (pp. 177-197). Houston, TX: Athelstan.

Zanettin, F. (1998). Bilingual comparable corpora and the training of translators. *Meta, 43* (4), 616-630.

---

[1] Système canadien d'appréciation de la qualité linguistique (Sical), Localization Industry Standard Association, (LISA), Canadian Translators,Terminologists and Interpreters Council (CTIC), American Translator Association (ATA).

[2] The following link describes the translation process for new apps developpers: https://developers.facebook.com/docs/internationalization/

[3] It should be mentioned that the authors were mostly focused on Bible translation.

[4] A collocation can be defined as is a co-occurrence of two or more words within a given span (distance from each other), while colligations are co-occurrences between specific words and grammatical classes, or interrelations of grammatical categories (Tognini Bonelli, 1996, p. 74). Collocations are therefore related to lexical or semantic relations, while colligations are co-occurrences of words and grammatical classes. Both of these features are related to the appreciation of naturalness in texts, as they point to the more frequent combinations in users' minds.

R U ready 4 new subtitles?
Investigating the potential of social translation practices and creative spellings

Alina Secară

University of Leeds

In this paper I investigate novel and creative linguistic features used in non-conventional subtitling settings such as fansubbing, arguing that they can be advantageously used in professional subtitling practices for a specific medium, such as the Internet. The integration of txt lingo in subtitling is supported by the recent explosion of social translation practices as a response to an ever-growing audience fragmentation as well as changes in technology which make the integration of several customised subtitling tracks possible. In an attempt to provide empirical evidence to support this argument I present the initial results of a pilot eye-tracker-based experiment to elicit data on the reception of "unregimented" subtitling when offered as an alternative to conventional subtitling from consumers in selected new subtitling contexts.

1. Change in the audiovisual translation landscape and scope for creativity in subtitling

The translation world has been going through dramatic changes over the last few years. They have seen the appearance of commercial online subtitled products, such as Vodafone's *Who Killed Summer?* (Vodafone, 2009), the first drama series to be played across social networks online and on mobile devices using professionally created multilingual subtitles. Advances in technology such as DTV (Digital TV) and Blu-Ray now offer new possibilities for data manipulation, linguistic or otherwise. Changes in information access habits of TV viewers and newspaper readers generally have led to content being made available not only online, but on demand as well. This was predicted as early as 1995 when Nicholas Negroponte, then Director of the Massachusetts Institute of Technology's Media Lab, described a future dominated by customised services where products such as newspapers would be personalised to fit the needs and preferences of individuals rather than the public as a whole (Negroponte, 1995). Moreover, the crowdsourced translation and subtitling sphere has grown in popularity with millions of users involved in online translation and subtitling activities, both as content producers and consumers.

Despite all these shifts, the provision of professional subtitling has, in general, attracted only minimal changes, remaining conventional in essence. This is even more surprising and, I would argue outdated, when the subtitled product is to be distributed on the Internet to an intended audience represented almost exclusively by young adults who have been reported to access and produce information using a variety of linguistic and technical media (Carrington, 2004; Crystal, 2006; Shortis, 2007). I believe that market changes need to be reflected in audiovisual translation and that social translation practices have the potential to become a rich source of inspiration for professionally-created audiovisual translations. This paper will explore only one such aspect, namely the integration of the so-called *txt lingo* in subtitling produced for Internet consumption. In this paper txt lingo refers to the creative spelling practices used in electronically-mediated communication (EMC) (Baron, 2010) to enhance group identity, overcome physical space constraints and simulate spoken language. I contend that market transformations need to be reflected in the way audiovisual translation in general, and subtitling in particular are conducted, requiring a variety of methods to cater for a corresponding variety of users and platforms. Accordingly, one would expect changes in the medium of delivery dictated by an increasingly fragmented audience to trigger changes in the form of the message as well.

I start from the premise that the use of *unregimented* (Shortis, 2007) and usually shorter types of spelling within subtitles—similar to those characteristic of the IM (instant messaging) and text message communities and fansubs (subtitles created by fans), for example C *u, frm, R, ☺*—not only allow a certain liberation from formal audiovisual translation constraints (e.g., maximum number of characters allowed per line), but also provide an alternative linguistic model appropriate for the channel in question. My assumptions are further grounded in the pioneering research by Nornes (1999) into *liberated practices* in subtitling, where he argues that a translation finds its strengths in its abuses, in its daring techniques and in its breaking with standard use. Before him, Lewis had also argued for a new approach "[…] that of the strong, forceful translation that values experimentation, tampers with usage, seeks to match the polyvalences and plurivocities or expressive stresses of the original by producing its own" (Lewis, 1985 as cited in Nornes, 1999, p. 18). Devices such as the use of modified font—getting bigger and bigger as the tonality of the actor rises—, creative spellings or the positioning of the subtitles on the screen to go hand in hand with the narrative are examples of "acts of violence" (Nornes, 2007, p. 156). They allow the audience to interact with and have direct experience of the foreign, by using an inventive approach and eliminating submissive practices ruled by codes, rules and norm. The abusive techniques need not be dominating or invasive, but creative. Nornes suggests that the first evidence of these new practices is to be found in fan communities and speculates on the advantages that these practices may have for other users as well.

These communities use devices that derive not only from the linguistic code but also from music and icons (e.g., the use of various symbols such as crescendo < and emoticons) which makes the communication multi-modal. Fansubbers and crowdsourcing subtitlers often use unconventional positioning of the subtitles, varied fonts, colours and customisable verbosity of the lines combined with non-standard spellings to create a collage of "distorted" practices in the overall discourse. The integration of creative subtitles that combine techniques used in fansubbing and txt language (Crystal, 2006; Díaz Cintas & Muñoz Sánchez, 2006; O'Hagan, 2008; Pérez González, 2006; Shortis, 1997) can be appropriate and more efficient than conventional subtitling, as some contexts require a more informal style that "does not create a clash of expectations" (McCarthy, 2003). A language needs diversity in order to survive the linguistic demands of a changing society (Crystal, 2009) so EMC with its txt lingo may well be a great opportunity for language revitalisation. Moreover, txt forms may provide a solution to the physical constraints which characterise subtitling, allowing more information to be conveyed within the same physical bounds thanks to condensed word forms. I contend this to be an effective alternative if offered to an audience already familiar with txt lingo. Finally, as signalled in Baron (2010), this study is further motivated by a change in focus in the research community from determining the characteristics of any such creative linguistic phenomenon to evaluating the actual impact it can have on human linguistic and social practices.

2. The diversity and richness of social communities

Research into fansubbing and crowdsourcing of translation (O'Hagan, 2008; Perrino, 2009), as well as studies in fields as diverse as patent reviews, journalism and computing (Howe, 2008) have investigated differences in practice between professional and non-conventional settings, and observed the richness of techniques and approaches used in the latter. Participants involved in the production of material in these settings create expectations about the content and the form of the message they are transmitting. Practices used in social translation communities such as Facebook and TED.com (a non-profit organisation committed to spreading innovative ideas about technology, entertainment and design) exhibit traces of both linguistic and typographical abuses described by Nornes (1999). In fansubbing, as mentioned above, this includes the use of varied fonts, emoticons, colours, and customisable verbosity of the lines combined with non-standard txt language spellings (Crystal, 2006; Díaz Cintas and Muñoz Sánchez, 2006; Pérez González, 2006; Shortis, 2007). The sheer number of participants involved in such non-conventional settings highlights the potential of these practices.

In a 2008 study, O'Hagan investigates the most salient feature differentiating a fan translator from a professional translator. She concludes that it is orthographic devices that are most frequently used to recreate the stereotypical profile of a source manga character. These typically consist of elongated vowels and consonants (*Reeeally, meee, I'llll*) to visually mimic their phonetic rendering or the tonality and emphasis put on them. These findings are also supported by Baron (2010), who writes that Internet language has the power to strengthen "the role of writing as a representation of informal spoken language" (p. 177).

These abusive techniques, as defined by Nornes (1999) can occur naturally in an environment which displays a powerful linguistic variety and identity. For example, the subtitles and translations produced online on an anime-dedicated platform are likely to display linguistic variations, creating a collage of "distorted" practices known and used in that community. This collage not only reflects the linguistic tradition of that community but it suits its expectations as well. Rather than investigating the various abusive techniques listed above, the present article concentrates on the use of txt language spellings when applied to the subtitles of a clip intended for Internet broadcast and specifically targeted at a generally young, txt-producing audience.

3. Investigating creative spellings

One of the reasons why studies on social media are growing in popularity is that more readers can identify with the very practices which are being researched. Just by navigating in one's phone SMS inbox one can quickly recognise the characteristics of language used in both the texts sent and those received. Expectations regarding the use of complex forms such as *btwn* and *b4* together with emoticons and instances where *2* is used instead of *to* will differ from person to person. Such individual differences raise a number of questions: Are these forms unique to your particular distance communication threads or do you share them with a wider linguistic community? Are you alone in using just a few creative forms in your messages? Is the frequency of emoticons in your texts indicative of your gender?

Based on a corpus of approximately 70,000 text messages, Fairon et al. (2006) investigated the special features of txt language in French and built a typology of techniques used. The techniques observed operate at both morphological and syntactic levels and include use of phonetic rendering of characters (*cette soirée* →*7sware*), phonetic orthographies (*quand*→ *kand*), expressive graphemes (*oooohhhhhh, aaaaaarghhh*), abbreviations, truncations, acronyms (*laugh out loud*→ *lol*) and truncated phrases.

A study investigating English txt language orthography (Shortis, 2007) lists similar devices, classifying them into three categories according to motivational principles. Firstly, features used for reasons of economy include omission of vowels *(good→ gd)*, letter and number homophones *(are→ r)*, and consonant reduction *(immediately→ imedtly)*. Secondly, to simulate spoken language, Shortis picks out devices such as pronunciation spelling *(going→ goin)*, reduplication to stretch sounds for emphasis *(Soooooooo)* and capitals to indicate paralinguistic details such as tonality. And finally, the incorporation of graphical and kinaesthetic devices such as emoticons, colours, movement and alphabetical constructions to shift the focus from the linguistic sign to the visual and graphical. Crystal (2006) provides an extensive classification of linguistic forms in identifying six features of textese, namely logograms *(@)* and pictograms *(☺)*, initialisms *(NP)*, omitted letters *(btwn)*, non-standard spellings *(thru)*, shortening *(mo)* and genuine novelties *(b4)*.

All three authors argue that, while several variations can co-exist for the same initial word, one form will always find greater popularity. One of the most interesting findings of these studies is that the use of creative spellings is less frequent than previously believed. This is supported by further studies carried out by Baron who investigates the "talk on IM" (2010, p. 45) and text messages, using undergraduates or very recent graduates at the American University, Washington D.C. Baron concludes that in IM abbreviations—which in her study include initialisms, omitted letters, non-standard spellings, and genuine novelties—"proved to be quite sparse" (2010, p. 45). "Out of 11,718 words, only 31 were EMC abbreviations" (Baron, 2010, p. 59). She also discovers a gender variation in the use of emoticons, with females using more than twice as many emoticons as males. For texting, emoticons were very infrequent and abbreviations were equally sparse.

EMC is shaped by using linguistic tools and technology to fit the topics, the platforms and the users. The characteristics of this writing are first informally created then replicated and further elaborated through immersion, giving the user an active role in the creation of this text practice. I believe the producers and recipients of written messages today have sufficient linguistic maturity to differentiate between txt lingo and standard language and select those contexts appropriate to each. As David Crystal highlights, EMC offers an unprecedented variety in the "communicative options available in our linguistic 'wardrobe'" (2009, p. 96) but the key point is knowing how to manage it to our advantage. I suggest that subtitlers could successfully manipulate these linguistic possibilities by providing creative subtitling solutions to Internet clips which display informal discourse and are aimed at a 20-40 year old technology savvy audience, producers and consumers of electronically-mediated information. The target group selection is motivated by prior studies investigating the age background of texters in several countries (Ling, 2005; Crystal, 2008). They report teenagers and young adults up to mid-20s to be the most enthusiastic group of users and highlight that texting is also very popular among individuals in the mid-30s to 40 category.

4. Cn y rd ths? Creativity and readability

The widespread belief that "a deviation from, and even more the conscious challenge of, orthographic norms has the potential of signalling distance from or negation of dominant culture" (Androutsopoulos, 2000, p. 515) seems too simplistic to define txt users' linguistic behaviour. As suggested by Androutsopoulos (2000, p. 515), even if a significant part of txting practices are consciously employed to mark an oppositional sociocultural stance, txting is also very frequently used for specific communicative purposes, such as attracting attention in an advertisement. The ability of txt language connoisseurs to participate easily in both conventional and new forms of text and literary practices is not simply a sign of negation but a negotiation of the orthography used for social functions and the context surrounding that communication. Myers explains that those creating and consuming linguistic products in such contexts "don't just create a genre, they create a social world" (2010, p. 21). One of the defining characteristics of this world is its linguistic diversity and this acts as a filter to guard against intruders. In subtitling, unregimented spellings should therefore be introduced only in those contexts and addressed only to those audiences capable and willing to decode them. Each community will create an identity based, among other factors, on linguistic choices. "The motivation to use them goes well beyond the ergonomic, as their playful character provides entertainment value as an end in itself as well as a means of increasing rapport between participants" (Crystal, 2009, p. 129). Crystal (2008, 2009) discusses the subject of txt lingo in great detail and demonstrates its creative aspect by providing an insight into the txt producing process and its history.

Not only are decisions concerning creative spellings consciously taken but txt forms are less frequent than previously believed (Shortis, 2007). Further evidence that decisions are consciously taken and that redundancy is well balanced by textese users is given by Crystal (2006), who reports preservation of apostrophes, regardless of the effort it takes to insert them. Nevertheless he stresses that apostrophes are inserted only when clarity is at risk—for example *we're* and not *were*, but *Im* rather than *I'm*. In addition, it could be argued that the choice is refined more locally depending on a user's preferences and the situation, as variations exist within txt lingo. The existence of local variation is supported by data from IM and text corpora (Baron, 2010; Fairon et al., 2006; Shortis, 2007; Tagg, 2009) which list several creative forms used for the same standard word form.

This awareness and ability to distinguish between boundaries of standard and non-standard makes it obvious that misuse and the danger of these practices permeating very formal contexts are relatively limited. Statistically-based studies report that abbreviations, acronyms, and emoticons are less prevalent in young people's IM and txt than previously suggested (Tagliamonte & Denis, 2008). The participants involved in this study were aged between 15 and 20 and were all born and raised in Canada. Moreover, speculations that non-standard spellings have a negative effect on children acquiring the standard spelling overlook the creative element that such spellings offer and the chance for users to experiment and identify with visual representations of language in ways that are not permitted in conventional settings. On several occasions Crystal (2006, 2009) reports research dispelling such myths that abbreviations are used routinely in school assessments or that children will start using txt lingo in all situations. Its use will always reflect the aims and intentions of the users as well as the medium. Therefore, if used in carefully identified contexts, these practices have the potential to help users overcome challenges, be they technical, such as the physical constraints encountered in IM or in subtitling, or linguistic, such as visually mimicking the phonetic rendering of a phrase.

So, is there a case for introducing txt lingo in subtitling? Are there similarities between text messages, IM and a subtitled product to allow for txt practices which are already established on the first two platforms to be incorporated into the third? The use of *squeeze text* (Carrington, 2004), another term for txt lingo, in subtitling can be motivated by three principles described by Werry (1996 as cited in Shortis, 2007) that apply to txt, IM platforms and subtitling environments. The first and most obvious one is represented by features of economy and text entry reduction, as all three contexts are regulated by strict space limitations that is, around 39 characters per line in subtitling and 160 characters per SMS while IM environments, even if not as strictly conditioned, seem to average in practice at around 5.6 words per transmission (Baron, 2010). Second, spelling by simulating spoken language has already been explored with some success for the translation of dialects in interlingual subtitling and the transfer of orality features in monolingual subtitling (Werry, 1996 as cited in Tagliamonte & Denis, 2008). Finally, all three environments feature a shift to multimodal visual and graphical effects and iconicity in which the linguistic sign is pushed into the periphery of meaning making. One aspect, i.e., the use of emoticons, has already been proposed and used with reasonable success in monolingual subtitling (Civera, 2005; Neves, 2005) and its use in SDH encouraged by the Spanish Standard UNE 153010 (Lorenzo, 2010, p. 134).

Having established the theoretical possibilities for integrating txt lingo into subtitling, I will now present the set-up and initial observations of an experiment to elicit data on the reception of "unregimented" subtitling when offered as an alternative to conventional subtitling, from consumers in selected new subtitling contexts such as Internet and mobile technology.

5. Experiment

Eye-tracking has been used successfully in neurolinguistic and psycholinguistic research into the study of reading processes (Rayner &

Pollatsek, 1989). More recently, diagnostic studies of audiovisual translation in language acquisition (d'Ydewalle et al., 1991; d'Ydewalle & De Bruycker, 2007), interlingual subtitling processing (Jensema et al., 2000) and reception of live subtitling (Romero-Fresco, 2009) have highlighted its versatility. The most frequent goal of eye movement analysis is to draw a map of its characteristics in terms of salient movements and their duration. Especially if it can be accompanied by user surveys, eye-tracking data is believed to be the best way of studying reading behaviour (Duchowski, 2003; Perego et al., 2010; Romero-Fresco, 2009;).

In the present experiment eye-tracking technology is used to monitor, assemble and analyse audience physiological response when viewing both conventional and creative (i.e., including txt lingo) subtitles. This includes observations about duration of fixations inside and outside the subtitling area, number of back and forth shifts or attention shifts (between image and subtitle) and regressive eye movements (in the subtitle) in two scenarios. This reading component is accompanied by post-experiment retrospective comments from the participants related to clip comprehension as well as appropriateness of the subtitling techniques encountered in an Internet environment.

This preliminary empirical study is designed to motivate reflections on the validity of integrating creative subtitles into specific environments as well as on the readability of textisms in subtitling.

5.1. Materials and design

The stimulus for the experiment consists of a short extract from a 2009 French documentary *Surfeurs du Paradis*. This source material was selected as the documentary itself originally targeted viewers belonging to an age group similar to that of my intended target audience, namely 20 to 40 and technology savvy, moreover the subject, surf championships, was also believed to be of interest to this group. Finally, the language style used made it appropriate to our target medium, Internet broadcast. Two English subtitle tracks were prepared for this clip following identical technical parameters. These were the same reading speed, i.e., 720 characters per minute, the same centre justification, a maximum of 39 characters per line and the same rules regarding timing over shot changes. The subtitle onset corresponded to the voice onset. The two subtitling tracks shared the same timing codes and presentation, since the creative subtitles were based on the standard, conventional subtitles. The variations included in the creative file consisted of the replacement of key terms from the conventional file with their txt lingo equivalents. Each creative subtitle contained one, two or several txt forms which, in their turn, could be simple logograms *(@)* and omitted letters *(hs, ths, smthg, cn, frm, yr, u, r)* or non-standard spellings *(dont, sum)* and genuine novelties *(b4, gr8)*. 53 one-line and two-line subtitles out of the 80 corresponding to the short clip underwent txt modifications and were therefore included in the analysis. As a result of the txt spellings applied the creative version displayed 5% fewer characters than the standard one, with 96 out of a total of 662 words affected. Only minimal creative spelling amendments were applied to the creative subtitling track since, for this study I particularly wanted to preserve identical presentation styles in the two subtitling files. D'Ydewalle et al. (1991, 2007) report proportionally more shifts recorded in two-liners and more viewing time spent on two-line as opposed to one-line subtitles, whose presentation is experienced as quicker. Therefore, the only variable in this experiment were the txt lingo amendments, and all other parameters remained constant.

Rayner et al. (2006) and Pollatsek and Rayner (2006) stress that the fixation of eyes on a location is also determined by word frequency. They also show that low frequency words often induce immediate regressions back to earlier parts of the sentence. The results of Moran's study (2008) show that the average fixation duration on subtitles which include high frequency words is lower than in the low frequency condition, and that the number of fixations in the non text area is higher in the high frequency condition. The influence of word frequency on reading speed is further documented by Jensema (1998) and other factors cited as having an effect on fixation are word length, lexical ambiguity, phonological coding, semantic relationships (Pollatsek & Rayner, 2006) and predictability of a word in that context. As the source clip and standard English subtitles did not contain any technical or exotic terms nor lexical ambiguities, it was essential that the txt subtitles match this level of familiarity. This was achieved by using corresponding high frequency txt forms and cohesive structures. I based my selection of txt variations to be included in the creative subtitle track on a corpus of 190,000 sms messages (Tagg, 2009). More specifically, the txt forms included in the subtitles came from the top 150 creative sms spellings in this corpus, therefore assumed frequent enough in this context. Since users of textisms are not constrained to follow a priori rules, and given that IM users and fansubbers can easily migrate from one practice to another as a result of careful reading of the social practices and circumstances (Bourdieu, 1990), these forms do not enforce any particular usage of creative language and subtitling techniques but simply provide examples of practice which are frequent and likely to be familiar to the members of these communities and therefore to the experiment participants.

5.2. Participants and experiment set-up

Four participants took part in this small-scale experiment and ethical approval was obtained in advance. The subjects were all native English speakers, with no knowledge of French, aged between 29 and 40 years. They had experience watching subtitled programmes, good vision and two were especially selected for their familiarity with txt language. Their reading skills were considered to be above average as all four participants had postgraduate qualifications. No participant took part in more than one experiment and they were tested individually. Two subjects were assigned to each of the two conditions in which the clip was shown. In Condition 1, the French clip was shown with French soundtrack and standard English subtitles. In Condition 2, the same clip was shown with French soundtrack and English subtitles which included creative spellings. As a reader's aim and perspective were shown to influence text processing (Kaakinen et al., 2003) I carefully designed the information provided to participants at the beginning of the experiment. Similar to other eye-tracking subtitling studies (Caffrey, 2009; d'Ydewalle & De Bruycker, 2007; Jensema, 1998) participants were told in advance that they would be taking part in an eye-tracking experiment. On the day they were told they were going to watch a subtitled French film and instructed to watch the material in the same way as they would at home. Telling the participants in advance that they are going to participate in an eye-tracking experiment and providing a brief description of the equipment, is not only ethical but it helps avoid any surprises or suspicions from the participants (Nielsen & Pernice, 2009).

On the day, they were seated in front of the computer, and after a short 5-point calibration of the eye-tracker to the individual subject the experiment begun. At the end of their session each participant was informed about the intent of the experiment and asked to comment on the experience. My post experiment session included questions to establish if they fully understood the content of the clip and to assess if they deemed acceptable the creative presentation of subtitles for the medium in question.

5.3. Apparatus

The equipment used was a Tobii X120 eye-tracker with its analysis software Tobii Studio, and the clips were shown on a 19 inch monitor at a viewing distance of 60cm. A non-invasive tracker, Tobii allows for binocular tracking, which minimizes the risk of data invalidation by continuing to track even if one eye is hidden from the field of view of the tracker due to head motion (head motion tolerance 30x22x30cm). This allows for a more natural behaviour of participants during the experiments. The tracker records the position of the eyes using X and Y coordinates and calculates the number and length of fixations. As a standard definition of fixation parameters does not exist, for this study I considered a fixation as having a minimum of 100 milliseconds, with a fixation radius, i.e., the smallest distance in pixels that can separate fixations, of 30, which is the recommended settings for situations with mixed content stimuli (Tobii Manual, 2006).

6. Analysis

Involving a number of cognitive processes, reading takes place at different levels with multiple processes occurring simultaneously. As first analysed by Emile Javal in 1880 and explained in Rayner and Pollatsek, reading is not linear but happens as "a series of jumps" (saccades) between which "the eyes remain relatively still, for about a quarter of a second, in what is referred to as a fixation" (1989, p. 6). In an audiovisual environment such as the one analysed here, the processing of information requires multiple attention shifts between text and images, different processing strategies for the two main visual sources of information, and the construction of meaning by putting all the information together (Perego et al., 2010, p. 247).

My experiment was to analyse the trade-off between image processing and text processing in the two conditions and how variations in the text forms might affect this exchange. Of particular interest to this study was to determine the fixation durations within subtitles, each defined as an individual Area of Interest (henceforth AOI), as opposed to the rest of the screen for the period of time a subtitle was displayed. One hypothesis was that the *squeeze text* subtitle version, with its fewer characters to process, would allow the viewer more time to focus on other parts of the screen as opposed to the standard subtitled clip experience, which would permit the viewer only short glimpses outside the subtitle area. My assumption is that when more cognitive resources are allocated to the reading of subtitles, the processing of the visual information outside the subtitling area suffers.

I analysed the resulting data using three relevant eye movement parameters as identified by Megaw and Richardson (1979), namely fixation duration, number of fixations and direction of eye movements, and compared gaze data across the two participant groups. For analysis purposes in Tobii Studio recordings need to be devided into segments called scenes. Using Tobii Studio, the four participants' gaze recordings were split into scenes, based on the original subtitle durations, and within every scene the corresponding subtitle was marked as an AOI. This was performed for all 53 subtitles analysed.

6.1. Fixation duration

The fixation duration (total or average length of fixations) represents the most frequent parameter used in eye-tracking studies. Previous eye-tracking studies on subtitling found that average fixation durations in audiovisual viewing tend to be shorter than those found in normal reading, with d'Ydewalle & de Bruycker (2007) reporting a mean fixation duration of 178 ms per word and d'Ydewalle et al. (1985) reporting a duration of 124 ms per word. These fixation durations are considerably shorter than the

Alina Secară

mean fixation duration for normal silent reading of English (i.e., text only) reported in Rayner (1998) of 225 ms.

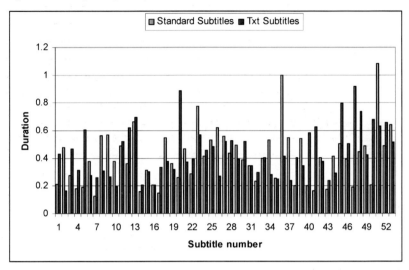

Figure 1: Mean fixation duration outside AOIs, per subtitle.

Figure 1 shows the duration in seconds, as mean of the two participants per condition, for all the fixations outside an AOI (i.e., subtitle) for the 53 scenes in the two conditions. The analysis of the data shows that in approximately 55% of subtitles, participants in Condition 2, i.e., txt subtitles, spent more time outside the subtitling area, than participants in Condition 1 viewing standard subtitles. This tendency seems to be accentuated from subtitle 40 onwards. The repetition of a low-frequency txt form which may not have been 100% recognised at the beginning, especially as many creative variations may exist for the same word, has a positive impact on the reading speed, as documented in numerous research papers (Chaffin et al., 2001, in Stab & Rayner, 2007; Rayner et al., 1995). Therefore, I suggest that a certain element of learning intervenes, thus increasing the participants' familiarity and reading ease with the txt forms used as they advance in the clip.

6.2. Number of fixations and mean fixation duration

Studies show that there is a correlation between the number of fixations and the subjects' reading experience (Anders, 2001; Chapman & Underwood 1998, both cited in Duchowski, 2003). The subjects who are more familiar with reading display an increased number of fixations and a decreased mean duration; by fixating for a shorter period of time, they can cover a wider area.

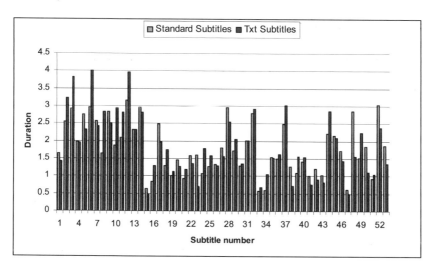

Figure 2: Mean fixation duration inside AOIs, per subtitle

In this experiment, in 28 out of 53 cases the txt subtitles had more fixations and their mean fixation length was, as shown in Figure 2, less than that of the participants in Condition 1. Even if it is not quantitatively significant overall, this trend is even more pronounced towards the end of the clip, as explained above. Moreover, analysis of the fixation duration inside the AOIs shows that peaks in the mean data, which might suggest difficulty when reading a particular creative word or cluster, are almost evenly shared between the two conditions. Pollatsek and Rayner state unequivocally that "one of the most robust findings in studies of eye movements and reading is that the ease or difficulty associated with understanding a word during reading clearly affects how long readers fixate on that word" (2006, p. 621). I therefore interpret the fact that the presence of creative forms did not trigger unusually long fixations and in more than 50% of cases where the mean was lower than in Condition 1, to indicate that frequent txt forms did not pose a significant challenge to the participants but allowed reading to occur naturally.

Alina Secară

Table 1: Means and standard deviations of the two parameters overall, inside and outside of the subtitling area

	Fixation Time Total (ms)			
	Mean		*Std. Dev*	
	Outside AOI	AOI	Outside AOI	AOI
C1	409.037	1890.339	201.263	746.930
C2	437.943	1857.094	179.838	886.792

Table 2: Fixation counts for the two parameters, inside and outside of the subtitling area

	Fixation Count			
	Total		*Mean*	
	Outside AOI	AOI	Outside AOI	AOI
C1	386	684	6	11
C2	370	793	6	12.5

Analysis of the means of the two parameters indicates that fewer fixations are recorded inside the AOIs for Condition 1 and the effect is significant ($F_{(2,53)} = 0.9804$, $p < 0.05$). The proportion of the fixation time devoted to the subtitled area did not differ significantly between the two conditions (C1: M = 1890.339, C2: M = 1857.094, t = 0.419) and the effect was not significant either ($F_{(2,53)} = 1.4095$, p = 0,1095). Therefore, no definite conclusion regarding the ease of processing text in C2 as opposed to C1 can be drawn. Nevertheless, as explained above, these preliminary results seem to indicate that the presence of txt forms did not impede the reading process, which followed a normal trajectory.

6.3. Direction of eye movements

Switching attention from the visual image to the subtitle area and reading the subtitles happens "effortlessly and almost automatically" (d'Ydewalle & De Bruyker, 2007, p. 196). Nevertheless, certain factors lead to disruptions in the reading of an audiovisual text. In a pioneering study carried out in the early 1980s, Baker singles out three situations which can trigger "false alarms" and therefore disrupt a normal subtitling reading process. The first type of false alarm happens when "the subtitle in question overruns a shot-change on the background video, and the viewer's point of regard is seen to regress to an early point in the subtitle" (Baker, 1982, p. 129). The second occurs when there is a lack of synchrony between the subtitle and the visual and audio, in particular when these predate the subtitle. The third kind of false alarm happens when a long subtitle display time leads the viewer to anticipate a new subtitle before it arrives, therefore only attracting re-reading of the subtitle with a long duration. Moreover, more recent studies established that the fixation of eyes on a location is also determined by how frequent the word is; so variations in the frequency of words also lead to disruptions in the reading process. Rayner et al. (2006) show that low frequency words often induce immediate regressions back to earlier parts of the sentence.

Shillcock (2007) found that "regressions are more likely to occur in a difficult text or during reinterpretation or to correct a long forward saccade" (p. 98). Such "corrective" regressions have nevertheless been shown to represent only 10% of the overall number of regressions (Stab & Rayner, 2007), therefore the majority of regressions can be considered linked to word frequency, length and predictability.

Table 3: Fixations (F), Regressions (R) and Shifts (S) per subtitle for C1 and C2

Subtitles C1	F	R	S	Subtitles C2	F	R	S
I'll be as quick as you are.	6	1	1	I'll b as quick as u r.	6	0	2
[I]f you don't do something just because you don't like it.	13	3	1	[I]f u don't do smthg jst cos u don't like it.	15	4	1
If I had to do that, I would.	8	0	2	If I had 2 do tht, I wud.	7	0	2

In the Table 3 above I present selected information on back and forth shifts (between image and subtitle) and regressive eye movements (in the subtitle), as a full analysis is beyond the scope of this article. These initial observations, suggest that the use of txt forms in subtitles did not disturb the viewing process as they did not induce a greater number of regressive movements in the txt subtitles than did normal subtitles. Moreover, the number of shifts was either maintained or increased, which suggests that both vertical (non-text area) and horizontal (subtitle) processing took place.

6.4. Questionnaire

These findings are also supported by the results of a short questionnaire distributed to the participants at the end of the eye-tracking experiment. The first two questions referred to content specific information to check comprehension and all four participants were successful in providing the correct answers. The third and fourth related to the display and the linguistic forms included. While all reported feeling comfortable with the display time and position of the subtitles, the participants in Condition 2 commented on their surprise at seeing txt lingo in subtitles. After the initial surprise reaction, they reported no problems reading and understanding the forms included. This is also supported by the eye-tracking data as explained above. Moreover, in answering the fifth and final question the two participants in Condition 2 expressed their enthusiasm regarding the introduction of creative practices for short online videos. One reason given was that these txt forms reflect the spoken and written practices they engage in daily and have become part of their linguistic identity. I can conclude from these remarks and the eye-tracking data that the txt language subtitles presented in this experiment were not only intelligible—the participants did not report difficulty in identifying the concepts the creative forms related to—but also presented a linguistic form viewers could easily identify with. As Crystal puts it "we are beginning to train a new generation of English speakers who are more aware of linguistic diversity and more tolerant of differences in linguistic behaviour" (Crystal, 2009, p. 48).

7. Further discussion and conclusion

The initial results of this experiment inspire confidence regarding the use of txt spellings in specially selected subtitling environments such as the Internet. Not only did the current study show that frequent creative spellings do not hinder the viewing process as a whole, but it also suggests that they might permit a fuller experience of the film, by allowing the viewers to spend more time fixating outside the subtitled area. It is known that traditionally this is only possible if time allows it as "caption reading dominates eye movement; viewing the screen action tends to be secondary" (Jensema et al., 2000, p. 284). In a recent study of a drama, Perego et al. (2010) claim that there is no trade-off between scene recognition and subtitle recognition. However, as indeed acknowledged later on in their study, this exchange may be age- and genre-dependent, therefore the results may be expected to differ for different age groups as well as a documentary or game show as opposed to drama. Moreover, the scene change investigated by Perego et al. (2010) is very much an aspect of the peripheral vision, which typically fails to make the identification of more subtle changes such as body expression of characters on screen possible. Therefore, comprehension of linguistic information aside, if more time is spent on the subtitles, less is available for the processing of aspects such as body language and expressions that contribute to the overall meaning of the audiovisual product. It could moreover be possible that txt forms may provide a solution to the physical constraints which characterise subtitling, allowing for more information to be presented or for less time to be allocated to the duration of subtitles.

Even if too limited to allow for generalisations regarding the processing of txt forms in general, this small-scale pilot experiment afforded a first glimpse of subtitles with txt lingo in action and, most importantly it allowed initial observations showing that participants were comfortable reading frequent txt varieties. In the hope that a more extensive analysis will benefit from the ground this first set of investigations has broken, I plan a more ambitious experiment exposing larger participant groups to even more diverse txt forms from emoticons to initialisms, skipped letters and letter and number homophones. As mentioned at the beginning of the article, I do not suggest that this type of subtitling be applied to all products, only that it should be considered as an alternative to professional subtitles for short clips which are aimed at a Internet-savy and txt producing audience of a certain age group.

As highlighted in MultiLingual Computing (2009), there is an increasing awareness of the richness of community translation contexts. It is my belief that the shift in position from periphery to centre and the growing attention social translation practices have been receiving over the last few years is a clear sign that they will, sooner or later, shape the way more conventional practices are carried out. Media such as IM and SMS are still novel and only with time will we be able to measure the impact they may eventually exert as suggested by Baron:

> If it took at least thirty-five years after the invention of the telephone to decide it was reasonable to issue a dinner invitation by phone, we should hardly be surprised that best practices for networked computers and mobile communication devices are far from worked out. (Baron, 2010)

References

Androutsopoulos, J. K. (2000). Non-standard spellings in media texts: The case of German fanzines. *Journal of Sociolinguistics, 4(4),* 514-533.

Baker, G. R. (1982). *Monitoring eye-movements While watching subtitled television programmes - a feasibility study.* London: Independent Broadcasting Authority.

Baron, N. S. (2010). Discourse structures in instant messaging: The case of utterance breaks. *Language@Internet, 7.* Retrieved from http://www.languageatinternet.de /articles/2010.

Bourdieu, P. (1990). *The logic of practice.* Cambridge: Polity Press.

Caffrey, C. (2009). *Relevant abuse? Investigating the effects of an abusive subtitling procedure on the perception of TV anime using eye tracker and questionnaire.* Unpublished doctoral dissertation, School of Applied Language and Intercultural Studies, Dublin City University. Retrieved from http://doras.dcu.ie/14835/1/ Colm_PhDCorrections.pdf

Carrington, V. (2004). Texts and literacies of the Shi Jinrui. *British Journal of Sociology of Education, Vol 25 (2),* 215-228.

Civera, C. (2005). Introducing emoticons and pictograms in SDHH. *Media for All conference.* Retrieved from http://www.fti.uab.es/transmedia/7-06-05.htm#

Crystal, D. (2006). *Language and the Internet.* Cambridge: Cambridge University Press.

Crystal, D. (2008). *Txting. The Gr8 Db8.* Oxford University Press.

Crystal, D. (2009). *The future of language.* London: Routledge.

Díaz Cintas, J., & Muñoz Sánchez, P. (2006). Fansubs: Audiovisual translation in an amateur environment. *The Journal for Specialised Translation, 6,* 37-52. Retrieved from http://www.jostrans.org/issue06/art_diaz_munoz.pdf

Duchowski, A. T. (2003). *Eye-tracking methodology: Theory and practice.* London: Springer.

d'Ydewalle, G., Van Rensbergen, J., & Pollet, J. (1985). Reading a message when the same message is auditorily available in another language: The case of subtitling.

Psychological Reports of Leuven University, 54. Leuven: Katholieke Universiteit Leuven.

d'Ydewalle, G., Praet, C., Verfaillie, K., & van Rensbergen, J. (1991). Watching subtitled television: Automatic reading behaviour. *Communication Research, 18*(5), 650-666.

d'Ydewalle, G., & De Bruycker, W. (2007). Eye movements of children and adults while reading television subtitles. *European Psychologist, 12*(3), 196-205.

eMarketer. (2008). *TV trends: Consumers demand control.* Retrieved from http://www.emarketer.com/Reports/All/Emarketer_2000499.aspx

Fairon, C., Kleind, J. R., & Paumier, S. (2006). *Le langage SMS.* Leuven: Presses Universitaires de Louvain.

Howe, J. (2008). *Crowdsourcing. How the power of the crowd is driving the future of business.* London: RH Business Books.

Jensema, C. (1998). Viewer reaction to different television captioning speeds. *American Annals of the Deaf, 143*(4), 318324.

Jensema, C., El Sharkawy, S., Danturthi, R. S., Burch, R., & Hsu, D. (2000). Eye movement patterns of captioned television viewers. *American Annals of the Deaf, 145*(3), 275-285.

Kaakinen, J., Hyönä, J., & Keenan, J. (2003). How prior knowledge, WMC, and relevance of information affect eye fixations in expository text. *Journal of Experimental Psychology: Learning, Memory, and Cognition, 29*(3), 447-457.

Kittur, A., & Kraut, R. E. (2008). Harnessing the wisdom of crowds in Wikipedia: Quality through coordination. CSCW 2008: *Proceedings of the ACM Conference on Computer-Supported Cooperative Work. New York: ACM Press.* Retrieved from http://kittur.org/research.html.

Ling, R. (2005). The socio-linguistics of SMS: An analysis of SMS use by a random sample of Norwegians. In R. Ling & P. Pedersen (Eds.), *Mobile communications: Renegotiation of the social sphere* (pp. 335-349). London: Springer.

Lorenzo, L. (2010) Subtitling for deaf and hard of hearing children in Spain: A case study. In A. Matamala & P. Orero (Eds.), *Listening to subtitles. Subtitles for the deaf and hard of hearing* (pp. 115-138). Bern: Peter Lang.

McCarthy, H. (1999). *Hayao Miyazaki: Master of Japanese animation.* Berkeley, CA: Stone Bridge Press.

Megaw, E. D., & Richardson, J. (1979). Eye movements and industrial inspection. *Applied Ergonomics, 10*(3), 145-154.

Moran, S. (2008, June). *The effect of linguistic variation on subtitle reception.* Audiovisual Translation: Multidisciplinary Approaches Conference, Montpellier, France.

MultiLingual Computing. (2009). Facebook applies for community translation pattent. *Multilingual Computing, 107 (October/November),* 8.

Myers, G. (2010). *Discourse of blogs and wikis.* Continuum.

Negroponte, N. (1995). *Being digital.* New York: Knopf.

Neves, J. (2005). *Audiovisual translation. Subtitling for the deaf and hard-of-hearing.* Unpublished doctoral dissertation. London: Roehampton University.

Nielsen, J. & Pernice, K. (2009). *Eyetracking methodology. 65 Guidelines for how to conduct and evaluate usability studies using eyetracking.* Retrieved from http://www.useit.com/eyetracking/methodology

Nornes, A. M. (1999). For an abusive subtitling. *Film Quarterly, 52*(3), 17-34.

Nornes, A. M. (2007). *Cinema Babel. Translating global cinema.* University of Minnesota Press.

O'Hagan, M. (2008). Fan translation networks: an accidental translator training environment?. In J. Kearns (Ed.), *Translator and interpreter training: Issues, methods and debates* (pp. 159-183). London: Continuum.

Perego, E. (2008). Subtitles and line-breaks. Towards improved readability. In D. Chiaro, C. Heiss & C. Bucaria (Eds.), *Between text and image: updating research in screen translation* (pp. 211-223). Amsterdam: John Benjamins.

Perego, E., Del Missier, F., Porta, M. & M. Mosconi, (2010). The cognitive effectiveness of subtitle processing. *Media Psychology, 13*, 243-272.

Pérez González, L. (2006). Fansubbing anime: insights into the 'butterfly effect' of globalisation on audiovisual translation. *Perspectives, 14*(4), 260-277.

Perrino, S. (2009). User-generated translation: The future of translation in a Web 2.0 environment. *The Journal of Specialised Translation, 11*. Retrieved from http://www.jostrans.org/issue12/art_perrino.php

Pollatsek, A., & Rayner, K. (2006). Eye-movement control in reading. In M. J. Traxler & M. A. Gernsbacher (Eds.), *Handbook of psycholinguistics, 2nd ed.* (pp. 613-657). San Diego: Elsevier.

Rayner, K. (1998). Eye movements in reading and information processing: 20 years of research. *Psychological Bulletin, 124*, 372-422.

Rayner, K., Liversedge, S. P., & White, S. J. (2006). Eye movements when reading disappearing text: The importance of the word to the right of fixation. *Vision Research, 46*, 310-323.

Rayner, K., & Pollatsek, A. (1989). *The psychology of reading* Broadway (US): Lawrence Erlbaum Associates.

Rayner, K., Raney, G., & Pollatsek, A. (1995). Eye movements and discourse processing. In R.F. Lorch and E.J. O'Brian (Eds.), *Sources of coherence in reading* (pp. 9-36). Hillsdale, NJ: Erlbaum.

Romero-Fresco, P. (2009). More haste less speed: Edited vs verbatim respeaking. Special issue of *Vigo International Journal of Applied Linguistics (VIAL)*, VI, 109-133.

Shortis, T. (2007). Revoicing txt: spelling, vernacular orthography and 'unregimented writing'. In S. Pasteguillo, M. J. Esteve & L. Geo-Valor (Eds.), *The texture of Internet: Netlinguistics in progress* (pp. 220). Cambridge: Cambridge Scholars Publishing.

Staub, A., & Rayner, K. (2007). Eye movements and on-line comprehension processes. In G. Gaskell (Ed.), *The Oxford handbook of psycholinguistics* (pp. 327-342). Oxford, UK: Oxford University Press.

Tagg, C. (2009). *A corpus linguistics study of SMS text messaging*. Unpublished doctoral dissertation, Department of English, University of Birmingham, UK.

Tagliamonte, S. A., & Derek, D. (2008). Linguistic ruin? Lol! Instant messaging and teen language. *American Speech, 83*(1) . Retrieved from http://americanspeech.dukejournals.org/cgi/content/short/83/1/3

Taylor, R. (2006). *Japanese comics go mobile.* Retrieved from http://news.bbc.co.uk/1/hi/programmes/click_online/4840436.stm

Vodafone (2009). *Who killed Summer?.* Retrieved from http://www.wks09.com/

TED. (2011). Retrieved from http://www.ted.com/.

Tobii X120 Manual, 2006.

Wong, Y., Grimm, S. M., Vera, N., Laverdet, M., Kwan, T. Y., Putnam, C. W., Olivan-Lopez, J., Losse, K. P., Cox, R., & Little, C. (2009). Community translation on a social network. *US Patent and Trademark Office*, Retrieved from http://tinyurl.com/mgtrxh.

V. IMPLICATION OF WEB 2.0 FOR TRANSLATOR TRAINING AND TRANSLATOR AWARENESS

Facebook me!: Initial insights in favour of using social networking as a tool for translator training

Renée Desjardins

University of Ottawa

This paper argues in favour of integrating and using online social networking, more specifically Facebook, within the translation classroom. This has numerous benefits in terms of aptly preparing trainees for the marketplace and also helping to foster a classroom community by encouraging a collaborative learning environment. A descriptive analysis of five undergraduate courses suggests that using online social networking as a teaching strategy has a significant impact: from engaging students through collaborative translation projects, to peer-reviewing assignments, to establishing 'telepresence', Facebook allows the trainer to 'connect' the classroom.

1. Introduction

Martin Weller argues that when it comes to integrating newer technologies into the classroom, specifically "internet-related technologies",[1] educators generally fall under one of the following two categories: e-learning detractors or e-learning enthusiasts (2007, p.6). E-learning detractors, who can be teachers and students alike, are, at times, "digital immigrants" (Prensky, 2001)[2]—individuals who have difficulty adapting to the 'language' of the 'digital natives'. Detractors opine that the decision to integrate new technologies, whether into their classroom routines or into their learning experiences, is often marked by a sense of insecurity and fear. Specifically, for educators, this "insecurity include[s] a level of 'not wanting to look foolish in front of students,'[who are increasingly "digital natives"] or be trapped by the technology with no options if the technology failed" (Schifter & Stewart, 2010, p.12). As an e-learning enthusiast, I am intrigued by the potential of using social networking sites, specifically Facebook,[3] as a tool for translator training rather than more "traditional" ("institutional") tools such as virtual learning environments (VLEs).[4] Drawing on my experience using Facebook in the context of teaching five undergraduate translation courses between 2005 and 2011 at the University of Ottawa in Canada, I will be assessing some of the benefits and drawbacks of incorporating social networking sites into translator training. Because the research is on-going at the time of writing, the observations discussed in this article are for the most part preliminary. Moreover, while some of the hypotheses make sense 'intuitively', they will require additional empirical data to support their relevance over the long-term. Nonetheless, I contend that some of my students' feedback, as well as my own personal observations, could provide some useful insight into future curriculum development in translator training. Using theoretical perspectives from cognitive constructivism and social constructivism, social presence theory, and insights from previous scholarship on translator training, I will argue that on the whole, there appears to be far more reason to include social networking in translator training than not.

First, I will map out a brief evolution of the Web (1.0, 2.0, 3.0) to illustrate how we are increasingly and inescapably living in a *networked, digitized, personalized* and *mobile* world. It is necessary to be aware of this evolution to understand the type of students (i.e. media savvy/media consumers) enrolling in and attending undergraduate translation programs – for the most part, these students are spending significant amounts of time interacting with technology and informal media (which include, for example, social networking sites). Krumsvick highlights key insights drawn from the British study *Personalisation and Digital Technologies* (Green, Facer, Rudd, Dillon & Humphreys, 2006):

> The study forecasts that today's [2008] British school-age child will, by the age of 21 [the approximate average age of an undergraduate student in Canada], have spent 15,000 hours in formal education, 20,000 hours watching television and 50,000 hours in front of a computer screen. Although this is merely a projection, it nevertheless provides an indication of the extent to which today's "screenagers" (Rushkoff 1996) or "millennium learners" (Pedro 2006) use the media Krumsvick 2009).[5]

In light of these statistical forecasts, it would seem a missed opportunity not to bridge institutionalized e-learning with students' online existences outside of the school's boundaries. Doing so would not only transmit course content but also impart increased digital competency and literacy as part of a complex learning strategy.[6] According to Peder Haug, who cites the work of Krumsvik and Jones (2007), "[...] in order to develop the students' digital competence, school should build on the students' needs and on their digital experiences from outside [school]" (2009, p.196). According to my observations, a significant amount of students' digital experiences outside school occur on social networking sites, making them a compelling locus for incorporating e-learning as part of translation competency.

Second, having identified that many translation students today are 'digital natives', I briefly argue in favour of incorporating social and cognitive constructivist approaches into today's translation classroom. I explain why I have chosen Facebook over traditional and institutional virtual learning environments (VLEs), in particular those provided by the University of Ottawa: Blackboard Vista / Virtual Campus / uoZone.[7]

Finally, I discuss some of the ways in which I have used social networking sites, particularly Facebook, in an attempt to enrich the translation training experience.

While I have my own biases as a translator trainer and fervent Facebook fan, in the final part of the article, I cite some of my students' personal observations and comments gathered over the period of experimentation as further support of using Facebook in translator training.[8] The overarching argument is in favour of social networking sites, however, negative aspects of these websites/web-based technologies will also be acknowledged throughout the article. These drawbacks should also be considered when choosing between an institutionalized VLE and a social networking site.

While training takes place in a variety of settings, five undergraduate courses serve as the training context for this particular case study. Arguably, the university classroom is not homogenous, but it does have certain characteristics that are not always present in other educational settings. For instance, students enrolled in an undergraduate translation course are not practising professionals with significant workplace experience; this is contrary to the state of affairs in professional workshops that cater to both professionals and trainees. Moreover, translation workshops often target a demographic that is already invested in the field of translation in some capacity, whereas this is not always the case for students in a first-year translation course who are trying to find their place in this new field.

2. The Web's evolution and its impact on teaching/learning

Without question, the Web and digital technologies have significantly altered many aspects of human interaction.[9] Moreover, these changes have been so rapid that it may seem nearly impossible to remember a time when we were not a "click away" from almost anything – an answer to a question, purchasing a product, booking a vacation and, in the context of translation, having access to a free, automatically translated text thanks to services such as Google Translate and Freetranslation.com. I would argue, however, that the Web has forcibly "digitized" our social interactions and that it is important to take a step back and take a moment to consider these shifts. After all, in terms of education and training, there is a direct correlation between the dissemination and implementation of digital technologies and the types of students populating today's classrooms. In fact, the use of digital technology and learning appear so increasingly intertwined, that some, such as Dr. Bruce D. Perry and Marc Prensky, argue that our brains have been altered as a result.

It is now clear that as a result of this ubiquitous environment and the sheer volume of their interaction with it, today's students *think and process information fundamentally differently* from their predecessors [...] "Different kinds of experiences lead to different brain structures," says Dr. Bruce D. Perry of Baylor College of Medicine [...]. It is very likely that *our students' brains have physically changed* [and] [...] we can say with certainty that their *thinking patterns* have changed (Prensky, 2001, p.1).

In the following paragraphs, I will briefly map out the Web's evolution and tie in these changes with some of the shifts that have occurred in pedagogy, and more specifically translation pedagogy.

The first "incarnation" of the Web is known as Web 1.0. Essentially, this was the "read-only web" where sought online content could have just as easily been found offline, for instance in a printed encyclopaedia or even on a CD-ROM. Content was uploaded online to be consulted 'passively' by users (read-only). In terms of modifying student behaviour and learning, Web 1.0 is likely the impetus behind the digital native habit of consulting the Web/Internet before consulting "offline" reference material (Prensky, 2001). Prior to the widespread use of Web 1.0, access to certain types of information/knowledge was generally restricted to experts and society's elite, which in turn justified a predominantly 'transmissionist' or 'instructivist' teaching model at the university level. Web 1.0 began to change this dynamic by democratizing access to information, which in turn modified the student/educator relationship. Students could access a wealth of information and find answers to virtually any question, bypassing the need for an in-person expert to 'transfer' content. That said, sifting through such a large body of information could cause 'content-overload', especially for students lacking certain digital competencies; the educator's role in the context of Web 1.0 was to help students navigate content and learn how to select valid, relevant sources. This shift from the trainer/educator as 'instructor' to 'guide' occurred roughly at the same period during which theories in education began to increasingly favour constructivist approaches; i.e. approaches that centered around the principles of "engagement, intelligibility and participation" (Weller, 2007, p.19). As Schifter and Stewart state: "As the technologies grew more multisensory, engaging, controllable and socially interactive [e.g. as Web 1.0 shifted to Web 2.0], elements of both the cognitive and social constructivist framework became apparent" (2010, p.14). Additionally, this led education theorists and educators alike to increasingly conceptualize the classroom as a "community" in which the student should be "enculturated" (Weller, 2007, p.19). "Community", at this juncture, generally implied the classroom community, not necessarily "community" in a broader sense (for example, the wider community of professional translators, the wider community of the university, the wider community at large, etc.).

Web 2.0 designates the Web's shift from a primarily read-only interface to a read-write interface. In other words, Web 2.0 meant that users could not only upload and disseminate content online; they could now interact with other users, as well as interact directly with Web-based content. Examples of Web 2.0 features include wikis (in which users can interact and modify online content),[10] online instant messaging (with which users can interact with each other in real-time), online forums (on which users can interact asynchronously), search engines (which use semantic searching mechanisms such as Google) and early incarnations of social networking sites such as Myspace, etc. Succinctly, not only could users 'congregate' virtually by consulting the same online content – creating a sense of "telepresence"[11] and "community"[12] – they could now collaborate digitally. Digital collaboration and sharing are two key Web 2.0 descriptors and they reinforce the notion of 'community' which is central to constructivist approaches in education. Thus, Web 2.0 technologies are particularly relevant tools in the context of e-learning. One example is the notion of peer-to-peer (P2P) collaboration. With Web 2.0, peer-to-peer collaboration can be exemplified through file sharing and instant messaging. In the context of constructivist strategies in education, peer-to-peer learning can take the form of discussion groups, tutoring and mentoring, both in and out of the classroom, as well as with collaborative assignments, etc. Evidently, this technology and these pedagogical activities can be combined so that students can use instant messaging to provide (peer)-mentorship and (peer)-tutoring in an online setting.

Another particularly important term associated with Web 2.0 is that of "online social networking". The adage "It's not what you know; it's who you know" was used before the Web; as such, it would be incorrect to claim that fostering a strong social network came about with the advent of the Web. However, it is interesting that most digital natives tend to associate any type of networking with online social networking, and this is largely due to the pervasiveness of social networking sites, especially, since 2006 with the mainstream use of Facebook. Indeed, such sites now constitute the backbone not only of major corporate marketing strategies, but are also ostensibly a main component of many universities' attempts at creating an online presence and branding strategy amongst potential and current students.[13] As a result, the connections that can be made between Web 2.0-style networking and education are numerous. In social constructivist theories, the belief is that learning is an inherently social practice; as such, social networking sites might offer a new locus for classroom activities (Selwyn, 2011, p.14). Social networking also promotes active participation or a participatory culture within shared communities, as well as a 'flattening the hierarchies' (cf., Kelly, 2005; Selwyn, 2011). Finally, "As Solomon and Schrum (2007) conclud[e] with regards to the second wave of 'social' internet applications that emerged throughout the 2000s, 'everyone can participate thanks to social networking and collaborative tools and the abundance of web 2.0 sites...The web is no longer a one-way street where someone controls the content. Anyone can control content in a web 2.0 world" (p. 8, as cited in Selwyn, 2011, pp.15-16).

Finally, the most recent incarnation, Web 3.0, also known as the semantic web,[14] focuses on customizing and personalizing the user's 'digital experience' through media and platform convergence. With the advent of more sophisticated and powerful mobile technologies (hardware such as smart phones and tablets, for instance, as well as software such as applications and widgets), digital natives are increasingly interested by platforms that allow them to consult and sift through all their data seamlessly. Web 3.0 caters to this request by allowing websites and other applications to 'talk to one another'; in short, data becomes interoperable and applications integrated—also known as convergence (Jenkins, 2006, p.282) so that users can now consult their e-mail on all their mobile devices, converge and upload multimedia files on social networking sites, etc. The notion of convergence, like the Web 1.0 and 2.0 notions of "digitized information" and "community", has also come to the fore in education scholarship, in particular with theories and approaches that foster "complex learning" (i.e., a convergence of skills) in which students are taught cross-disciplinary skills that include critical thinking, synthesis and metacognitive skills (Weller, 2007, p.20).

While the main goal of this paper is not to extensively outline the Web's evolution in any greater depth, this overview lists some of the web-based technological 'advancements' used by today's translation trainees and trainers.[15] Due to the Web's increased presence in the lives of students, the use of technology in the classroom appears inescapable. Moreover, if trainers do not want to seem like antiquated 'digital immigrants', ideally they will favour the use of up-to-date technologies, even if at first this can be intimidating. Furthermore, today's undergraduate student is largely the product of a social and cognitive constructivist education (from K-12, or what is also known as "compulsory schooling"),[16] meaning that transmission-style lectures are also viewed as being archaic and out of sync with students' previous educational experiences and currently favoured pedagogical approaches. In her book *A handbook for translator trainers: A guide to reflective practice*, Dorothy Kelly (2005) discusses many of the challenges trainers and trainees face. Because training is generally split between university professors and translation professionals (retired translators, government employees, freelancers), teaching styles can vary tremendously. Kelly affirms "As professionals with little time to devote to reflection on how to organize teaching and learning, many early trainers limit [...] class activity to asking for on-sight translation of journalistic and literary texts, with little or no prior preparation on the part of the students" (2005, p.11). Her assertion echoes Kiraly's (1995) earlier observations, and while Kelly claims that progress has been made since the publication of Kiraly's work (her publication arriving nearly a decade later and overviewing the work of prominent translation pedagogues),[17] I would argue that as a graduate of the School of Translation and Interpretation's undergraduate program (graduating class of 2005), I have attended lectures that were taught in a similar fashion to that previously described: that is to say, translations carried out by students in class, with no prior contextual information and/or preparation – a context that left my peers and me feeling completely disengaged. Moreover, students of my graduating class were even deterred or barred from using the Web by some professors who felt that using such technology was unprofessional, unscholarly and even deemed, in some extreme cases, to be a form of cheating. In the context of today's competitive marketplace, it would be unreasonable to suggest that one could not have access to the Web in order to carry out one's work, especially in the context of professional translation praxis in which quick turnaround and speedy information retrieval are deemed essential to the translator's skill set.

Given that the role of training is to prepare trainees for the marketplace that awaits them upon graduation, it follows that translation training must ideally incorporate these technological changes into the classroom, whether in terms of using the technologies in the context of practical/professional translation or as part of the teaching methodology. Certainly, translation technology courses are one way of doing this (teaching *wiki*-technology in the context of a translation technology course in the same way as computer-assisted translation tools or translation memory software would allow translator trainees to have a better command of wiki-technology in the context of localization, for instance), but I also contend that there is something to be said about the actual teaching of translation through some of the interfaces and tools provided by Web 2.0 and Web 3.0[18]—which is why I justify a move to Facebook.

3. Using Facebook as a Pedagogical Translation Tool—preliminary observations

3. 1 Why Facebook?

The first question that arose when I first started presenting my preliminary hypotheses (Desjardins, 2010, 2011) pertaining to the use of Facebook in translator training was why I had chosen this particular platform instead of a more 'conventional' and academically 'acceptable' VLE. There are two answers to this question. The first is rather simple: from 2006 to 2011, at the beginning of each semester and with each new group of students, I polled the students anonymously, asking them to choose between having our class group on WebCT or on Facebook.[19] In total, of the approximately 200 undergraduate students I have taught, only 5 of these students have significantly opposed the use of Facebook, and this was either due to an altogether refusal to use the site or due to a lack of an existing Facebook profile at the time (2 of the initial detractors eventually created profiles, while the other 3 maintained their ideological stance).[20] Evidently, given the overwhelming majority favoured the use of Facebook, the use of the site was deemed consensual. Because the use of Facebook was initially an "add on" to the courses' mandatory core content, important notifications were always conveyed either in-class or through a mandatory e-mailing list so that all students, regardless of Facebook membership, would be contacted. However, as semesters would progress, initially sceptical or reluctant students would generally hear of the benefits and sign up.

The second answer is slightly more complex. First, while some claim Facebook's status as a commercial company and classroom distraction (Bugeja, 2007) blurs the lines between 'laudable' academia and corporate culture and consequently has no place over more widely-accepted VLEs such as WebCT and Blackboard, I personally fail to see the difference. For instance, to suggest that Blackboard is any less of a commercial entity than Facebook seems unjustified; advertising and branding may be less obvious with the tools provided by the former company, but authors such as Selwyn tend to place both companies on an equal playing field stating that "a multitude of commercial providers and IT industry actors are responsible for 'selling' [...] educational technologies to schools" (2011, p.11). This runs parallel to Giroux's description of the university acting increasingly like a corporation:

> Anyone who spends any time on a college campus [...] these days cannot miss how higher education is changing. Strapped for money and increasingly defined through the language of corporate culture, many universities seem less interested in higher learning than in becoming storefronts for brand-name corporations – selling off space, buildings, and endowed chairs to rich corporate donors. (2007, p.105).

Furthermore, universities are even branding themselves in order to 'sell' their programs over those of other universities' (Giroux, 2007); ironically, one of the main strategies of this type of corporate branding strategies is marketing via Facebook.

From a pedagogical perspective, I would be tempted to argue that VLEs still place the educator at the 'center' of course content dissemination: VLE moderation can in most cases only be granted to the course's lecturer or professor. If using Facebook, however, the educator may be the one who creates the courses' online discussion groups, but then can grant administrative functions to any and all group participants, thus eliminating an online hierarchy between educator and students in terms of uploading content. In my experience, this has fostered increased online group/discussion participation and has also increased my "telepresence" with students, simultaneously creating a heightened perception of "being there" and "being with" (Schifter & Stewart, 2010, p.18). Moreover, Facebook was not an innocent choice; the site is used nearly ubiquitously by students and incorporating the site into one's course structure meant permeating into students' social lives. Whereas students could easily claim "forgetting" to check the institutional VLE, students tend to log onto Facebook daily (if not more frequently), and as such, it was a strategic medium to stay connected with them. On the whole, I would say that my students have found my use of Facebook "surprising" and "cool", and have framed me as a more "approachable" and "up-to-date" lecturer because of it.[21] Instructivist and constructivist approaches argue that one of the fundamental roles of the educator is to connect with students offline and online; I have found that my use of a Facebook group has ostensibly favoured both offline and online connections.

The final part of the answer lies in the symbolic connotation associated with VLEs: Facebook is an inherently social interface, and as such, student contributions to the group are not generally seen in the same light as 'homework', which bears a negative connotation; rather, contributions to Facebook's discussion threads—whether achieved by posting videos, sharing news articles, etc.—become part of a social experience. As some of the previously cited social constructivists have argued, reframing learning as socialising has a lot more currency for digital natives and certainly promotes the view of the trainer as 'cognitive coach'. VLEs are perceived by students as institutional tools that are regulated and that promote and value certain types of interactions over others. Finally, as a trainer, I wonder about the universities' rationale behind implementing institution-wide VLEs; while I would be tempted to think this is to foster e-learning, to cater to diverse learning styles and to optimize student/teacher contact, one might instead get the impression that these environments benefit the corporate strategies of the institutions rather than meeting purely academic goals. To explain briefly, let me use the example of WebCT's 2003 sales pitch (as cited in Weller, 2007, p.8): "E-learning technology is a proven way to expand an institution's enrolment capacity without the capital outlays for new construction. Institutional infrastructure can be built virtually rather than physically, often at lower cost". Keeping costs at a minimum seems to be a recurrent trend for universities seeking to maximize the bottom line which is also achieved by "replacing full-timers with part-timers and temps and by subcontracting everything from food services to the total management of physical plants, but also by substituting various schemes of computerized instruction" (Ohmann, 2002).

Given the scope of this article, I will not delve into more of the reasoning behind choosing Facebook over the University of Ottawa's Blackboard Vista; I hope the previous arguments will prove sufficient for the time being.

4. 1 Facebook, Social Networking and Translator Training—a few examples

Communities are formed around a sense of belonging and shared practices (Weller, 2007; Stewart, Schifter, & Selverian, 2010). If learning is a social process, it follows that we should create disciplinary communities that primarily use shared social practices. In my estimation, the Facebook group is a tool that achieves this quite successfully. Not only does the Facebook group easily facilitate the possibility of peer-to-peer networking (which includes group and private instant messaging, asynchronous discussion threads, and the possibility of classmates becoming Facebook "friends"), but it also creates a link with the larger professional translation community. For instance, by encouraging students to use online social networking in their translation practice, the translation trainer implicitly trains students to talk about translation with others (peers, fellow students, other translators, other Facebook users, etc.). Doing so forces the trainees to utilize translation's metalanguage and concepts regularly, which helps them become 'fluent' in the language of professional translation and is likely to better prepare them to face some of the adversity professional translators face in the workplace. For instance, a trainee who has become accustomed to discussing their reasoning behind certain terminological choices is far more likely to convince a client than one who has never had this opportunity. And while such an exercise could be carried out in the classroom, the synchronous/asynchronous feature of the Facebook group allows students the time to reflect and come back to the exercise rather than having to perform on demand, which can be especially intimidating for introverted students. To encourage the active discussion of translation both online and offline is to prepare students for the marketplace in that they will be able to talk about what it is that they are doing. Passive learning, the type that Kiraly (1995) and Kelly (2005) both strongly denounce, does not empower students to think of themselves as professionals able to speak about their profession and skills. Moreover, discussing translation and supplementing this discussion using media rich content (videos, sound clips, mash-ups, pictures, applications, etc.), which is easily integrated into the Facebook group (and does not have to go through the trainer to be uploaded), has the added advantage of situating the translation student in the larger translation community. For example, being able to easily and instantaneously post online news articles pertaining to current affairs involving translation tells students that what they are learning is directly related to real-world events.

Additionally, the social nature of Facebook deters student disengagement. Because translation is a highly subjective practice and involves a much broader skill set than most lay people and incoming undergraduates realize, in my experience, beginner trainees often feel discouraged after they have received their first evaluations. Students can be encouraged to post some of their solutions on the Facebook group's discussion wall ("board"), and may discover, to their surprise, that many of their peers had similar solutions. Not only is this form of peer-to-peer sharing invaluable in terms of creating a sense of classroom community (through shared practice/share experience), but the posts act as a sort of collaborative translation. Students may build upon each other's ideas and rework their translations. From an educator's perspective, these posts provide insight with regards to students' learning curves, their aptitudes, and the areas that need improvement without the detrimental effect of punitive evaluation which is invaluable in terms of providing ongoing assessment and feedback for students. Though some of these exercises and features are available through VLEs, in my experience, participation has always been more positive and more active via Facebook.

Finally, professional translation praxis is increasingly becoming collaborative and "digitized" in nature. Though translators have always worked in tandem with other specialized professionals (subject-field experts, for instance) and clients, new technologies and digitization have created new challenges and novel types of translation projects that require a full command of digital competencies. For instance, Ubisoft, an educational software and videogame company, employs translators/localizers to work alongside programmers and software engineers in order to create localized versions of their products. The localization strategy inevitably includes the translation of marketing campaigns, which, unsurprisingly, often incorporate social media (Facebook and Twitter). The more translators find ways of integrating and using social media in their professional translation practice, the more savvy they will be in terms of translating content destined for these platforms. For instance, a 2011 guest lecture at the School of Translation given by freelancer and videogame localizer Baris Bilgen included some examples of localizers having to translate Twitter "tweets" for promotional purposes. Tweets are 140-character micro-blogs (or micro-messages) that can be used to "publish" quick, instantaneous updates—in short, they are an extremely condensed version of larger-scale social networking profiles and pages. 'Tweets' are commonly used by companies to launch new products, and thus, localized versions of these 'tweets' have become central to international marketing campaigns. Students who are well-versed in online social media understand the relevance and structure of these updates and as a result, they are also better suited to translate them in an efficient and effective manner. In light of these types of campaigns, educators can incorporate online social media into translation exercises such as the localization of tweets. For example, a "Translation Challenge" posted on a class' Facebook group wall might consist of translating 140-character posts and the student who could respond the fastest (exemplifying the translator's ability to provide quick turnaround time) with the most effective target version (based on in-class lectures on what parameters constituted "most effective" or "most functional") would "win". Not only does this exercise implement a number of constructivist principles (role-playing, simulation, collaboration, etc.), but it demonstrates that social networking sites are not simply used for professional networking—they are also being translated. Facebook's statistics page boasts that the site is translated and localized in 70 different languages.

5. Student Comments

Given certain challenges with regards to ethics clearance, screenshots of students' Facebook contributions could not be included in this article. While this is certainly a substantial drawback, it does suggest some avenues for more thorough research in the future as well as the possibility of collecting additional empirical data to support some of the tentative hypotheses presented here. Fortunately, many students share their opinions regarding the use of Facebook using the University of Ottawa's teaching evaluations which take place every semester. Student feedback is anonymous and given to the professor only after the final marks have been submitted to the administration.

Overall, response to Facebook was positive. Students enjoyed feeling that they could easily contact the professor and found that while it was unconventional to discuss course content via Facebook's features, it made them feel as though they could more easily relate to the professor and vice versa. Moreover, they appreciated that they had been exposed to the networking potential of social media in professional translation praxis. They thoroughly enjoyed creating promotional Facebook pages for fictional translation companies, translating 'tweets' and 'status updates', uploading YouTube videos of newer translation technologies (for example, tutorials for Google Translate and Word Lens), and participating in what came to be known as the "translation classroom community". Shy students enjoyed using Facebook, stating that while conventional VLEs were helpful in terms of accommodating their personalities and learning styles, being able to use online social media made them feel "more extroverted" and "more connected" to the rest of the group. Students with lower level of linguistic proficiency, either in the L1 or L2, expressed that they had started using Facebook in different languages in order to increase their linguistic proficiency—an unintended benefit which certainly merits additional study.

In short, student commentary tended to support two main hypotheses I had when initially considering the use of social networking sites in translator training: (1) such media easily enable trainers to implement and devise social and cognitive constructivist approaches; (2) the possibilities for finding links between these sites and professional translation are only beginning to come to the fore—as mentioned previously, not only can social networking sites themselves be translated (link with practical translation/professional translation), but they can also become tools for translator training and professional networking.

6. Conclusion

Initially, investigating how Facebook could play a positive role in translation pedagogy was simply a means to find an alternative to conventional VLEs. In other words, Facebook seemed a more convenient way of conveying course-related content to students in a way that would appeal to them. After having used Facebook for nearly 5 years, I now realize the repercussions of using these websites and they far exceed expectations, both in terms of the benefits, and especially in terms of the potential ethical and pedagogical drawbacks that authors like Selwyn (2011) have so aptly discussed in their critical assessment of digital technologies in schools. Particularly worthy of further analysis and discussion are the issues of privacy and security, and while a detailed position on the matter falls slightly out of the scope of this preliminary set of observations, suffice to say they cannot be disregarded. Hacking, content copyright, and students' and educators' privacy settings are a few examples of parameters that would require more investigation.[22] Moreover, the idea that Facebook can be a tool in education is certainly not novel, and has increasingly been discussed in second-language education (Roblyer et al., 2010; Kabilan et al., 2010; Blattner & Fiori, 2009), thus far, however, there seems be relatively little research on social networking sites, particularly Facebook and their relevance in and for Translation Studies. I hope this article has begun to fill that void.

By no means do I believe these observations to be conclusive, especially given the transient nature of the Web and digital technologies, but nevertheless contend that future research that links online social networking, translation training and professional translation will become indispensable. Facebook may often be framed as a distraction rather than a potentially rich educational space; this is unfortunate, particularly because excluding these tools from our classrooms represents a missed opportunity when they are so pervasive on the outside. Social networking sites can be incorporated in ways that foster complex learning provided students are taught to use them judiciously. If this can be achieved, then I would argue that we are effectively helping students to navigate the social, academic and professional spheres, both physical and virtual, in which they invariably interact. And is that not the goal of higher education as a whole?

References

Anderon, C. (2006). *The long tail: Why the future of business is selling less of more.* New York: Hyperion.

Blattner, G. & Fiori, M. (2009). Promises and possibilities. *International Journal of Instructional Technology and Distance Learning. 6*(1), 17-28.

Boyd, D.M. & Ellison, N.B. (2007). Social networking sites: Definition, history, and scholarship. *Journal of Computer-Mediated Communication, 13*(1), 210-230.

Bugeja, M. (2007). Distractions in the wireless classroom. *The Chronicle of Higher Education.* Retrieved from http://chronicle.com/article/Distractions-in-the-Wireless/46664.

Charron, M. (2005). Plus vite, encore plus vite : la traduction à l'heure de la mondialisation. *Translation Studies in the New Millennium, 3*, 15-27.

Chickering, A. & Gamson, Z. (Eds.). (1991). *Applying the seven good principles for good practice in undergraduate education.* San Francisco: Jossey-Bass.

Delisle, J. (2003). *La traduction raisonnée : manuel d'initiation à la traduction professionnelle.* Ottawa, Canada: University of Ottawa Press.

Delisle, J. (2005). *L'enseignement pratique de la traduction.* Ottawa, Canada: University of Ottawa Press.

D'eon, G. (Director/Writer) (2011, October 28). *Facebook follies.* CBC *Doc Zone.* Toronto, Canada: Canadian Broadcasting Corporation.

Desjardins, R. (2011, April). How Facebook can revamp translator training. *Forum 2011: Innovations in Translator, Interpreter and Localizer Education.* Symposium conducted at the Monterey Institute of International Studies, Monterey, CA.

Desjardins, R. (2010, March). Facebook me!: Arguing in favour of social networking websites as pedagogical translation tools. *9th Edition of Voyages in Translation Studies.* Colloquium conducted at Concordia University, Montreal, Québec, Canada.

Findlay, S. (2010, March 1). Who needs a prof? *Maclean's.* Retrieved from http://oncampus.macleans.ca/education/2010/03/01/who-needs-a-prof

Gane, N. (2005). An information age without technology? *Information, Communication and Society 8*(4), 471-476.

Gile, D. (1995,2009). *Basic concepts and models for interpreter and translator training* (2nd ed). Amsterdam: John Benjamins.

Giroux, H.A. (2007). *The university in chains: Confronting the military-industrial-academic complex.* Boulder, CO: Paradigm Publishers.

Gouadec, D. (2007). *Translation as a profession.* Amsterdam: John Benjamins.

Green, H., Facer, K., Rudd, T., Dillon, P., & Humphreys, P. (2006). *Personalisation and digital technologies.* London: Futurelab.

Jenkins, H. (2006). *Convergence culture.* New York: New York University Press.

Kelly, D. (2005). *A handbook for translator trainers: A guide to reflective practice.* Manchester, UK: St. Jerome.

Kenny, D. (1999). CAT tools in an academic environment: What are they good for? *Target 11*(1), 65-82.

Kiraly, D. C. (1995). *Pathways to translation: Pedagogy and process*. Kent, OH: Kent State University Press.

Krumsvik, R. (Ed.). (2009). *Learning in the network society and the digitized school*. New York: Nova Science.

Kussman, P. & Tirkonnen-Condit, S. (1995). Think-aloud protocol analysis in Translation Studies. *TTR: traduction, terminologie, rédaction, 8*(1), 177-199.

Lévy, P. (2001). *Cyberculture* (R. Bononno, Trans.). Minneapolis, MN: Minnesota University Press.

Lombard, M. & Ditton, T. (1997). At the heart of it all: The concept of presence. *Journal of Computer-Mediated Communication, 3*(2). Retrieved from http://jcmc.indiana.edu/vol3/issue2/lombard.html

McDonough, J. (2007). How do language professionals organize themselves? An overview of translation networks. *Meta: journal des traducteurs/Meta: Translators' Journal, 52*(4), 793-815.

Nord, C. (1991). *Text analysis in translation* (C. Nord & P. Sparrow, Trans.). Atlanta, GA: Rodopi.

Ohmann, R. (2002). Citizenship and literacy work: Thoughts without a conclusion. *Workplace*. Retrieved from http://louisville.edu/journal/workplace/issue7/ ohmann.html

Pedro, F. (2006). *The new millennium learners: Challenging our views on ICT and learning organisation for economic co-operation and development*. Retrieved from: http://www.oecd.org/dataoecd/1/1/38358359.pdf

Perkins, D. (2009). *Making learning whole: How seven principles of teaching can transform education*. San Francisco: Jossey-Bass.

Prensky, M. (2001). Digital natives, digital immigrants, part II: Do they really think differently? *On the horizon, 9*(6). NCB University Press, 1-9.

Prensky, M. (2006). Listen to the natives. *Educational Leadership, 63*(4), 8-13.

Prensky, M. (2007). How to teach with technology. *BECTA's Emerging Technologies for Learning, 2,* 40-46.

Robinson, D. (2003). *Becoming a translator: An introduction to the theory and practice of translation*. London: Routledge.

Roblyer, M. D., McDaniel, M., Webb, M., Herman, J., & Witty, J. V. (2010). Findings on Facebook in higher education: A comparison of college faculty and student uses and perceptions of social networking sites. *Internet and Higher Education. 13*(3), 134-140.

Rushkoff, D. (1996). *Playing the future: What we can learn from digital kids* New York: Riverhead Books.

Selwyn, N. (2011). *Schools and schooling in the digital age: A critical analysis*. London: Routledge.

Shih, C. (2009). *The Facebook era: Tapping online social networks to build better products, reach new audiences, and sell more stuff*. Boston: Pearson Education/Prentice Hall.

Solomon, G. & Schrum, L. (2007). *Web 2.0: New tools, new schools*. Washington DC: International Society for Technology in Education.

Stewart, C.M., Schifter, C.C., & Markaridian Selverian, M. (Eds.). (2010). *Teaching and Learning with Technology: Beyond Constructivism*. London: Routledge.

TechTerms. (2011) *Wiki definition*. Retrieved from http://www.techterms.com/definition/wiki.

Weller, M. (2007). *Virtual Learning Environments: Using, choosing and developing your VLE*. London: Routledge.

Wenger, E., White, N., & Smith, J. (2009). *Digital Habitats: stewarding technology for communities*. Portland, OR: CPsquare.

---

[1] "The US-based *Learning Circuits* magazine (http://www.learningcircuits.org/glossary) defines it as 'a wide set of applications and processes, such as Web-based learning, computer-based learning, virtual classrooms, and digital collaboration. It includes the delivery of content via internet, intranet/extranet (LAN/WAN), audio- and videotape, satellite broadcast, interactive TV, CD-ROM, and more.' [...] So, for the purpose of this book I will define e-learning as any learning experience that utilizes internet-related technologies to some extent. This definition emphasizes the internet as the primary medium with regards to e-learning but does not exclude blending with other media and approaches (for example DVD, face-to-face, print, etc.), but by focusing on the internet, some key features of the medium, and how these relate to learning and teaching can be examined" (Weller, 2007, p.5).

[2] Prensky uses the terms "digital immigrants" and "digital natives" to make the distinction between those who were born before and after the mainstream use of digital technologies: "What should we call these *"new"* students of today? Some refer to them as the N-[for Net]-gen or D-[for digital]-gen. But the most useful designation I have found for them is *Digital Natives*. Our students today are all "native speakers" of the digital language of computers, video games and the Internet. So what does that make the rest of us? Those of us who were not born into the digital world but have, at some later point in our lives, become fascinated by and adopted many or most aspects of the new technology are, and will always be compared to them, *Digital Immigrants*. The importance of the distinction is this: as Digital Immigrants learn – like all immigrants, some better than others – to adapt to their environment, they always retain, to some degree, their "accent,", that is their foot in the past. The "digital immigrant accent" can be seen in such as things as turning to the Internet for information second rather than first [...]" (2001, p.12).

[3] As of May 2008, Facebook was ranked the world's most frequently consulted and used social networking site (Balagué &Fayon, 2010, p. 14). According to Facebook's own statistics page (http://www.facebook.com/press/info.php?statistics), at the time of writing, the social networking site has a total of more than 750 million active users.

[4] I follow Weller's definition: "For our purposes, we will define a VLE and LMS [learning management system] as 'a software that combines a number of different tools that are used to systematically deliver content online and facilitate the learning experience around that content'. This definition is sufficiently broad to encompass most recognized VLEs, regardless of

whether they have an underlying pedagogy associated with them. It does, however, deliberately exclude bespoke websites, or specific tools that may be used in a learning context but do not in themselves constitute a VLE. The point about a VLE is that it is an enterprise, institution-wide system used by a variety of educators to deliver a range of courses; it is not specific to one course or one function" (Weller, 2007, p.5).

5   Prensky states: "Today's [2001] average college grads have spent less 5,000 hours of their lives reading, but over 10,000 hours playing video games (not to mention 20,000 hours watching TV). Computer games, email, the Internet, cell phones and instant messaging are all integral parts of their lives" (2001, p.1).

6   Weller explains that complex learning is "an approach that focuses on the type of learning that takes place across or between courses. It is concerned with the development of complex skills such as critical thinking, analysis, synthesis and evaluation as well as metacognitive skills. These go beyond an appreciation of the particular subject matter and require considerable time to develop [...]. They are also the type of skills that employers frequently say they require of graduates" (2007, p.20). In my estimation, this falls in line with some of the suggestions Donald C. Kiraly listed in his "New Pedagogy of Translation", in which translator training goes beyond simply translating texts and seeks to encourage students to utilize a broader skill set to solve translation 'problems' and tasks (1995, p.18-19 and p. 33).

7   The University of Ottawa's portal ("web-based system for non-course related information" (Weller, 2007, p.58) is called uOzone. uOzone, as defined by the University, is the "gateway to your uOttawa web applications, personalized information and alerts from your professors, faculty and department...all in one central, single sign-on environment" (http://uozone.uottawa.ca/en/faq). From this portal, students can access "Virtual Campus" which houses the University of Ottawa's virtual learning environment, Blackboard Vista (previously, the University of Ottawa used WebCT as its primary VLE; Blackboard acquired WebCT through a merger that took place in 2005-2006).

8   In compliance with research ethics, student feedback was offered voluntarily and anonymously in the "Additional Comments" section of the University of Ottawa's Teaching and Course Evaluation Questionnaire. As such, these data can be included in academic research without asking explicit consent from individual students.

9   Nicholas Gane further describes these changes and states: "It would seem to me that internet-related technologies have directly altered the patterning of our everyday life, including the way we work, access and exchange information, shop, meet people, and maintain and organise existing social ties. These technologies have dome more than 'add on' to existing social arrangements; they have radically altered the three main spheres of social life, the spheres of production, consumption and communication" (2005, p.475).

10   "A wiki is a Web site that allows users to add and update content on the site using their own Web browser. This is made possible by Wiki software that runs on the Web server. Wikis end

up being created mainly by a collaborative effort of the site visitors. A great example of a large wiki is the Wikipedia, a free encyclopedia in many languages that anyone can edit. The term "wiki" comes from the Hawaiian phrase, "wiki wiki," which means "super fast." I guess if you have thousands of users adding content to a Web site on a regular basis, the site could grow 'super fast'." (TechTerms, 2011, *wiki* definition)

[11] According to Schifter and Stewart, "telepresence is the "perceptual illusion of nonmediation" (Lombard and Ditton, 1997). "Perceptual" refers to the real-time reaction of the individual through sensory, cognitive and affective systems to stimuli. The "illusion of nonmediation" occurs when the individual no longer recognizes that the sensory stimuli are introduced or produced through a medium" (2010, p.18). In short, Web 2.0 blurred the lines between our virtual and real lives in that even though social interaction is filtered through the medium of the screen and the Web itself, users still perceive the "real presence" of their interlocutors.

[12] "In retrospect, looking back at the development of the internet, it makes sense that such technology would profoundly affect the potential of communities because the interactivity and connectivity it enables are so aligned with the ways communities of practice function as a context for learning" (Wenger et al., 2009, cited in Wenger, 2009, p.xv).

[13] For example, the University of Ottawa has a Facebook page: http://www.facebook.com/pages/Universit%C3%A9-dOttawa-University-of-Ottawa/ 34877449140.

[14] "The Semantic Web provides a common framework that allows data to be shared and reused across application, enterprise, and community boundaries. It is a collaborative effort led by W3C with participation from a large number of researchers and industrial partners." (http://www.w3.org/2001/sw/SW-FAQ)

[15] While I generally maintain an optimistic and positive view of Web technologies, I am aware that it is important to consider some of the negative consequences and effects these technologies can also have. In fact, more and more recent scholarship has presented the 'untold story' of academic digitization which tends to paint a far less utopian picture. This body of research suggests that digitization presents an "illusion of novel progress" (new = better) (c.f. Selwyn, 2011) and is largely premised upon "corporate education" (cf., Giroux, 2007).

[16] "i.e. the elementary and secondary schooling that is provided free of charge by the state and is generally mandatory for all children and young people" (Selwyn, 2011, p.8)

[17] Cf., Delisle (2003), Nord (1991), Gile (1995), Kiraly (1995) and Robinson (2003).

[18] Using technology both in terms of practical translation and as part of the teaching method has the "double advantage of giving students the practical skills they will require in the workplace

and of generating new knowledge of how technologies impact on translation practice" (Kenny, 1999, p.73).

[19] This was prior to the University of Ottawa's implementation of *Blackboard Vista.*

[20] Correspondence with these students was maintained using alternative solutions such as in-person meetings or e-mail.

[21] Comments excerpted from my teaching evaluations.

[22] A recent Canadian documentary produced by the CBC (Canadian Broadcasting Corporation) titled *Facebook follies* addressed some of these issues, using recent examples from the corporate and public sectors, as well as examples from individual's private lives. Security experts weighed in on the issues and suggest that social media literacy is a competency that many lack. These observations add weight to the argument that social media literacy should be part of media literacy, and taught as part of core content in today's classrooms.

An empirical study of professional translators' attitudes, use and awareness of Web 2.0 technologies, and implications for the adoption of emerging technologies and trends

Joanna Gough

University of Surrey

This questionnaire-based study was conducted as a part of an MA Dissertation in the summer of 2010 (Gough, 2010a). It examines the trends within the translation industry which have developed in response to the evolution of the Web from Web 1.0 (the information web) to Web 2.0 (the social web) and places professional translators against the backdrop of these trends. The developments based on the principles of sharing, openness and collaboration associated with Web 2.0 can be seen as affecting the tools used by translators and the processes in which they engage. This study examines professional translators' awareness and perception of the new open, collaborative tools and processes and the degree of tools usage and process participation. The key findings of this study highlight translators' vague awareness and insufficient understanding of these trends, marginal use of the open tools and little engagement in the collaborative processes. The underlying factor determining translators' awareness, perception and the use of these tools and processes is their attitude towards adopting new technologies, with an indication that professionals with innovative attitudes are more inclined to embrace the new trends and developments.

1. Introduction

Since the birth of the World Wide Web in the 1990s, we have witnessed a galloping "webolution" enabled by the various technological advancements in Information Technology. This webolution seems to be accelerating more and more rapidly. No sooner does a concept become widely recognised and acknowledged, than it changes, evolves or morphs into another one, causing academic research to become outdated faster than ever before. This study is focused upon Web 2.0 and the issues it presents to today's translators. It is relevant to the technological challenges of the present day; however it is cognisant of further changes from evolving new technologies, e.g., those associated with Web 3.0.

Traditionally, technology has not been perceived by translators as a vital part of the translation process, mainly because the process of linguistic and cultural rendition has always been exclusively tied to the cognitive and creative skills, which are deemed essentially human. For this reason, as Bergman (n.d.) observes, professional translators might not generally have been associated with tech-savviness or fast adoption of trends and developments in the field of translation technology. Admittedly, the adoption of Computer Assisted Translation (CAT) technology increased in the last decade and Shuttleworth and Lagoudaki (2006) rightly point out that "translation professionals seem to have achieved a certain level of sophistication as computer users and greater familiarity with TM systems" (n.p.). However, new trends and technologies emerge faster than ever before and with the lack of empirical studies assessing the adoption of these trends and technologies by professional translators it is difficult to gauge the current status. This research has therefore been motivated to provide such evidence.

2. The significance of Web 2.0

The Internet is undoubtedly the biggest technological revolution of our time. The early Internet, now labelled Web 1.0, had a fairly static form, with books, news, music etc. being merely posted on-line in a digital format. It was akin to a one-way street. As the adoption of the Internet increased and feedback loops were formed, the evolution of technology began to encompass the two-way communication desires of the end users. The arrival of Web 2.0 applications which enabled this two-way communication (such as Wikipedia, Twitter or YouTube), encouraged active participation, allowing users not only to socialise, generate content and share ideas, but also to engage in work practices on-line, with the benefit of instant, global communication. Closer to the translation field, sites like ProZ have benefitted from the interactive features of Web 2.0 such as KudoZ network or the job posting board. No longer a narrow one-way street, the Internet has become a superfast, multilane, two-way highway. The underlying "collaborative" characteristic of Web 2.0 spawned a new generation of Internet-enabled technologies which have had a tremendous impact on the translation industry and the ensuing practices of professional translators. This impact is observable in the tools used by translators and the processes they engage in.

The major changes affecting the architecture of modern internet tools, including translation tools, are twofold. On the one hand, there is the collaboration-driven, open source movement which is affecting software applications and undermining the proprietary model, and on the other hand, there is a shift in emphasis on the value of data as opposed to the value of applications per se. The translation tools market, hitherto filled exclusively with proprietary, inflexible and expensive software has been permeated with various open, often free of charge tools offering a greater degree of flexibility and customization. The market dominance of closed-environment desktop tools has diminished in favour of their web-based counterparts which allow collaboration, cloud-based resource sharing in real time and offer a better, XML based architecture and a higher degree of interoperability (Gough, 2010b). The underlying data-driven approach of Web 2.0 (which benefits from the abundance of data on the Internet) has not only brought about the rapid development of statistical machine translation but highlighted the issue of data sharing.[1]

Workflows, referred to in this paper as 'processes', too, have been subjected to a radical change. The traditional, sequential, Gutenberg-based TEP (translate, edit, proofread) model has been undermined by a PCTP (plan, coordinate, translate, publish) model, supercharged on today's broadband-distributed collaborative network (Beninatto & DePalma, 2007), with added steps allowing for machine translation and crowd/community contribution. Various collaborative processes enabled by Web 2.0 technologies, such as crowdsourcing and community translation, have disturbed the status quo and are changing the traditional landscape of the translation workflow. According to Garcia and Stevenson (2008, 28) these processes "are going to shake the profession in a [...] radical way". As the translation industry is undergoing dramatic changes, translation in the globalised society is emerging as a "standard feature, a ubiquitous service, [...] a basic need of human civilisation" (Van der Meer, 2011a, n.p.). Translation tools and processes are constantly adapting to these changes to fit in with our changing lifestyles, preferences and habits and to meet the growing demand for translation services. But these changes are disruptive and as such affect the human workforce of the industry the most. Professional translators are the human core of the translation industry and therefore are very likely to feel the immediate effects of such disruptive innovation. This study examines how professional translators are responding to the recent changes affecting the translation industry.

3. The questionnaire

For the purpose of this study, a questionnaire comprising of 21 questions was developed (see Appendix). It aimed to examine professional translators' awareness of the new open and collaborative tools and processes, establish to what degree translators use these tools and participate in the processes, and investigate what is their perception of these tools and processes. It also briefly examined how professional translators are adapting to the changing landscape of the translation industry.

The questionnaire was distributed in English via numerous forum groups such as LinkedIn, ProZ and Translators Cafe as well as websites (e.g., www.translatorstraining.com), newsletters (e.g., Translation

Automation User Society (TAUS)), e-mails, blogs and Twitter. It was circulated for 6 weeks, from 12 July until 22 August 2010 and yielded 224 usable responses from professional translators. Whilst 42 countries were represented, the sample was dominated by respondents from European countries (67%), with small samples from the Americas (14%), Asia (6%) and Africa (1%). 12% of respondents did not disclose their place of residence. 65% of the respondents were female, and all ages were represented in relatively equal proportions. Translators with 3-5 years of experience accounted for a third of the sample, representing the largest single group while over 50% of the respondents indicated experience in excess of 6 years (see Figure 1). The respondents were asked to classify themselves with regard to adopting new technologies. The following classification was used:

(1)   Innovator/early adopter—looking for innovative solutions and picking up new technologies as soon as they emerge

(2)   Fast follower—careful attitude but accepting change more quickly than the average

(3)   Late majority—sceptical attitude and using new technologies when the majority are using them

(4)   Traditionalist—only accepting new technologies when they have become commonplace tradition.

Almost half of the respondents declared to be fast followers and one third classified themselves as late majority.

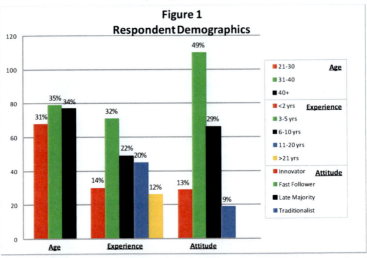

Figure 1: Respondent demographics in terms of age, experience and attitude

82% of respondents were freelancers, 20% held in-house positions, 27% worked for agencies or language service providers, 37% worked directly with clients and 12% worked in other roles.

The survey data were analysed in the subsequent sections according to the following categories *age*, *experience* and *attitude* towards adopting new technologies.

4. The results

4.1. Awareness of concepts related to Web 2.0 technologies

The respondents were asked to state the level of their familiarity with various concepts related to Web 2.0 and translation technology such as cloud computing, crowdsourcing/community translation, collaborative translation, open source collaborative translation tools, translation memory (TM) sharing, and the convergence of machine translation (MT) with TM (see legend of Figures 2a and 2b).

The results revealed that translators display a certain degree of awareness of general concepts related to the technological developments and trends, and to those pertaining to the industry. However, this awareness seems to be lacking in depth, with answers 'heard about it but don't know the details' and 'quite familiar' scoring the highest. Figure 2 illustrates the relationship between the specific concepts and the level of translators' awareness of them, with Figure 2a showing the less known concepts and Figure 2b showing concepts with which the respondents were more familiar.

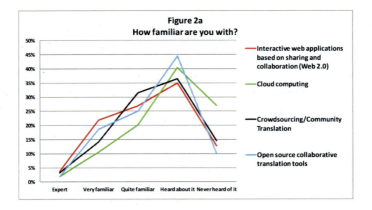

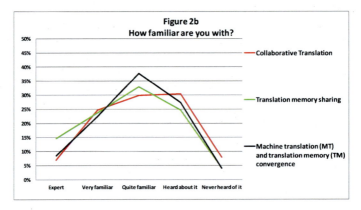

Figure 2: Awareness of concepts related to Web 2.0 and translation technology

The biggest aggregation of 'vague' awareness is displayed in relation to Web 2.0, cloud computing, crowdsourcing/community translation and open source tools (Figure 2a). Three in four respondents showed various degrees of familiarity with concepts involving TM, such as MT/TM convergence and TM sharing. Higher awareness is therefore verified in the areas linked with tools or processes translators are already using or engaging with (Figure 2b). Therefore, unsurprisingly, professional translators seem to have more awareness and knowledge about specific developments within the translation industry such as MT/TM convergence or data sharing than about the overall technology trends such as Web 2.0 or cloud computing. As an American sociologist, Beniger suggests, "we may be preoccupied with specific [...] events and trends, at the risk of overlooking what only many years from now will be seen as the fundamental dynamic of our age" (Beniger, 1986, p.3). The respondents were next asked whether they keep up with the latest technological developments in the translation industry. Interestingly, only 6% declared that they do not and 62% confirmed that they keep up to some extent (see Figure 3a). Figure 3b shows that the 32% of the respondents who claim to keep abreast with the trends and developments are mostly innovators/early adopters and fast followers.

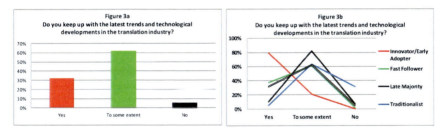

Figure 3: Keeping up with technology

3040% of the respondents who feel they keep up with the developments consider professional associations, professional literature, training, conferences, seminars and workplace to be good sources of information. However, the results show that the biggest source of information about the developments is the Internet. Nearly 70% of those who try to keep abreast with technology use discussion forums and other social media such as blogs, LinkedIn and Twitter for this purpose

The main reasons for not keeping up with technological developments were financial constraints, the lack of time, and the lack of need (56, 37 and 30% respectively for all respondents—for range of choices provided see question 9 of the questionnaire). 27% of the respondents feel that keeping up with these developments is too difficult from a technological point of view or that training takes too much effort. Interestingly, although only 6% of the respondents admit to not keeping abreast with developments, 95% have given reasons why they don't. This could mean that although the majority of the sampled translators try to keep up with the technological developments, in reality, there are too many constraints hindering them from doing so. This would explain the discrepancy found between the relatively high numbers of translators declaring that they keep up with the developments and the relatively low levels of awareness and uptake.

When analysing data in search of a "profile" of translators who display the greatest awareness of the latest developments in the field of translation technology, it transpired that age was not a determining factor (Figure 4a). Experience played an influential role in the case of translators who practiced for less than two years, as discussed later. However, it became clear that attitude towards technology was the biggest differentiator. The Figures 4a and 4b below illustrate this.

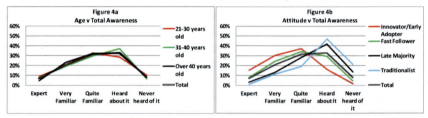

Figure 4: Awareness of Web 2.0 technology related concepts as affected by age and attitude[2]

The respondents who self-proclaim to be innovators or early adopters are clearly the most familiar with the latest developments, followed by fast followers, late majority and traditionalists. Therefore, it would transpire that the more pro-active and positive attitude towards technology, the more acute awareness of the trends and developments within the industry.

An interesting observation can be made in relation to experience affecting technology awareness. The least experienced translators showed the least awareness, which would imply that knowledge about the developments comes from practical experience, and not necessarily from current education. On average, 40% of translators coming fresh to the market with the benefit of having just completed their courses are unaware or vaguely aware of the developments within the translation industry despite 80% of them holding Masters or PhDs (see Figure 5). For further reading regarding the issues of translator education/training and the industry see Gough (2010c).

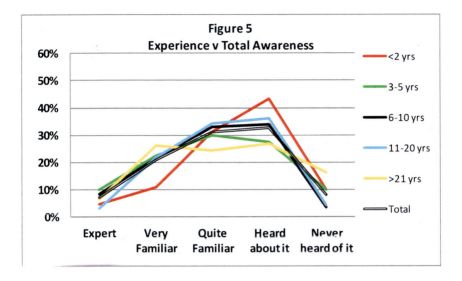

Figure 5: Familiarity with web 2.0 technology related concepts as affected by experience

The translation industry is on the cusp of a powerful transitional change and as Vashee (2010, n.p.) observes,[3] "larger forces that are driving structural changes are an observable fact of the translation landscape today". This transformation has global roots, but manifests itself on different levels such as social practices involving translation (e.g., crowdsourcing or community translation) or on the level of translation technology. The relatively low levels of awareness of the recent trends might indicate that the realisation of what this change means and entails and an understanding of what it might bring to the world of professional translators has not been fully realised, and the impact has not yet been felt by translators responding to this survey.

4.2. Use of tools and processes

4.2.1. Use of tools

The findings of this study reveal that over 80% of surveyed translators are using proprietary CAT Tools, with three out of four using them on a regular basis. Open tools (including open source translation tools such as Omega T[4] and various open translation or sharing platforms such as TAUS search (TAUS Data Association)[5], MyMemory,[6] Worldwide Lexicon[7] or Open

TM2)[8] are used by 25% of the respondents, with 6% using them on a regular basis. Interestingly, despite the low current usage of open tools, 75% of translators taking part in this survey expressed a likelihood of using open tools in the future. This corresponds to the 'awareness score' for open tools, which was highest by far on the 'vague awareness' point (see Figure 2a).

As in the case of translators' familiarity with technology concepts, attitude seems to be the most discernible factor when it comes to the use of tools in general. The same pattern was observed for both proprietary and open tools with regard to attitude. In both cases the biggest users were innovators, followed by fast followers, late majority and traditionalists respectively. Traditionalists stand out with nearly 70% not using proprietary CAT Tools at all and only 2% using open tools, as shown on Figures 6a and 6b below.

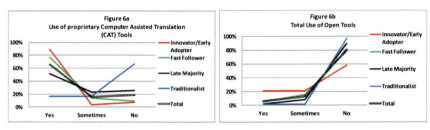

Figure 6: The use of proprietary and open tools as affected by attitude

Data gathered in this study corroborates a rational principle whereby the more readily people adopt new technologies and follow technological developments, the more tools they use and the greater the variety of software they tend to explore. Therefore, translators with innovative attitudes towards technology will naturally seek to explore alternatives to standard solutions more enthusiastically than translators with more conservative approaches.

4.2.2. Participation in processes

With regard to involvement in crowdsourcing or community translation, it was empirically shown that 12% of professional translators are contributing to these collaborative processes today. However, there is an indication that participation might increase, with nearly 40% of respondents declaring they would consider getting involved in the future.

The degree of participation seems to be affected by all three factors – age, experience and attitude (see Figures 7a, 7b and 7c respectively). There is an indication that in future the collaborative processes are likely to attract younger translators with little experience, possibly as an opportunity to practice newly acquired skills or self-promote their services. Attitude seems to affect the involvement in these processes, with four times more innovators taking part than even fast followers. The Figure 7c below illustrates this.

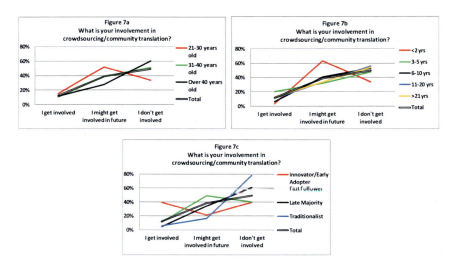

Figure 7: Collaborative processes as affected by age, experience and attitude

To summarise, the survey results suggest that so far the new tools and processes have only been embraced by professional translators with the most innovative attitudes; however there is a strong indication that a greater number of translators might be using the open tools and intending to participate in the collaborative processes in the future.

4.3. Perception of tools and processes

The respondents were asked whether their work practice had changed in the last few years due to advancements in technology. Nearly half of the respondents admitted that their work practice had changed significantly and a quarter reported that it changed dramatically. Only 3.6% of the respondents did not notice any change (see Figure 8).

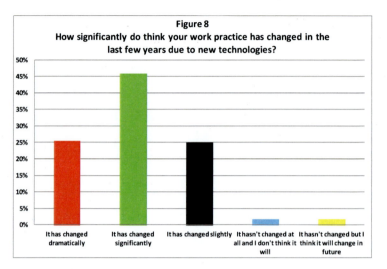

Figure 8: Change in work practices in the last few years due to new technology

Whilst it transpires that the majority of surveyed translators have felt the impact of new technologies on their work practices, the opinions regarding these technologies seem to be either divided or not yet fully formed, as illustrated in the following sections.

4.3.1. Perception of tools

TM sharing is a relatively well known concept, with 70% of the respondents displaying various degrees of familiarity. When asked about the potential benefits of sharing translation memories, opinions were mostly divided between 'agree' and 'no opinion' (see Figures 9a, 9c & 9e). However, when considering TM sharing as a potential threat, translators were almost equally divided between those who agree, disagree and have no opinion, which would point to the fact that the benefits of sharing are thought to outweigh the threat (see Figures 9b, 9d, 9f). Interestingly, translators with the most experience display the highest levels of 'no opinion'.

It could therefore be concluded that although professional translators are starting to recognize the potential of sharing their linguistic resources, confirmed by the very low rate of 'disagree' responses, they seem to be divided on the subject of sharing. On average, 30% of the respondents are willing to share and recognise the fact that they can benefit from having access to translation memories of other translators (see Figures 9a, 9c and 9e). The remaining respondents either feel uncomfortable about freeing their assets and are inhibited by the fear of losing competitive advantage or hold no view at all (see Figures 9b, 9d and 9f below).

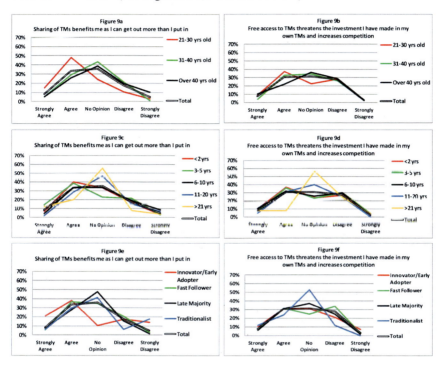

Figure 9: Positive and negative aspects of TM sharing as affected by age, experience and attitude

With regard to the collaborative tools, the respondents' perception seems to tally with their awareness of these tools. Since over half of the respondents do not have much knowledge of the open tools, there is a strong presence of 'no opinion' regarding these tools, especially amongst the more mature translators displaying conservative attitudes towards technology (see Figures 10a, 10b, 10c, 10d, 10e and 10f).

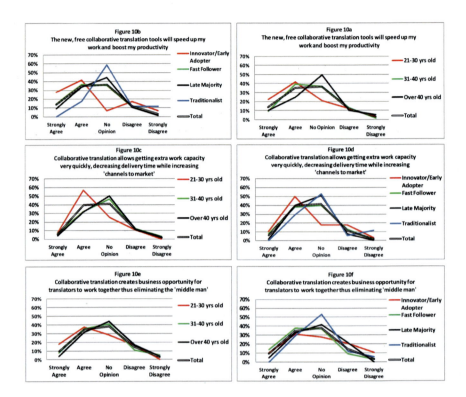

Figure 10: Perception of collaborative tools as affected by age and attitude towards technology

However, on average, the total number of translators in agreement is much higher than those in disagreement, which seems to point to the fact that the alternative, collaborative translation workflows might be gaining popularity.

To summarise, it is clear that with regards to the perception of collaborative tools, the younger translators generally hold stronger opinions, whether positive or negative, and there is a significant perception gap between traditionalists and innovators. However, despite the apparent, overall division between agreement and no opinion, there seems to be no vehement opposition or any discernible critique of the collaborative tools. This most likely stems from the respondents' insufficient knowledge or awareness of these tools, thus preventing them from forming an educated opinion. Professional translators with innovative attitudes seem to be more readily attracted to the open tools, which tallies with their higher knowledge of these tools.

4.3.2. Perception of processes

The concepts of crowdsourcing and community translation seem to be the least known of all the concepts examined in this study (see Figure 2b); however, they attract relatively strong opinions.

Respondents were asked to give an opinion to statements reflecting negative and positive aspects of the collaborative processes, as listed in the legend of the Figure 11 below.

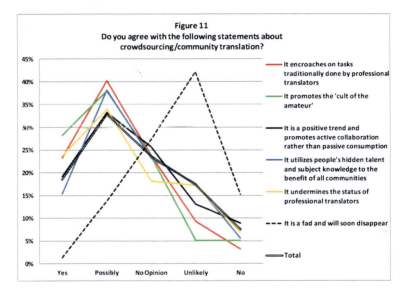

Figure 11: Perception of the collaborative processes – positive and negative aspects

On average, 50-60% percent of the respondents are in an agreement with both the positive and the negative statements (15-28% saying 'yes', and 33-40% 'possibly'). This could mean that, as in the case of TM sharing (Figure 9), professional translators seem to recognise the social values of these trends, such as utilizing people's hidden talents or promoting active collaboration rather than passive consumption. However, on a personal level they might feel threatened by them as they might undermine their professional status or encroach on tasks traditionally done exclusively by professional translators. Nonetheless, taking into account that only a small percentage of the respondents were actually familiar with the concepts of crowdsourcing/community translation (see Figure 2a) and only 12% of the surveyed translators actually participate in these initiatives, it would appear that these opinions might not necessarily be based on an informed perspective.

Joanna Gough

Rather interestingly, the only question that prominently stands out is the one concerning the future of collaborative processes. The majority of the respondents agreed that the collaborative processes in the form of crowdsourcing or community translation are not a fad and are here to stay. When analysing questions related to the various aspects of collaborative tools and processes (such as productivity, scalability, delivery time, channels to market, creativity or innovation) against the age, experience and attitude of the respondents, there appears to be a consistent pattern. Innovators and fast followers seem to outnumber late majority and traditionalists in recognising that collaboration with other translators through open tools could bring potential benefits (see Figures 10b, 10d & 10f).

An interesting result emerged with regards to the effectiveness of quality assurance based on peer-review, which is used in a typical voting system in the collaborative models of translation such as crowdsourcing or community translation, but would make perfect sense in the case of collaborative translation between language professionals. There seems to be almost unanimous agreement to this question, indicating a high potential for more collaborative translation patterns to emerge in the future, with peer-review being an important component of this kind of process.

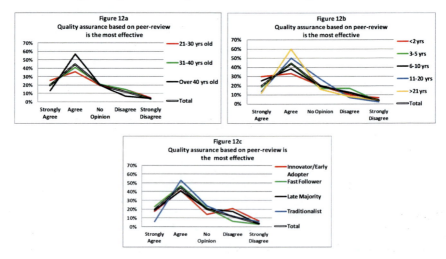

Figure 12: Perception of the effectiveness of quality assurance based on peer review as affected by age, experience and attitude

To summarise, with the exception of the young innovators, there seems to be an absence of opinions regarding the open tools and collaborative processes or, if present, they appear to be based on insufficient knowledge. This perhaps reveals a rift between professional translators' appreciation of the benefits these new technologies and their applications can bring, and apprehension caused by lack of knowledge.

4.4. Future

When asked about the possible ways of adapting to the changing nature of their work, professional translators who responded to this survey generally expressed willingness to re-position themselves, with only 20% declaring they would leave the industry. The most interesting finding points to the fact that 85% of the respondents would prefer to adapt using conservative ways such as specialising or changing position within the current establishment (see Figure 13). Only a small percentage would look into innovative solutions such as crowdsourcing and, unsurprisingly, the majority of the respondents who chose this option had labelled themselves as innovators and fast followers.

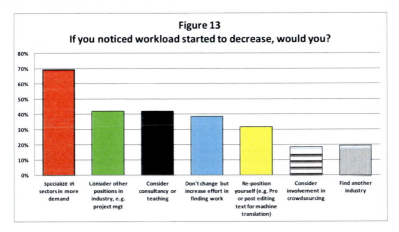

Figure 13: Future alternatives for professional translators

With regard to the relationship between translators and the industry, the main finding revealed that 59% of the respondents feel that professional translators are not being educated about the changing nature of the industry and about the possible ways of adapting to the new challenges of the market.

4.5. Openness, sharing and collaboration

Professional translators were asked whether they subscribe to the latest trends of sharing, openness and collaboration. Currently 26% of the sampled translators subscribe to these trends; however, over half of the respondents declare that they might do in future. The results unambiguously show that openness to these trends does not depend much on age or experience (see Figures 14a and 14b), although the youngest translators do seem to have a much higher rate of future commitment than the more mature ones. However, the most important finding points to the fact that it is the attitude towards technology that determines to what extent translators embrace these trends (see Figure 14c).

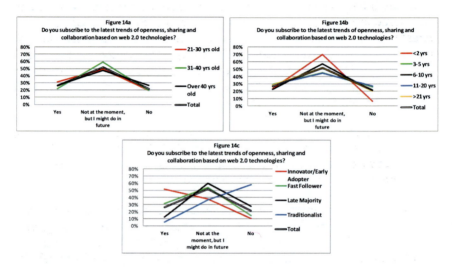

Figure 14: Openness towards the trends of oppenness, sharing and collaboration as affected by age, experience and attitude

5. Conclusion

This study, undoubtedly, is bound by certain limitations. Capturing a representative picture of professional translators' awareness, usage and perception of the new technological trends proves extremely difficult given the fragmented nature of the translation industry, the limitations of the chosen method, as well as a perceived general lack of time, enthusiasm or interest on behalf of some professional translators with regard to participating in surveys, especially ones carried out by students.[9] The sample was largely dominated by respondents from European countries and due to the fact that the questionnaire was primarily administered through various on-line media, it is likely that it would have attracted translators who are frequent Internet users, and therefore could have potentially been more technology aware. Also, the fact that the questionnaire was circulated only in English would have prohibited non-English speakers from contributing. During the time the questionnaire was circulated, another limitation was pointed out, mainly the fact that the age groups were not well represented, especially at the both ends of the spectrum. Subsequently, since there were no respondents under 20 years old, this category was dropped during the analysis.

 The findings of this study demonstrate that professional translators responding to this questionnaire have neither fully grasped the driving concepts behind the Web 2.0 nor embraced the technology that employs these ideas and depends on them. The concepts of openness, sharing and collaboration and their utilization through translation tools and processes remain in the realm of varied, mostly vague awareness, resulting in marginal use of the open tools, little engagement in the processes and reluctance to adapt to the new reality through innovation. This seems to imply that the changes are happening to translators rather than with translators. Gouadec (2007) observes:

> information technology and dedicated applications are now having a major impact on the profession, and are beginning to create a rift between those who are able and willing to make full use of the resources available, and those who are not. (p. 279)

Multilingual communication is now an instant, global phenomenon and translation is often only one part of a larger, information management workflow. According to Garcia and Stevenson (2008, p.28), "translation is about the only obstacle left in the way, and accordingly translators will be among the first to feel the effects as the planet tries to dismantle Babel and reach a universal 'dialogue continuum'".

Translators are a part of the translation industry's eco-system where the same rules of nature apply to all its organs. Automation and collaborative approaches are often perceived by professional translators as threatening and phrases such as 'eat or be eaten' (TAUS: online) or 'collaborate or perish' (Schmidt, 2009: online) found in the recent industry discourse point to this threat. Although the extinction of professional translators is not predicted any time soon, their role within the eco-system could be weakened or, possibly, they might be left to perform only highly specialised functions. The relatively slow uptake of trends and technology by professional translators and the possible difficulties in seeing the potential opportunities that technology might bring could greatly contribute to this diminished role of professional translators in the future.

One of the key findings of this study is the fact that the underlying factor determining translators' awareness, perception and use of tools and processes is their attitude towards adopting new technologies, with an indication that the professionals with less experience and innovative attitudes are more inclined to embrace the new open tools and collaborative processes. On the other hand, the results show that formal education and training are not necessarily the source of awareness and knowledge about the recent issues and trends, with nearly 60% of the sampled translators feeling they are not being educated or informed about the changing nature of the industry and the possible ways of adapting to the new challenges of the market.

If attitude is the X-factor which determines translators' alignment with the latest trends and willingness to embrace them, then this factor can be promoted, fostered and cultivated to enable translators to actively engage in the affairs of their industry, rather than feeling that they are sidelined, threatened and exploited.

In order to achieve this, the translation industry needs to feed the latest trends into the education system as soon as they become apparent to facilitate a more comprehensive training of translators and to present them with a realistic view of the industry and career possibilities. On the other hand, the education system should embrace these trends quickly and provide future-oriented courses with the relevant technology modules built in into their existing programmes. Furthermore, an open dialogue between the industry, professional translators and educational bodies would be advantageous for the benefit of all concerned with the future of the translation industry.

In the meantime, a new 'layer' of more sophisticated and far-reaching technology associated with Web 3.0, which could have an even bigger impact on the shape of future translation processes and indeed, the technological infrastructure supporting them, is already permeating the Internet.[10] Although there are indications that professional translators might draw nearer to the full understanding and participation in the technological offerings of Web 2.0 in the future, the speed with which Web 3.0 is approaching would suggest that it could be even more difficult to catch up with the developments in the future.

Sociologists Brinkerhoff, White, Ortega and Weitz (2008, p. 378) argue that "technology defines the limits of what a society can do [and therefore] technological innovation is a major impetus for social change". They go on to say that "currently, new technologies are developing to meet new needs created by a changing culture and society [resulting in a] never ending cycle in which social change both causes and results from new technology" (ibid). As the development of tools naturally determines/influences the processes within which these tools are used, it would appear that social change is the underlying cause driving both technology and process advancement and that these advancements/new capabilities may indeed influence the next step in social change. The rate of trends and technology adoption by professional translators might be an indicator of the pace of the social change within the community of professional translators.

References

Beniger, J. R. (1986). *Control revolution: Technological and economic origins of the information society.* Cambridge, Massachusetts: Harvard University Press.

Beninatto, R., & DePalma, D. (2007). The end of localization taylorism. *Global Watchtower.* Retrieved from: http://www.commonsenseadvisory.com/Default. aspx?Contenttype=ArticleDetAD&tabID=63&Aid=1209&moduleId=391

Bergman, F. (n.d.) *Project/Open - Technology adoption and competitive advantage in the translation industry.* Retrieved from http://www.slideshare.net/Samuel90/ technology-adoption-and-competitiveness-in-the-translation

Bohn, R.E. & Short, J.E. 2009. *How much information? 2009 report on American consumers.* Global Information Industry Centre, University of California, San Diego. Retrieved from http://hmi.ucsd.edu/pdf/HMI_2009_ConsumerReport_ Dec9_2009.pdf

Brinkerhoff, D. B., White, L. K., Ortega, S. T., & Weitz, R. (2008). *Essentials of sociology.* Belmont: Thomson Wadsworth.

Garcia, I., & Stevenson, V. (2008). Translation trends and the social web. *Multilingual,* April/May 2008, 2831.

Garcia, I. (2009). Beyond Translation Memory: Computers and the Professional Translator. *The Journal of Specialised Translation,* Issue 12, 199214. Retrieved from http://www.jostrans.org/issue12/art_garcia.php

Gouadec, D. (2007) *Translation as a profession.* Amsterdam: John Benjamins.

Gough, J. (2010a). *The implications of Web 2.0 technologies based on openness, sharing and collaboration for professional translators and their future.* Unpublished MA Dissertation, University of Surrey

Gough, J. (2010b). Troubled relationship - the compatibility of CAT Tools. *TAUS.* Retrieved from http://www.translationautomation.com/technology/a-troubled-relationship-the-compatibility-of-cat-tools.html

Gough, J. (2010c). Imagine you are a translation graduate. *TAUS.* Retrieved from http://www.translationautomation.com/perspectives/imagine-you-are-a-translation-graduate.html

Schmidt, E. (2009). Collaborate or perish. *What Matters.* Retrieved from http://whatmatters.mckinseydigital.com/organization/collaborate-or-perish

Shuttleworth, M., & Lagoudaki, E. (2006). 'Translation memory systems: Technology in the service of the translation professional'. In *Proceedings of 1st Athens International Conference of Translation and Interpretation,* Athens, Greece, 13-14 October 2006. Retrieved from http://translation.hau.gr/telamon/ files/ MarkShuttleworth_ElinaLagoudaki_PaperAICTI.pdf

TAUS (2010). Retrieved from http://archive.constantcontact.com/fs023/1101329149450 /archive/1103591034195.html

Van der Meer, J. (2011a). TAUS Annual Plan 2011. *TAUS.* Retrieved from http://www.translationautomation.com/about-taus/annual-plan.html

Van der Meer, J. (2011b). The future for translators looks bright, but they will have to reinvent the profession first. *TAUS.* Retrieved from

http://www.translationautomation.com/perspectives/the-future-for-translators-
    looks-bright-but-they-will-have-to-reinvent-the-profession-first.html

Vashee, K. (2010). Falling translation prices and implications for translation
    professionals. *eMpTy Pages*, 27 April 2010. Retrieved from
    http://kvemptypages.blogspot.com/2010_04_01_archive.html

---

[1]   Statistical Machine Translation relies on a statistical analysis of large amount of parallel
        bilingual data as opposed to sets of language-specific rules which form the core of Rule Based
        Machine Translation.

[2]   Total awareness refers to an aggregated awareness of all the concepts listed in the legend of
        Figures 2a and 2b

[3]   The driving factors behind this change could be summarized as:

-       a change in the way we communicate - the shift from Web 1.0 to Web 2.0 technology which
        enabled great advancements in global communication and collaboration (Gough, 2010a)

-       a change in the amount of information consumed by people - the increased, general demand for
        knowledge and information (which in America has grown 6% per year in the last 28 years,
        adding up to a 350% increase over 28 years (Bohn, R.E. & Short, J.E., 2009: online))

-       a change in the amount of information produced for our consumption and the pace of the
        delivery of this information - the increased volume of content to be translated and pressures to
        deliver in shorter timescales (Garcia, 2009: online)

-       a change in nature and formats of this content, especially on the Web - dynamic content
        requiring constant updating in a variety of formats (Van der Meer, 2011: online)

-       a change in translation technology as a result of the above pressures - stress on value of data,
        opening up of the resources, increased automation (Gough, 2010a; Garcia, 2009: online)

-       a change in the working patterns as a result of the above pressures - alternative, collaborative
        workflows, often involving non-professionals (Garcia 2009: online).

[4]   http://www.omegat.org/en/omegat.html

[5]   http://www.tausdata.org

[6]   http://mymemory.translated.net

[7]   http://www.worldwidelexicon.org/home

[8]   http://www.opentm2.org

---

[9] This observation has been made on the basis of discussions which accompanied the survey on-line, as well as the ratio of the number of people viewing the questionnaire versus the number of respondents. For discussions see: http://www.linkedin.com/groupItem?view=&gid=145268&type =member&item=24916093&trk=group_search_item_list-0-b-ttl&goback=%2Egna_145268

http://www.proz.com/forum/off_topic/176524-why_do_we_hate_questionnaires-page2.html

[10] Web 3.0, also called the Semantic Web, is a solution for enriching the information on the Web with a new 'semantic layer'. This new Web 'dimension' is created by linking up entities on the Web in terms of their relationships and properties, so that computer applications can understand not only the syntactic, but also the semantic layer of the information contained on the Web pages. At present, the Web contains countless documents contained in about trillion pages, but computers cannot 'understand' this content and intensive human processing is needed to find the most relevant information. The Semantic Web will alleviate this problem by enabling the so called 'intelligent agents' to search for, gather, process or transform data in a meaningful and useful way by following the links established within the semantic layer. This will open up endless possibilities for technology to evolve towards more intelligent systems and certainly will have direct implications for language technologies, including translation.

Professional Translators and web 2.0 Technologies Based on Openness,

1. Introduction

This questionnaire has been developed to provide data for my MA dissertation. It focuses on professional translators and aims to ascertain how they react to and embrace the current trends of openness, sharing and collaboration; not only in their social aspect, but more importantly as a business solution for the future.

Not much research has been carried out in this area and I would very much appreciate it if you take the time to complete this questionnaire. On average it takes about 10 minutes to complete.

This survey is confidential. You can choose to provide contact details should you agree to follow up this questionnaire with an inteview and/or would like to receive the results of this questionnaire.

Thank you,
Joanna Gough

2. Professional Translator's Profile

1. Which country do you normally live and work in?

2. What is your age and sex?

	-20	21-30	31-40	41+
Male	☐	☐	☐	☐
Female	☐	☐	☐	☐

If you belong to the age group of 51-60 or 61+, please feel free to indicate your age group

3. What is the highest level of your education qualifications? (You can tick nearest equivalent or qualifications in progress)

- ○ None
- ○ Secondary education
- ○ First degree
- ○ Master's degree
- ○ Doctorate

Other translation-related education or certificates, please specify

4. Do you: (You can tick multiple boxes)

☐ Freelance

☐ Have an in-house position

☐ Work for a translation agency/Language Service Provider

☐ Work directly with clients

Work as a translator in any other way - please specify

```
```

5. How long have you been working as a translator?

○ Less than 2 years

○ 3-5 years

○ 6-10 years

○ 11-20 years

○ Over 21 years

6. What type of translation do you do? You can tick multiple boxes.

☐ Business/Economic

☐ General

☐ Legal

☐ Literary

☐ Technical/Scientific

3. Professional Translators and Technology

7. Do you keep up with the latest trends and technological developments in the translation industry?

○ Yes

○ To some extent

○ No

8. How would you classify yourself with regard to adopting new technologies?

○ Innovator and early adopter (looking for innovative solutions and picking up new technologiues as soon as they emerge)

○ Fast follower (careful attitude but accepting change more quickly than the average)

○ Late majority (sceptical attitude and using new technologies when the majority are using them)

○ Traditionalist (only accepting innovative technologies when they have become commonplace or tradition)

9. If you don't keep up with the latest technology trends and developments in the translation industry, please explain why. You can tick multiple boxes. Skip if you feel you keep up with the developments.

☐ Lack of time

☐ Don't feel the need

☐ Can't see the benefits

☐ Financial constraints (e.g. expensive tools, training, seminars, subscriptions etc.)

☐ Technological constraints (too difficult to use, takes a lot of effort to train etc.)

Other reasons - please specify

[text box]

10. If you do (or to some extent) keep up with the latest trends and technological developments in the translation industry, how do you achieve it? You can tick multiple boxes. Skip if you feel you don't keep up with the developments.

☐ Professional associations

☐ Professional literature

☐ Conferences/seminars

☐ Training

☐ Discussion Forums

☐ Workplace

Other ways you keep up - please specify

[text box]

11. How familiar are you with:

	expert	very familiar	quite familiar	heard about it but don't know the details	never heard of it
Interactive web applications based on sharing and collaboration (Web 2.0)	○	○	○	○	○
Cloud computing	○	○	○	○	○
Crowdsourcing/Community Translation (collaboration between non-professional and possibly professional translators)	○	○	○	○	○
Collaborative Translation (collaboration between professional translators)	○	○	○	○	○
Translation memory sharing	○	○	○	○	○
Open source collaborative translation tools	○	○	○	○	○
Machine translation (MT) and translation memory (TM) convergence	○	○	○	○	○

4. Professional Translator and the Ideas of Sharing, Openness and Collaboratio...

12. Do you use:

	yes	sometimes	no
Proprietary Computer Assisted Tools (CAT) (Trados, DejaVu etc)	○	○	○
Open source translation tools (OmegaT etc)	○	○	○
Open TM platforms (TAUS search, MyMemory, etc)	○	○	○
Open source collaborative translation platforms combining MT with TM (Worldwide Lexicon etc)	○	○	○
Open source translation management systems (GlobalSight, Open TM2)	○	○	○

13. Do you intend to use in future:

	yes	very likely	quite likely	not very likely	no
Proprietary tools	○	○	○	○	○
Open source tools	○	○	○	○	○

14. What is your involvement in crowdsourcing/community translation?

○ I get involved

○ I might get involved in future

○ I don't get involved

If you get involved, please specifiy which projects you have worked on.

```
                                                          ▲

                                                          ▼
```

15. Do you agree with the following statements about crowdsourcing/community translation?

	yes	possibly	don't have an opinion	unlikely	no
It encroaches on tasks traditionally done by professional translators	○	○	○	○	○
It promotes the 'cult of the amateur'	○	○	○	○	○
It is a positive trend and promotes active collaboration rather than passive consumption	○	○	○	○	○
It utilizes people's hidden talent and subject knowledge to the benefit of all communities	○	○	○	○	○
It undermines the status of professional translators	○	○	○	○	○
It is a fad and will soon disappear	○	○	○	○	○

16. Do you subscribe to the latest trends of openness, sharing and collaboration based on web 2.0 technologies?

○ Yes

○ Not at the moment, but I might do in future

○ No

17. How significantly do think your work practice has changed in the last few years due to new technologies enabling the use of on-line tools, dictionaries, glossaries, multilingual databases, exchanging information via forums, etc?

○ It has changed dramatically

○ It has changed significantly

○ It has changed slightly

○ It hasn't changed at all and I don't think it will

○ It hasn't changed but I think it will change in future

18. Do you agree with the following statements?

	strongly agree	agree	don't have an opinion	disagree	strongly disagree
The new, free collaborative translation tools will speed up my work and boost my productivity	○	○	○	○	○
Sharing of TMs benefits me as I can get out more than I put in	○	○	○	○	○
Free access to TMs threatens the investment I have made in my own TMs and increases competition	○	○	○	○	○
Collaborative translation allows getting extra work capacity very quickly, decreasing delivery time while increasing 'channels to market'	○	○	○	○	○
Quality assurance based on peer-review is the most effective	○	○	○	○	○
Collaborative translation creates business opportunity for translators to work together thus eliminating the 'middle man'	○	○	○	○	○
Crowdsourcing together with open source collaborative translation tools open up channels for creativity and innovation	○	○	○	○	○

5. Professional Translators and their Future

19. If you noticed that the amount of work you were receiving started to decrease, would you: (You can tick multiple boxes)

☐ Re-position yourself and consider for example pre-editing text for machine translation or post-edit machine translation

☐ Specialize in sectors/content types that may be in more demand

☐ Look into alternative positions within the industry, e.g. project management, translation memory maintenance, technical writing etc.

☐ Decide not to change the way you work and put more effort into or find different ways of looking for work?

☐ Consider consultancy or teaching translation or a language

☐ Consider involvement in crowdsourcing (eg. management of projects based on crowdsourcing)

☐ Find another industry

Can you identify other ways of adjusting to the situation?

[text box]

20. Do you agree with the following:

	strongly agree	agree	don't have an opinion	disagree	strongly disagree
Professional translators are not being educated about the changing nature of the industry and about possible ways of adapting to the new challenges of the market	○	○	○	○	○
Clients are not being educated about the level of professionalism required to deliver quality translation and are therefore accepting alternatives more easily	○	○	○	○	○
Professional translators are not being engaged in discussions about the future of the translation industry	○	○	○	○	○
Translation industry should cooperate with professional translators in developing their technologies	○	○	○	○	○

21. If you are not familiar with the recent developments or feel you don't know enough, would you:

○ Try to find out more

○ No, I'm happy with my knowledge base

22. Would you be willing to follow up this questionnaire with a short interview using Skype or other medium chosen by you?

○ Yes

○ No

23. Thank you for taking the time and effort to complete this questionnaire. Would you like to receive the results of this questionnaire?

○ Yes

○ No

Please provide your e-mail address to receive the results. You e-mail address will not be used for any other purpose.

BOOK REVIEWS

Merkle, D., O'Sullivan, C., van Doorslaer, L., & Wolf, M. (Eds.). (2010). *The power of the pen. Translation & censorship in nineteenth-century Europe (Representation – Transformation 4).* Wien/Berlin: LIT Verlag, 298p.

This collection of essays by scholars from different European countries addresses various aspects of the intricate bond between *translation* and *censorship* in different nineteenth-century European contexts.

In their introduction the editors define censorship as "blockage of a cultural product from entry into a cultural space, the elimination of a product from a cultural space or its modification through attenuation or cutting." (p. 14). However, such interventions/manipulations (blockage, elimination, modification) must not always be regarded as censorship: "While censorship is a manifestation of manipulation, not all manipulation is censorship" (p. 14). Censorship happens when the manipulation of a cultural product "is motivated by a desire either to protect the vulnerable [...] or to create and maintain a religious, cultural or political system [...]" (p. 14). One might add: or by the desire to challenge, protect or gain (structures or positions of) power within such systems. In other words, whether or not an act of manipulation qualifies as censorship depends as much—if not more—upon the intended effect of the manipulation as upon the act itself.

The link between censorship and translation is obvious: "As a form of traffic between cultures, translation [...] has an important role to play in sustaining or subverting cultural blockage" (p. 15). Quoting Holman and Boase-Beier, the editors hold that "the activities of translator and censor are in many ways related. Both are gatekeepers, standing at crucial points of control, monitoring what comes in and what stays outside any given cultural or linguistic territory." (p. 12).

The idea of the translator as gatekeeper is further elaborated in the first case study by Norbert Bachleitner and Michaela Wolf ("ÜbersetzerInnen als "gatekeepers?" (Selbst-)Zensur als Voraussetzung für die Aufnahme in das literarische Feld der späten Habsburgermonarchie"), which draws on Pierre Bourdieu's concept of 'structural censorship' to demonstrate how self-censorship affected different nineteenth-century German translations of Gustave Flaubert's *Madame Bovary* and Giuseppe Garibaldi's *Clelia*.

The second case study, by Luc Van Doorslaer, focuses on the selection policy of serial prose translations in three nineteenth-century Flemish newspapers. It opts for a purely quantitative approach—"(F)or the purpose of this study the content of the cultural news is not pertinent,"(p.66) the author writes—to argue for the existence of a "relationship between the ideological orientation of the newspaper and the source language or source culture of the translated literary texts." (p. 64).

In the third case study Ibon Uribarri examines the reception of Immanuel Kant's writings in nineteenth-century Spain. In his very informative contribution, Uribari demonstrates how a repressive, intolerant Catholicism hampered the translation and assimilation of Kant's magnum opus *Kritik der reinen Vernunft* (1781) into Spanish culture. More generally, Kant's work suffered from "a sort of structural preventive censorship" which "was working through symbolic violence that imposed the dominant national-Catholic discourse and excluded and silenced foreign, modern, secular ideas from the public sphere" (p. 92).

A fourth case study, by Denise Merkle, examines how and why a translator rather than a translation can provoke heavy cultural resistance to the point of being excluded from the literary field altogether. Merkle compares the first Victorian translations of Gustave Flaubert's erotic text *Salammbô* (1862), one by the American feminist author Mary French Sheldon and one by John S. Chartres, published in 1885 and 1886 respectively. While Chartres' translation was received quite positively, Sheldon's was not. Merkle holds that "French Sheldon's translation was censured if not censored by the literary translation field" (p. 107) due to Sheldon's limitations as a translator: "(S)he seemed not to be aware of the linguistic failings of her work and not to have the requisite mastery to recreate linguistic transgression." (p. 111).

A fifth contribution, by Carol O'Sullivan, examines a more straightforward case of censorship in Victorian England, namely the modified translations of six "Extra Volumes" in Henry Bohn's Standard Library, published between 1846 and 1855. Drawing (as many authors in this volume do) on Pierre Bourdieu's concept of 'structural censorship' and on Phillips Davidon's "third-person effect hypothesis", O'Sullivan demonstrates how Bohn's translations of texts by (among others) Rabelais, Boccaccio and Cervantes obviated blockage by omitting certain passages deemed inappropriate or by publishing them in French or Italian.

These five examples of "Forms of Cultural Blockage" as the first section of this volume is called, are followed by four essays on "The Permeability of Institutional Censorship". In a first case study Elisabeth Gibbels concentrates on the complete ban of Social Democratic writings in Bismarck Germany ("Zensur und Translation in Deutschland zwischen 1878-1890: Das 'Sozialistengesetz' und die Exilzeitung der Sozialistischen Arbeiterspartei."). In a piece entitled "Translation, Censorship and Romanticism in Portugal, 1800-1850", Rita Bueno Maia produces "documentary evidence of preventive and repressive censorship and its consequences for the delayed development of Portugese Romanticism" (p. 170). Censorship in nineteenth-century Portugal also affected translation policies, especially when it came to French literature. Canonical Portugese Romantic authors and translators preferred moralistic literature by second-rate authors over acknowledged masterpieces by Jean-Jacques Rousseau or Voltaire, for instance. "(S)everal Portuguese writers and intellectuals of the period still pointed to the potential for corruption inherent in such translations, for all French novels were considered to be a danger to good conduct." (p. 175-176).

In a similar vein, Maria Eugenia Perojo Arronte examines the role translation and censorship played during Spanish Romanticism ("Spanish Romanticism and the Struggle for Legitimation: Translation, Censorship and the Development of the Movement."). Brian James Baer concludes this section with an essay that explores "how the liberal-minded elite in Russia around the time of the Decembrist uprising of 1825 developed strategies for evading censorship of translated texts in order to introduce into Russia a civic-minded literature and to construct the poet as an important public figure." (p. 213).

The third and final section, variously called "Censorship and Norms" and "Censorship and social convention", contains an essay by Benoit Léger about "censure and censorship in the case of Dante's *Divine Comedy* during the French Second Empire (1851-1870) and a piece by Outi Paloposki about two Finnish translators, Carl Niclas Keckman and Samuli Suomalainen, who worked as censors in nineteenth-century Finland. Paloposki returns to the notion of the translator/censor as cultural gatekeeper and stresses "the need to contextualize the work of past translators not only within institutional and historical frameworks but also within an experiential framework, taking into account the ethnography of translation." (p. 281).

The Power of the Pen contains many illuminating and thought-provoking essays—case studies as well as more general, historical overviews—about the ways in which nineteenth-century translations and translators either endorsed or challenged multiple kinds of censorship.

Frank Albers, Department of Translators and Interpreters, Artesis University College Antwerp

Peeters, J. (2010). *Traduction et communautés***. Arras: Artois Presses Université. 212 p.**

Traduction et communautés regroupe treize contributions, en français et en anglais, issues d'un colloque qui s'est déroulé en 2006 à l'Université de Bretagne-Sud. La question qui avait retenu l'intérêt des chercheurs concerne l'identité sociale des traducteurs. Partant du constat que, ces dernières années, l'identité subjective des traducteurs avait souvent été envisagée dans les études traductologiques, les auteurs de ce recueil ont voulu analyser plus avant les liens entre les actants de la traduction et différentes communautés.

L' « Introduction » de Jean Peeters ouvre le volume de façon tout à fait convaincante. Ce chapitre introductif propose une analyse approfondie de la problématique et la situe dans un cadre plus large. Il détaille tous les angles de recherche qui permettraient de s'atteler à l'étude de la question annoncée. Loin de se limiter à la synthèse des contributions, Peeters propose une véritable analyse et suggère de nombreuses réflexions qui éclairent les points de rencontre et d'écart entre les articles.

Plusieurs articles s'engagent dans la réflexion sur le traducteur comme acteur engagé et parfois militant. Il s'agit de situations où l'on peut distinguer des langues minoritaires et majoritaires, dominées et dominantes et où la traduction « témoigne de relations de pouvoir asymétriques entre les langues. » (p. 11)

Ainsi la réflexion de Paul F. Bandia dans « La traduction aux carrefours de la mondialisation : voyage entre l'oralité et l'écriture » est à situer dans un contexte de « cohabitation dichotomique des communautés issues de la colonisation et des communautés issues des puissances coloniales » (p. 23) et pose la question de la traduction comme voie médiatrice entre la tradition et la modernité. Bandia rappelle la spécificité de la littérature africaine en langue européenne qui a été, à de nombreuses reprises, comparée à la traduction dans un sens figuré. Il souligne également l'importance des textes euro-africains qui se caractérisent par un style innovateur et explosif et pointe la problématique de la traduction de ces textes en une autre langue européenne.

La situation sud-africaine est illustrée par Ilse Feinauer dans « Antjie Krog, author and translator: the twain does meet ». Comme l'indique le titre de l'article, l'approche ici part du cas d'un traducteur individuel, Antjie Krog. L'analyse démontre l'influence que peut avoir un individu comme Krog, un auteur considéré dans son pays et à l'étranger, pour ce qui est des traductions dans des situations de pouvoir asymétriques. L'article pointe aussi la manière dont l'écrivaine sud-africaine exprime sa sensibilité par rapport aux différentes communautés linguistiques dans son pays : elle a en effet traduit en afrikaans des œuvres écrites en anglais (e.a. l'autobiographie de Nelson Mandela), en néerlandais et en langues africaines indigènes existantes ou disparues. Sa méthode de traduction, c'est ce que constate Feinauer, fait preuve d'un grand respect de la voix de l'Autre. L'engagement politique qu'elle a déployé dans son œuvre personnelle se traduit donc de la même façon dans son travail comme traductrice, dans la mesure où elle est « interested in bringing alternative perspectives on South African history into the domain of Afrikaans » (p. 53)

Si l'objet dans « Traduction et médiation, les incontournables de l'intercommunautaire : cas du Lexique Foncier Franco-Malgache dans la sécurisation foncière à Madagascar » de Lucie Raharinirina Rabaovololona semble de prime abord essentiellement terminologique, l'auteur démontre très vite que la transposition d'un lexique adéquat d'une langue majeure vers une langue mineure peut avoir pour enjeu les relations heureuses entre différentes communautés ethniques et culturelles. La problématique ne relève pas seulement d'un écart linguistique entre la majorité (75%) de la population malgache qui est rurale, analphabète et malgachophone et les services de l'Etat, malgachophones, mais qui utilisent des documents français. L'opposition fondamentale concerne surtout la notion même de propriété. Si la conception juridique de celle-ci est largement d'inspiration française, les Malgaches en général « donnent un caractère quasi sacré à la terre » et perçoivent leur patrie comme « un ensemble de terres léguées par les ancêtres. » (p. 166) À partir de cette constatation fondamentale, l'auteur explique concrètement comment il a été procédé pour élaborer le lexique concerné.

« The Scandal Translates Back. La dernière offensive des langues vaincues : traduire le majeur par le mineur » de Giovanni Nadiani prend comme point de départ le phénomène, constaté actuellement partout en Europe, mais plus spécifiquement en Italie en Allemagne, de la traduction d'œuvres poétiques et théâtrales écrites dans la langue nationale vers les nombreuses langues mineures dialectales. Sans développer plus avant des exemples spécifiques, Nadiani entend analyser ces pratiques de traduction que l'on pourrait qualifier de « redondantes », « anachroniques » et « linguistiquement et culturellement afonctionnelles » (p. 39). Il souligne l'importance de ces traductions, aussi bien pour la langue mineure, que pour la langue majeure. Ainsi le « majeur local » apprendra en effet que « les rapports entre les langues les cultures différentes seront toujours des rapports de force symétriques et [...] un jour, ils pourront également [l'] intéresser. » (pp. 45-46)

« Le traducteur : équilibriste des frontières » de David ar Rouz apporte une autre approche encore concernant les rapports entre langues majeures et mineures et concerne la perception qu'a le traducteur de la communauté dont il fait partie. Au moyen d'une enquête auprès d'une vingtaine de traducteurs vers/du breton se dessinent en effet un certain nombre de caractéristiques et de points de vue de ce groupe étudié. L'analyse montre qu'il s'agit le plus souvent d'hommes (82%) néo-bretonnants qui voient leur travail surtout comme une façon de promouvoir la langue bretonne. Ar Rouz pointe le manque de formation et de considération professionnelle ainsi que les problèmes terminologiques auxquels les traducteurs bretons ont à faire face.

Il convient de souligner que la contribution de Nadiani, plus générale et théorique sur la traduction littéraire vers les variantes dialectales des langues européennes, et celle de Ar Rouz sur les traducteurs bretons, permettent une intéressante lecture en pendant.

La question que pose Thomas Buckley dans « Le traducteur littéraire est-il prisonnier ou créateur de l'image du pays-source dans le pays-cible ? » est tout à fait intéressante et porte sur la façon dont nous recevons les traductions d'œuvres étrangères et surtout sur la manière dont elles confortent ou mettent en question nos préjugés concernant la culture de départ. L'auteur s'intéresse également à quelques exemples de traductions de textes qui ont vu le jour en Albanie, en Lituanie, en Russie, en Turquie et

Union soviétique, mais ce sont essentiellement les rapports entre le France et les États-Unis qui sont analysés. Si le questionnement proposé est on ne peut plus pertinent, la méthodologie adoptée par le chercheur convainc nettement moins. Il est fait usage de l'*Index Translationum* et de certains comptes rendus de *Momus* et *The Guardian,* mais les constatations de l'auteur ne sont pas le fruit d'une analyse exhaustive à partir de sources clairement identifiées. L'intérêt de cet article est donc programmatique : la question de recherche mérite en effet d'être traitée de façon plus structurée.

Erwan Sommerer, dans « Peut-on traduire les idéologies politiques ? L'exemple de la diffusion du fascisme au Brésil et en Argentine », s'intéresse à la traduction de concepts et de discours politiques. Sa contribution est à situer dans le domaine qui relie celui de la traduction à la communication interculturelle. Selon Sommerer, ce n'est pas tant la dénotation des concepts politiques, que leur connotation, leur surplus de sens, dont il convient d'étudier le passage d'une communauté à une autre. Ses exemples concernent la traduction du fascisme (d'origine italienne) au Brésil et en Argentine et montrent, entre autres, la problématique de la traduction d'une idéologie nationaliste, celle-ci étant par essence cantonnée à l'intérieur de certaines frontières et celle-là appelée à les franchir.

Certaines contributions insistent sur l'importance de la traduction dans l'établissement et le renforcement de la communauté-cible.

Ainsi, dans « The Role of Literary Translation in the Survival of Hungarian Language and Culture or One of the Ways for a Nation to Maintain Its Identity », Ágnes Somlé donne un aperçu historique, du Moyen-Âge au XXe siècle, du rôle qu'a pu jouer la traduction dans la survivance de la langue et de la culture hongroises. Somlé montre que la traduction n'a pas seulement permis d'établir des relations entre la communauté hongroise et les autres langues et cultures, mais qu'elle a également servi à légitimer l'identité communautaire même.

Le parti pris de Michèle Laliberté est fascinant. Dans « Paris, Berlin, New York en chansons traduites : l'affectivité du traducteur face à l'altérité », elle entend montrer combien le psychisme du traducteur, qui est nécessairement influencé par le contexte sociopolitique, ne se présente pas nécessairement comme ce qui est le plus individuel, le plus personnel, mais relève bel et bien du communautaire. Partant d'un corpus de chansons françaises et américaines, dont elle étudie les traductions anglaises, allemandes et françaises entre 1910 et 1960, elle affirme que la part du psychologique (collectif) n'a pas été assez étudiée en traductologie et présente une démonstration convaincante pour pallier ce manque. Reste qu'il est dommage que les sources utilisées dans l'article—et parmi les plus intéressantes— ne se retrouvent pas dans la bibliographie et que, inversement, celle-ci contient de très nombreuses références que le lecteur ne retrouve pas dans le corps du texte.

Ce sont des traductions « du plus francophile des tous les écrivains tchèques de la fin du XIXe siècle » (p. 105) que présente Miroslava

Novotnà dans « Le sens et l'effet des adaptations des chansons médiévales françaises par Julius Zeyer ». L'analyse proposée, plutôt littéraire que purement traductologique, entend montrer comment les adaptations des chansons de geste françaises par Zeyer ont permis de relier le passé de la communauté des chevaliers médiévaux à la réalité poétique et politique tchèque de la fin du 19ième siècle. Les adaptations de Zeyer nourrissent en effet autant la poésie fin-de-siècle que les idéaux de renaissance nationale tchèques.

Dans « Réception des traductions et appartenances communautaires : étude de trois collections de catalogues éditoriaux espagnols », Claudine Lécrivain évalue comment les éditeurs créent des appartenances communautaires et « catégorisent le même et l'autre » (p.15). Par une analyse détaillée et à l'aide de tableaux, l'auteur montre que l'épitexte éditorial crée également les attentes de la culture-cible.

« Hégémonie culturelle, choix traductionnels et relations intercommunautaires : étude d'un cas » de Simos P. Grammenidis présente des cas très intéressants de traductions en grec de textes écrits en français, mais comportant des éléments ottomans. Grammenidis étudie le passage de ces éléments relativement exotiques dans le texte français vers le grec et distingue deux attitudes de la part des traducteurs : la « loyauté » et la « servilité ». Parfois les éléments exotiques dans le texte français, souvent accompagnés d'explications et de marquages typographiques spécifiques, sont éliminés dans le texte-cible grec. Ce changement s'explique évidemment par le fait que le passage de la traduction leur a conféré un statut endogène. Dans d'autres cas, ces éléments sont rendus tels quels et constituent donc des explications plus ou moins circonstanciées de concepts tout à fait familiers au lecteur grec. C'est surtout le regard de la communauté grecque sur celui que porte sur elle la communauté française qui est analysé.

Le groupe social virtuel des traducteurs est analysé par Freddie Plassard dans « Les communautés des traducteurs communautés réelles, communautés virtuelles en traduction ». C'est la constitution d'une communauté par le biais de listes de diffusion professionnelles qui est étudiée à partir des cas concrets de la liste des traducteurs de l'Institute of Translating and Interpreting et de celle de la Société Française des Traducteurs. Plassard y argumente de façon fort convaincante qu'une communauté peut se construire sur un territoire dématérialisé et porte un regard nouveau sur des communautés de traducteurs.

L'intérêt de ce recueil est entre autres de montrer combien la traduction joue avec les frontières entre identité et communauté et les brouille par la même occasion. Les traducteurs ainsi que les lecteurs de traductions se positionnent dans un territoire qui est en même temps séparé et solidaire d'autres aires linguistiques, culturelles et idéologiques. Le traducteur comme être « social [qui] participe de plusieurs groupes en

même temps et [qui] est acteur de communautés différentes » (p. 7) est mis
à l'honneur dans cette publication.

**Katrien Lievois, Department of Translators and Interpreters, Artesis
University College Antwerp**

Franco, Eliana, Anna Matamala and Pilar Orero. (2010). *Voice-over
Translation: An Overview.* **Bern/Berlin/Bruxelles/Frankfurt am
Main/New York/Oxford/Vienna. 248p.**

One of the main challenges facing the authors of this extremely useful
volume was to work through the terminological confusion that surrounds its
subject, voice-over translation. The authors provide a valid definition of this
concept, taking into account previous discussions by Translation Studies
and Film Studies scholars, but distancing themselves from them. More
specifically, they remind us that in Film Studies (as in filmmaking), voice-
over is usually understood in the sense of "a disembodied voice"
(Wikipedia) or "the voice of an unseen narrator" (Merriam Webster) and is
therefore distinct from the practice of revoicing a text in another language,
which is the topic of this book. Further, in an original move, the authors
differentiate between voice-over, which is always superimposed over an
audible voice in a different language, and narration/commentary, which
fully replaces the language of the original audiovisual product. They are
thus able to define voice-over translation as "oral or spoken rendering that
is delivered simultaneously and in synchrony with original speech length,
recognisable words and images" (p. 43). Having pinned down the identity
of their research object, the authors are in a position to explore its main uses
and features from various professional and scholarly perspectives.

The outcome of their effort is an innovative book in many ways. The
problem of terminological inconsistency referred to above is symptomatic
of the lack of any comprehensive study of voice-over translation. This book
clearly aims to fill this gap. It constitutes an "Overview", as per its title, in
the sense that it accounts for the history of voice-over translation, explains
the current state of research into that topic, examines voice-over translation
in relation to the professional structures and workflows within which it
takes place, associates this practice with specific film genres, and covers a
range of languages and national traditions from Eastern Europe to South
America. The three authors (one of whom, Eliana Franco, completed the
first ever doctoral thesis on voice-over translation in 2000), follow a
structured approach through which the theoretical and technical
complexities of this particular type of translation are gradually revealed. A
singular strength of the book is that it is largely based on actual professional

experience and offers an impressive amount of genuine examples from practice.

In the first chapter, the thorny issue of terminology is addressed. The decision to define voice-over as "the translation voice on top of the original voice, which remains audible" (p. 39) is not without risks. The authors' concern with establishing voice-over translation as a unique recognisable research object is legitimate, and an unambiguous definition of that object is crucial to that effect. However, by excluding commentary from that definition, and by relegating it to the status of "off-screen dubbing" (pp. 41-42), the authors perhaps unnecessarily narrow down their scope of primary reference. Meanwhile, commentary and narration continue to be common practices carried out by voice-over translators and voice-over talents, regardless of academic distinctions. The relevance of commentary is indirectly acknowledged in the book, since small sections in Chapters 3 and 4 are dedicated to it.

Another potential problem ensuing from the strict definition of voice-over translation in this book is that it could alienate Film Studies scholars who, as the authors' research shows, understand voice-over in a less prescriptive manner. Indeed in a rather simplistic statement, the authors refer to the "good and bad influence of Film Studies on voice-over translation" (p. 42), as if the latter were an abstract notion that needs to be protected from conceptual contamination rather that a flexible and evolving practice that needs to be understood and described as it actually happens.

Chapters 2 and 3 are dedicated to voice-over for post-production (once the source audiovisual product has been completed and is ready for translation for a new audience), while Chapter 4 focuses on voice-over for production (where voice-over translation is an integral part of the product.) Working conditions are described in detail, with an emphasis on the variety and unpredictability of situations that translators may find themselves faced with. Specific issues that relate to the genre of source materials (fictional products, documentaries), the typology of audiovisual texts (narration, interviews, on or off-screen speakers), and the main difficulties encountered in the process of translation (orality, accents, synchrony, terminology etc.) are addressed systematically and with constant reference to indicative examples. The semiotic analysis of synchrony in voice-over translation is based on an older paper by Orero, but remains extremely insightful, relevant and useful (Orero, Pilar. (2006). 'Synchronization in Voice-over', in Bravo, J. M. (ed.) *A New Spectrum of Translation Studies*. Valladolid: Publicaciones de la Universidad de Valladolid. 255–264).

It would of course not be possible to cover all possible typologies and working conditions in one volume. It is worth noting, however, that the experience of translating for voice-over can be widely different from that described in this book. In the UK, for instance, where translation projects tend to be large, multilingual and centrally managed, translators often download their material from ftp servers, have some of the factual research done for them by the agency, have their work proof read, and are sometimes asked to oversee the recording process. It is also increasingly common to work with short commercial videos for the Internet, rather than with longer documentary productions. Thus, while the main principles of voice-over translation remain as described in this book, it is important to acknowledge that professional contexts and practices merit further scholarly attention, as they evolve constantly and vary from place to place.

Chapter 5, "Training in voice-over", discusses the specific competences and skills that voice-over trainees ought to develop. The authors draw on existing literature on the didactics of Translation and on their own experience of setting up the first ever course on voice-over translation in the Universitat Autònoma de Barcelona, in 2001. This clearly pioneering course offers theoretically informed and systematic training at postgraduate level, and its description here is intended as a model for similar courses elsewhere. There are examples of voice-over translation exercises, a useful discussion of assessment methods, and a brief presentation of the same University's online course in voice-over translation - a further innovation in the field of translator training.

The special emphasis placed in this book on translator education is demonstrated by the authors' decision not only to devote an entire chapter to voice-over training, but also to supplement each chapter with "suggested exercises". These encourage trainees to think on theoretical aspects of voice-over translation, to investigate the audiovisual landscape of their country, to develop research skills, to respond to tricky translation problems that may well occur in actual situations, and generally to begin thinking as professional translators faced with real voice-over assignments.

The authors turn their attention back to "practitioners and academics" in Chapter 6. Here "a global survey on voice-over" is offered, based on a questionnaire which was designed to record existing perceptions on the nature and main features of voice-over translation. The 43 respondents (a number which, in fairness, hardly justifies the qualification "global", with only three responses from Asia and one from Africa, for instance) answer both closed and open questions, and it is the latter ones that incite the most informative and critically aware responses. The authors do excellent work in analysing these responses, ultimately showing that voice-over translation is an "underestimated mode of translation lacking [...] serious study", despite the fact that it is "widely used" and is sometimes backed by "very strong tradition[s]" (p. 186).

The book closes with a "commented bibliography on voice-over" (Chapter 7), which is arguably the most comprehensive account of existing literature on this topic. That the entire body of literature on voice-over translation (at least in Catalan, English, French, Italian, Polish and Spanish) consists of around 70 titles, most of them journal articles, can only serve to prove the main point advanced by the authors, namely that this is an enormous field of practice and study that awaits to be properly researched.

There are further merits to this book. In terms of content one could point out the brief reference to "Gavrilov translation" (§2.1, the main technique for revoicing feature films for TV broadcast in many Eastern European countries), which is also gaining recognition as a separate research topic. In terms of presentation, one could mention the many images, screenshots and tables used to illustrate the abundance of examples offered by the authors.

Unfortunately, there are major shortcomings too. The absence of an index is deplorable, especially for a volume that aspires to be a reference work in the field of Audiovisual Translation. Readers who wish to look for a specific term, for example, "audio subtitling", would have to do plenty of guesswork, before they can locate that term (it is on p. 49).

There is, however, an even more important problem with this publication, which will hopefully be mended in a future revised edition. The problem consists in the lack of good linguistic editing. Careless writing and a plethora of typos and syntax errors very often render the reading of this book a daunting task. Here are a few examples:

–   "In addition to [exercises and hard work], the student is also believed [*sic*] to reap the rewards from the benefits of the interaction between. [*sic*]" (p. 144).
–   "But Darwish [...] analysed the text and discovered that while the first Arabic words of the excerpt below are audible the English, the voice-over does not match. [*sic*]" (p. 118).
–   "The concepts in the text have not elaborated on [*sic*] in too much detail [*sic*]" (p. 88).
–   "Six years later, [...] Orero provided an updated [*sic*] on the amount of research performed" (p. 20).

The list of similar errors is long; while in most cases the intended meaning can be deduced, in others - such as the first two examples above – this is not possible. It is a great shame, especially in view of the fact that the book is authored by professional translators and academics and is intended for the benefit of trainees.

Despite these faults, Franco, Matamala and Orero's book remains a valuable and necessary one. It constitutes the most comprehensive and most updated overview of voice-over translation available, and it will be essential reading for students, teachers and scholars working in this under-researched field.

Dionysios Kapsaskis, University of Roehampton, London

Rundle, C., & Sturge, K. (Eds.). (2010). Translation under fascism. Basingstoke: Palgrave Macmillan, 285p.

Among the different readings that this book invites, especially two have retained our attention. First, this work offers an excellent overview of historically oriented translation research in four countries during twentieth century dictatorship (Hitler, Mussolini, Franco and Salazar). The collected overview essays and case studies can be read independently of the whole, although the authors never lose sight of the common thread (translation under fascism). A second reading would start from the idea expressed in the title and look, throughout the chapters of the book, for specific translation strategies and mechanisms under a fascist regime. This, however, is a more problematic reading as the editors very well realize. The challenge posed by the title has been solved conveniently by surrounding the overview essays (Part II) and case studies (Part III) with an Introduction (Part I) and Response (Part IV). For this review, let us start with the 'unproblematic' reading, which considers the distinct contributions of the volume as independent units.

Part II consists of four overview essays dedicated to translation policies and practices in four countries: Italy, Germany, Spain and Portugal. According to the chronological landmarks of the regimes under consideration, the time spans of the studied periods vary considerably. Whereas the Italian and German cases end with the defeat of fascism in 1945, the Spanish and Portuguese cases continue into the post-war period, entering the cold war and finally coming to an end in the 1970s. Even without taking into account the conceptual problem raised by the use of 'fascism' as an overarching label for the four historical cases, it is obvious that the differences in time span and international context make any comparison between the four cases extremely difficult, also because of the fact that each author has used a different methodological approach.

In the first essay, *Translation in Fascist Italy: 'The Invasion of Translations'*, Christopher Rundle focuses on the attitude of the Italian fascist regime towards translation in light of an emerging translation industry. An interesting date is the role played in the debate on cultural (including translation) policies by the statistical information on translation rates and flows as facilitated from 1932 by Index Translationum along with national publishing figures. Rundle's analysis clearly shows that even under a fascist regime, the political attitude towards translation does not necessarily mean effective intervention in the publishing industry or in translatorial practice, an insight that also applies to the other case studies presented in the volume. For fascist Italy, the 'invasion' of foreign literature through translation was first and foremost a matter of 'loss of face', the painful awareness of the gap between the fascist imperial dream and the subalternized cultural reality.

In her essay on translation in Nazi Germany *('Flight from the Programme of National Socialism'? Translation in Nazi Germany)*, Kate Sturge privileges a specific genre (i.e., translated fiction) as the focus of analysis. This shift in focus offers insights that complement those presented in Rundle's essay. Sturge explores the margins of tolerance of Nazism towards an activity, translation, which by definition runs counter to the *völkisch* protectionist concerns of the regime. As the different levels of analysis reveal—from the microlevel of the text to the macrolevel of the market—translation under a fascist regime does not differ in an *absolute* way from translation in other historical and political contexts. Rather, the specificity should be seen as a matter of *degree*.

The Spanish case is treated by Jeroen Vandaele, who, firstly, reflects on what translation studies can offer to the study of Francoism, and, secondly, provides an overview of existing translation research on the Franco period. This second section of the chapter is organized according to 'realms of discourse' or genres (press, prose, film, etc.) in combination with countries of origin or source languages. As a valuable contribution of Translation Studies to our understanding of Francoism, Vandaele points to the *non-dits*, the unveiling of the 'negativities' of cultural politics, which leads the author to the remarkable conclusion that "Francoist culture in general was what it was *not*" (p.113).

In *Translation in Portugal during the Estado Novo Regime*, Teresa Seruya is forced to cope with a double handicap. Firstly, the lack of research on Portuguese translation history, and secondly, the fact that Portugal has been absent, up to now, from research on translation under fascist regimes (see the landmark conference held at Forli (Bologna) in April 2005, *Translation in Fascist Systems: Italy, Spain, Germany*). From her disadvantaged position, Seruya tries to fill this double gap by sketching an overall picture of the place of translation within the cultural politics of the *Estado Novo* regime. Seruya records some specific conditions strange to the ideology of the regime that influenced the translation policy and practices under Salazar and Caetano. As such, she acknowledges the huge illiteracy rate among the Portuguese people, the cultural dominance of the neighbouring country Spain, as well as the proficiency of the Portuguese elite in foreign languages, which explains the presence of non-translated books available to a small minority and out of the regime's concern.

Part III (Case Studies) is less systematically structured than the former part. Spain disappears from the scene in favour of a strong interest in the Italian case, beside Germany and Portugal. The first case study analyses the interaction of two fascist regimes, Germany and Italy, from the viewpoint of literary exchange, viz. German literature in Italian translation. In a second case study, Francesca Nottola reveals the many inconsistencies of Italian fascist policy on translations by focusing on an emblematic anti-fascist publishing house, Einaudi. Frank-Rutger Hausmann sheds light on how the Franco-German border was crossed during the heydays of the Second World War through translation of poetry. The publication of a French-German and a German-French Poetry Anthology in 1943–1945 presents the editor with a double challenge of 'translating the untranslatable', as a result of both the ethnic ideological constraints—the essentialist view of the uniqueness, and hence untranslatability of the *Volk*—and the literary discursive constraints imposed by the inseparability of form and contents in poetry. This case study still needs some further elaboration, which the author acknowledges in his conclusion ("A full history of German-French and French-German poetry anthologies has yet to be written", p. 210), and we can only hope that a full discussion of this exciting case will.be undertaken very soon. Finally, in a fourth case study, Rui Pina Coelho studies Shakespeare translations and performances during nearly half a century of Portuguese 'Salazarism' (1926–1974). If we take into account the specificities of cultural life in twentieth-century Portugal as discussed in Seruya's overview essay, the question arises as to the extent to which Pina Coelho's findings are to be ascribed to the political context of Salazarism itself. Shortly after the Carnation Revolution of 25 April 1974, the theatre professionals described themselves in a manifesto as a "generation that was sacrificed by the outgoing regime during their most creative years" (p. 229). In light of this assertion, it would be interesting to extend Pina Coelho's analysis to present-day translations and stage performances of Shakespeare in Portugal to assess, from a comparative point of view, the true impact of the former dictatorial regime on cultural life.

As stated at the start of this review, a second reading of this book—bearing in mind the title *Translation under Fascism*—is more problematic. The editors are well aware of this difficulty and offer some valuable interpretive tools to cope with this problem in Part I, Chapter I (*Translation and the History of Fascism*) and Part IV, Chapter 10 (*The Boundaries of Dictatorship*). In their introduction, Rundle and Sturge contend that translation practices are "a prime area of interest for scholars of fascist cultural policy" (p. 4), a contention which is convincingly demonstrated throughout the volume. However, what remains less convincing is why the editors so eagerly adhere to the problematic use of the term *fascism* as a common label for the selected regimes and countries. In the introduction, Rundle and Sturge argue that their "use of the term is informed by a body of historical research which, while making all the necessary distinctions, includes these regimes in the debate on comparative fascism" (p. 5). Nevertheless, Jeroen Vandaele opens his overview essay on Spain by stating that "[i]t would be wrong to call Francoism a fascist regime" (p. 84). The discomfort about the choice of the term *fascism* as a common feature accompanies the reader until the final chapter, which happily broadens the perspective by abandoning the problematic label of *fascism* in favour of dictatorship, a perspective that better fits the scope of the volume, which includes also post-fascist Francoism and Salazarism. In his highly illuminating 'Response', Matthew Philpotts clearly shows how the insights into translation policies, rhetoric and practices as revealed in the essays of the volume contribute to our understanding of the 'boundaries of dictatorship'. As translation is by definition a border-crossing activity, translation research can be, for the cultural historian, a privileged tool to scrutinize the porosity of the dictatorial boundaries.

Finally, if we try to define the specificity of fascist dictatorial regimes with respect to translation as it appears throughout the essays collected by Rundle and Sturge, we would say that this specificity lies in the fact that such regimes have to deal with the same paradox as the translator. It is the paradox created by the need to conciliate two antagonistic objectives: to translate or not translate itself, and to exoticize or domesticate the foreign. While the fascist dream of imperial regeneration depends on translation as a means of increasing the nation's cultural capital, the dictatorial 'fear of the invasion of the foreign' fiercely condemns translation as a source of ethnic contamination. This paradox probably explains the many inconsistencies in translation rhetoric and practices recorded by the authors of this volume and distinguishes—as far as translation is concerned—a fascist dictatorship from other dictatorships.

Christiane Stallaert, Department of Translators and Interpreters, Artesis University College Antwerp / Department of Social and Cultural Anthropology, Catholic University of Leuven

Gambier, Y., & van Doorslaer, L. (Eds.). (2010). *Handbook of translation studies (Volume 1)*. Amsterdam: John Benjamins. (printed edition (p. 458) & online version)

The broad selection of contributions found in the *Handbook of Translation Studies* (*HTS*) makes an all-inclusive book review problematic in the spatial limitations imposed on book reviews in this section. Consequently, this book review will adopt a different approach. It consists of two sections: a general introduction to the edited *HTS* and a discussion of some carefully selected themes of importance in the *HTS*.

In the introduction to the 74 contributions that make up the *HTS*, editors Yves Gambier and Luc van Doorslaer state the following: "The *HTS* aims at disseminating knowledge about translation and interpreting studies. It is an academic tool, but one that is also directed at a broader audience. It addresses the needs of students (who often prefer to surf the net, to skim and make do with short texts rather than studying long monographs), researchers and lecturers in Translation Studies and practitioners, as well as scholars and experts from other related disciplines (linguistics, sociology, history, psychology, etc.)" (p. 1). It is in this light that all of the contributions should be read and evaluated. The handbook adopts a dictionary-style format with 74 discrete overview articles on a wide range of translated-studies-related topics (e.g., Audiovisual translation, Conference interpreting, Journalism and translation, Language learning and translation, Quality in translation), which are discussed in alphabetical order in 500 to 6000 words per entry (based on the relevance of the topic in the field) by "specialists in the different subfields" (p. 2). In addition, the *HTS* is available in both a print edition and a slightly adapted online version, which offers hyperlinks to the Translation Studies Bibliography available at http://www.benjamins.com/online/tsb/. It is the piecemeal approach adopted in both the printed edition and the online version that makes it difficult to discuss every single contribution in a traditional book-review format. Consequently, the remainder of this book review will highlight the following three overarching themes of importance in the *HTS*: (1) broad readership and accessibility, (2) breadth of scope and (3) editing.

Broad readership and accessibility: as is visible in the introduction to the *HTS* (see quote above), the editors had in a mind a relatively broad readership ranging from students, researchers and lecturers in translation studies to practitioners, scholars and experts from other related fields. However, writing for such a broad readership often results in an unpleasant mismatch between information that is too general and information that is too specialised. In turn, this mismatch often results in a choppy reading experience, resulting in a distance between the author and the reader. To my surprise, the editors of the *HTS* have been extremely successful in ensuring that most of their specialists wrote their contributions using a relatively consistent writing approach. This writing approach consists of introductory information about specific translation-studies-related topics followed by selections of key concepts and developments related to the topics that are being written about. This writing approach has resulted in contributions that can be read and processed relatively easily by the intended readership. Some people will inevitably find specific contributions too simplistic and too introductory but because of the vast array of topics on offer in the *HTS*, there is undoubtedly something for everyone interested in getting to grips with essential concepts in the field of translation studies. The general idea behind the *HTS* is not to provide highly specialised readers with in-depth information and findings about specific research topics. Although such information is extremely important and useful, it would be misplaced in a book such as the *HTS*. Readers who are looking for such specialised information should turn to the multitude of highly specialised books in the field of translation studies. In addition to providing factual introductory information about key topics, most contributions in the *HTS* also provide the readers with reference lists and some contributions even provide lists with books for further reading.

Breadth of scope: the breadth of scope is a feature which makes the *HTS* tremendously useful to a vast array of readers (see above). However, it is also a feature which can lead readers to experience the contents of the *HTS* as fragmented. The approach adopted by the editors of the *HTS* is not the approach that you typically find in other books which are referred to as *handbooks*. Most handbooks adopt more thorough investigations of a smaller, unified set of topics, providing detailed insights into the selected topics. The editors of the *HTS* have consciously decided to broaden their investigation scope by accepting contributions on 74 topics. However, this does not mean that the 74 topics are 74 unrelated topics. There are clear links between certain topics (e.g., Conference interpreting–Consecutive interpreting–Interpreting studies–Media interpreting–Relay interpreting– Simultaneous interpreting) but the links are not always made explicit, which may be necessary for readers who are not at all familiar with the diversity found in translation studies.

Editing: editing a book is without a doubt a challenging task. Editing a book with no fewer than 74 contributions, most of which have been written by different authors, may appear to many as too tall an order for the best of editors. However, Gambier and van Doorslaer have done a remarkably good job. It is obvious that the collaboration between both editors required planning, strategy and precision. The fact that most of the contributions follow a relatively consistent writing approach is testimony to the synergy between the editors, on the one hand, and the contributors, on the other hand. However, there are quite a few language- and style-related inaccuracies, which the editors (and possibly proofreaders) did not manage to filter out. A few examples of such inaccuracies are (in alphabetical order) the following: *associated to* (instead of *associated with*), *bilingual* <> *bi- lingual*, *to practice* (AmE) <> *practising* (BrE) *professionals*, *compare to* (instead of *compare with*), *consists in* (instead of *consists of*), *don't* (instead of *do not*), *grammar-translation method* <> *grammar translation method*, *- ise* <>*-ize*, *non-verbal* <> *nonverbal*, order of some of the in-text references (neither chronological nor alphabetical), *programme* <> *program* (outside of IT contexts) and *South-Africa* (instead of *South Africa*). Luckily most of the inaccuracies do not lead the reader astray by creating intractable ambiguities or incomprehensible stretches of discourse. The editors may want to consider tackling such problems if they are considering an updated version of the book.

Overall, the *HTS* is a publication which successfully manages to introduce a wide range of topics which are currently being investigated in the field of translation studies to an extremely broad readership. The editors have done a wonderful job of combining the numerous contributions in the handbook in a relatively consistent way and of making the handbook available in a printed version and an online version, the latter of which they intend to keep updated. For any future editions of the printed version or for

any changes to the online version, the editors would do well to filter out any
language- and style-related inaccuracies.

**Jimmy Ureel, Department of Translators and Interpreters, Artesis
University College Antwerp**

Baer, B. J. (Ed.). (2011). *Contexts, subtexts and pretexts: Literary
translation in Eastern Europe and Russia.* Amsterdam: John Benjamins.
332p.

This volume on *Literary translation in Eastern Europe and Russia* in the
prestigious *Benjamins Translation Library* series is entirely dedicated to the
Other Europe, as Eastern Europe is frequently referred to by scholars from
Western Europe. I would have written *Central and Eastern Europe* as I
usually do when mentioning the region, but the editor has good reason not
to use the concept of *Central Europe*, as he explains in the *Introduction* (pp.
2–3), following the recommendations in the paper by Charles Sabatos (see
below).

For some years now the classical viewpoint of Western translation
studies scholars has shifted towards more *exotic* regions and cultures. As
editor Baer correctly points out, non-Western translation traditions are
becoming "increasingly visible in recent years as a reaction to hegemonic
Western models of translation and the general Eurocentrism of
contemporary translation studies" (p. 1). However, renouncing
Eurocentrism in translation studies usually involves a turn towards Asian
and African translation topics. Despite the impressive papers by, for
instance, Russian, Czech and Slovak scholars (p. 5) in the theory of
translation studies, the eastern part of Europe is largely neglected in most
recent Western publications on the subject, which led to the big gap that
this volume partly tries to fill.

The collection of translation studies-related articles *Contexts,
Subtexts and Pretexts* is an attempt to cover most of the region of Eastern
Europe. The majority of languages and cultures in the region (not only the
Slavic languages that the area is too often associated with) are represented
in the volume and only the Russian topics (8 papers) clearly outnumber the
other themes which might, however, reflect fairly realistically the
respective weight of these languages and cultures in contemporary
translation studies. Besides Russian, only one Slavic culture is dealt with
twice in the volume, for one of the great representatives of Czech literature
is present as the metaphorical *alpha and omega* of the volume: Milan
Kundera, an author with a more than moderate interest in translation, has
the honour of opening and closing the volume. Other languages discussed

in the volume are Ukrainian, Romanian, Croatian, Serbian, Slovenian, Hungarian, Bulgarian, Polish and Latvian.

The volume not only geographically covers most part of the Eastern European region, it also addresses a broad range of different translation-related topics, with papers on various aspects of translation. However, most of the papers look at translation from a cultural-studies angle, emphasizing the roles that politics and ideology have played and still play in the development of culture in Eastern Europe and Russia, especially during the twentieth century. Most of the papers deal with what André Lefevere (1992) calls "patronage outside the literary system" (p. 15), that is, political and ideological pressure. Geographical borders, linguistic colonialism and the consolidation of cultural identity are key concepts in nearly all of the articles in this volume.

As the title of the volume suggests, the papers are divided into three sections, the first of which, *Contexts*, deals with "the broad cultural and political contexts that helped shape the choice of texts for translation, the translation approach taken, and the reception of translated texts in the various cultures represented by Eastern Europe and Russia" (p. 10). This is the largest part of the volume with 7 papers on 5 different Eastern European languages. In the opening paper, a key question in Slavic studies is touched upon, that is, the existence, or rather the alleged non-existence, of a conceptual *Central Europe*. Charles Sabatos relates the history of Kundera's essay on the "Tragedy of Central Europe" (1984), in which the author claimed the existence of a transnational Central European identity, based on "*small nations* rather than languages, including Austria but not Germany, and even [...] Slovenia and Croatia" (p. 25). However, Sabatos explains why he is not convinced by Kundera's ideas.

Nation building and the development of national culture is the common theme in the next two papers as well. Vitaly Chernetsky addresses the problem of "shaping [...] modern Ukrainian culture" (p. 33) and investigates this process as a reaction to what he calls Ukraine's *colonial* history. In Chernetsky's view, literary translation should be considered a "conscious project of resistance" (p. 34) against the domination of Russian language and culture. Literary translations from languages other than Russian, frequently funded by Western institutions, mark, according to the author, a double process of globalization and strengthening of national identity in Ukraine. David L. Cooper, on the other hand, shows how the Russian nation had similar doubts about its own identity, albeit in another period, namely the beginning of the nineteenth century when Russia was in search of *narodnost'* (national originality) and its own voice in world literature. Cooper illustrates the polemics about translations and the concept of originality in Russia through the work of author–translator Vasilij Žukovskij and a reaction from colleague writer Nikolai Gogol.

Translation and the nation's cultural identity play an equally important role in Sean Cotter's paper on the thinking of the Romanian philosopher, essayist and poet Constantin Noica. Cotter deals with Noica's "international nationalism" (p. 80) and his ideas about Romania as "Europe's translator" (p. 80). Noica is convinced that translation activities benefit only "the translator, not the public that reads them" (p. 86) and therefore Romania should play its role of Europe's translator, wedged as it is between three large empires (Austro-Hungary, Russia and the Ottoman empire).

Susmita Sundaram brings the reader back to Russia with an article on Konstantin Bal'mont's translating activities. Bal'mont was one of the free spirits among the poets of Russia's Silver Age, who showed great interest in ancient and exotic cultures (the Mayas, India, Egypt) and considered himself a *cultural mediator* between Russia and various distant cultures. At a higher level, the writer saw Russia as a mediator between East and West (p. 113), providing the nation with a specific mission in the world. Sundaram extensively illustrates Bal'mont's Indophilia (p. 107) and his love of oriental motifs.

Sibelan Forrester investigates, in her paper, how Croatian and Serbian authors used translations of Russian avant-garde writers from the early twentieth century "in order to shape his or her own bibliography and literary personality" (p. 117). Forrester pays tribute to writer–translators Sever, Kiš, Vrkljan and Ugrešić, who continued to recommend Russian literature to their Croatian and Serbian audiences in a period (the 1970s and 1980s) when Russian (Soviet?) literature "appeared as stunted as the economy" (p. 119) and the number of literary translations from Russian rapidly dropped in favour of translations from English.

The last paper of the *Contexts* part deals with a more practical translation topic: the problem of translating "theoretical categories and social types for which there are no Slovenian counterparts" (p. 137), especially lesbian, gay, bisexual and transgendered literature and non-fiction. The author, Suzana Tratnik, is a translator of "seminal Western works of gay and lesbian fiction and queer theory" (p. 137) herself, and she recounts her own struggle to find translations for this special type of *realia* since much of the required terminology has not yet been developed in Slovenian.

The second part, *Subtexts*, has 5 papers in 3 different languages, dealing with "the various ways in which politics has mediated the theory and practice of translation in Eastern Europe and Russia" (p. 11). This part is dominated by *Russian* papers that afford insights into the position of translation against the background of politics, ideology and censorship in the former Soviet Union. For instance, Susanna Witt investigates the probably largest ever "coherent project of translation" (p. 149)—the history of literary translation in the Soviet Union, that, according to Witt, remains "still basically unwritten" (p. 167). She is convinced that a closer look at the Soviet translation project could even supply "new perspectives on such key concepts, such as source language, target language, authenticity and translation agency" (p. 168).

The next two papers examine the ideas and translating practices of three well-known names in the Russian history of literary translation. Brian James Baer relates how two coryphaei of Russian literary translation, Roman Jakobson and Vladimir Nabokov, became theoretical opponents in the Cold War period. The polarization between these great thinkers became obvious in the context of a proposed joint translation project of the famous *Slovo o polku Igoreve* (The Lay of Igor's Campaign), which Nabokov saw foremost as a pure work of art, while Jakobson apparently wanted to use the Russian origin of the anonymous text for patriotic political and ideological concerns. Yasha Klots, in his paper, illustrates how ideological censorship can also contribute to a poet's artistic completion. In the case of Nobel Laureate Iosif Brodskij, for instance, "the process of reconciling [...] aesthetic predispositions to the ideological demands of the state-owned publishing industry" (p. 187) forced the poet to refine his own poetics. Translations from a broad range of languages gave Brodskij the opportunity to create a kind of *pure poetry*, independent of the source language in which the poetry had been written, and strengthened his idea about the poet being the instrument of an ultimate *Ur*-language, rather than the *Ur*-language being the instrument of the poet (pp. 200–201).

The effects of (communist) censorship on the practices of literary translation are the leitmotif running through the next two papers as well. László Scholz explains the reasons behind "the surprising uniformity of translations" (p. 205) of Latin American narrative texts into Hungarian in the postwar period. Scholz blames the practices of planned art for being "by nature old-fashioned" (p. 216) and therefore averse to the stylistic experiments of modernity. As Vitana Kostadinova points out in her paper on literary translations (or rather the absence of translations!) of Byron in Bulgaria, literary and historical contexts can have a great influence on translation practices. In describing the reasons for not translating Byron in three different periods of Bulgarian cultural history, she clearly illustrates why "the absence of translations in a given culture can speak as loudly as the translations themselves" (p. 219).

The third part of the volume, *Pretexts*, on "the secondary status traditionally attributed to translated texts" (p. 11) with a special focus on contemporary translation, is more heterogeneous than the previous ones. This section presents the reader with another 6 papers dealing with 4 different Eastern European cultures. The first two papers touch upon contemporary translation practices in Russia. Vlad Strukov focuses on the cultural authority of film translator *Goblin* and deals with questions of intellectual property in a globalized world. Strukov relates how Goblin gradually introduced new forms of film translation by first thoroughly domesticating discourse in his earlier works and transforming translation into parody later on in his work. Aleksei Semenenko discusses a more traditional, even canonical, topic—the translation of Shakespeare's *Hamlet* into Russian. Semenenko investigates and compares no fewer than six twenty-first-century translations of *Hamlet* and concludes that all the translations, however different they might be, share some common, typically postmodern features (p. 261). All six translators tend to modernize the text and even "strive not to translate the text, but to give an original interpretation of individual passages" in order to write their "names in the history of *Hamlet*" (pp. 261–262).

The expectations of the postmodern reader are dealt with in Natalia Olshanskaya's paper on the translations of Russian dystopias into English. By its nature, the dystopian narratives of Evgenij Zamjatin and Vladimir Vojnovič contain a more than average amount of *untranslatable* vocabulary, used to depict the dystopian worlds created by the authors. Olshanskaya investigates translators' decisions and concludes that contemporary literary translators tend to "over-domesticate" the target texts "in part because of the inability of the general readership to relate to the dual nature of specifically Russian cultural references and the hidden implications of the Russian absurd" (p. 273). Allen J. Kuharski addresses another topic of *translatability* in his paper on "translating classical tragedy into Polish theater" (p. 277). Kuharski focuses on stage director Zadara's recent attempts to revive "neglected Polish and foreign classics" (p. 277) by adapting the dramas of Racine and Kochanowski and performing them on the twenty-first-century stage in Poland. He illustrates Polish concerns about, on the one hand, the will to integrate culturally into a larger European tradition and, on the other hand, the fear of losing its own cultural identity.

An even stronger concern about cultural and linguistic identity is seen in Latvia, where first German and later Russian were the dominant languages and where nowadays "70% percent (sic) of the texts consumed by the average Latvian are translations", mainly from English (p. 295). Gunta Ločmele and Andrejs Veisbergs observe in their paper a rapid "shift in norms and conventions" (p. 295) in Latvian, directly affected by English norms, not only at the levels of lexis and semantics, but also in grammatical constructions, spelling norms and even the phonetic system (p. 307), thus illustrating globalizing tendencies as a result of translation practices.

Milan Kundera not only opens this volume on literary translation in Eastern Europe and Russia, he is also the theme of the closing paper, written by Jan Rubeš, on the author's "problematic relationship" with "the translation of his work" (p. 317). Hardly any writer shows more interest in literary translation than Kundera, who sees translation as his "entrée onto the world stage" (p. 317) but who is, at the same time, rather hesitant about the loss of control that the translation process contains. In the case of Kundera, Rubeš points out, the situation is even more complex because his early (Czech) novels have been translated into French, while the author himself is writing in French at the moment and "refuses to authorize the

Czech translation of his books written in French" (p. 322). The whole complexity of authorship and the status of translated texts could not be illustrated more strikingly than in this closing paper to volume 89 in *Benjamins Translation Library*.

   Contexts, Subtexts and Pretexts is a real must-have for all translation researchers working on that 'Other Europe', but for whom a lot of sources written in 'minority languages' remain unreadable, as well as for researchers in Slavic studies dealing with translation. So it seems all the more annoying to me that such an inspiring collection of papers has been rather carelessly compiled, for a lot of typographical and formal errors have made it into the final version of the text. Apparently, not all proper names in the papers have been checked, as I find Norvid instead of Norwid (pp. 198–199), Brian De Palmo instead of Brian De Palma (p. 238) and Norwegian instead of Norway (p. 320). Moreover, the editor apparently made no use of a style sheet either for bibliographical references, or for the transcription or transliteration of the Cyrillic alphabet. The different contributors to this volume all use their own system, which results in various inconsistencies in the bibliography. For instance, Marina Cvetaeva (I prefer the ISO R/9 system myself) is referred to twice in the bibliography, once as Cvetaeva (p. 324) and once as Tsvetaeva (p. 331) without any cross-references between the two. The same goes for Majakovskij and Mayakovsky (p. 328), while Černov is cited next to Chernyshchevsky (sic—this name does not contain a "shch") on page 324. Even more confusing is the reference to a Meirkhol'hold (sic) on the same page, an obviously wrong transcription for Mejerhol'd (ISO R/9) or at least Meyerhold (in English transcription), to whom a reference is made in one of the papers (p. 165), without this name being added to the bibliography.

   Despite these formal inconsistencies *Contexts, Subtexts and Pretexts* touches upon some essential and *hot* topics in literary translation in Eastern Europe and Russia and should be recommended to a broad public of translation scholars and students.

Reference

Lefevere, A. (1992). *Translation, rewriting and the manipulation of literary fame*. London: Routledge.

Piet Van Poucke, University College Ghent / Ghent University

Nord, C. (2011). *Funktionsgerechtigkeit und Loyalität. Die Übersetzung literarischer und religiöser Texte aus funktionaler Sicht.* **Frank & Timme, Berlin 2011, 302p. (In der Reihe: TransÜD Arbeiten zur Theorie und Praxis des Übersetzens und Dolmetschens.)**

Dieser Band in der Reihe *TransÜD Arbeiten zur Theorie und Praxis des Übersetzens und Dolmetschens* bündelt 17 Artikel, die Christiane Nord in den vergangenen 30 Jahren in verschiedenen wissenschaftlichen Zeitschriften und Büchern veröffentlicht hat. In diesen Beiträgen behandelt sie Themen zur Übersetzung literarischer und religiöser Texte aus dem Blickwinkel der funktionalistischen Translationstheorie.

Christiane Nord hat insbesondere mit ihrem Modell der funktionalen Textanalyse und Translation und ihrem reformerischen Einsatz für die Translationsdidaktik Namen gemacht. In zahlreichen Publikationen zur Ethik und Didaktik des Übersetzens und zur Notwendigkeit einer translationsorientierten Textanalyse entwickelt sie ihre Translationstheorie anhand von Beispielen aus der Praxis und prägt sie den Begriff der *Loyalität*, der die vagere Vorstellung der *Treue* innerhalb der Translationskritik ersetzen soll. Nord diskutiert und untersucht in ihren Beiträgen, ob die Kriterien der funktionalen Translation für die Übersetzung von literarischen und religiösen Texten gültig gemacht werden können.

Diese Diskussion ist innerhalb der Translationswissenschaft längst nicht abgeschlossen und bewegt sich auch oft im etwas dogmatisch angehauchten Gebiet der kreativen Handlung, die von funktionalen Aspekten und Zielsetzungen keineswegs gestört werden dürfe. Nord sucht in ihren Beiträgen eine Antwort auf die ewige Frage, ob nun "Kopf" oder "Bauch" die Translation lenken sollten. Klar ist, dass in der funktionalen Translationswissenschaft die Antwort zugunsten des Kopfes ausfällt.

Innerhalb der literarischen Translationskritik hat die funktionale Vorgehensweise jedoch zahlreiche Gegner. So nennt zum Beispiel der deutsche Literatur- und Translationswissenschaftler Rainer Kohlmayer die funktionale Translation "eine wissenschaftlich argumentierende Anleitung zur Herstellung von Trivialliteratur" (Kohlmayer, 1988, S.34). Nord bekämpft diese Art von Kritik mit einschlägigen Argumenten: „Diejenigen, die von [...] dem Ideal einer „treuen" Abbildung des AT durch den ZT ausgehen, dürften sehr bald an die Grenzen der Übersetzbarkeit stoßen" (Nord, 1989, S.101).

Nord sucht einen Ausweg aus der Sackgasse der literarischen Translationspraxis, indem sie eine Strategie entwickelt, die verschiedene Sichtweisen konsolidieren und insbesondere die Übersetzung literarischer und religiöser Texte aus einer Art der Regellosigkeit herausholen könnte.

Die funktionalistische Translationstheorie, die den Schwerpunkt von *Bedeutung* auf *Funktion* verlagert, soll den Translator als Experten, der eine translatorische Handlung erbringt, sichtbar machen. Dieser handelt nach einem Entscheidungsprozess, der vom *Skopos*, von der *Funktion* oder *Absicht* des Textes - großenteils vom *Initiator* oder Auftraggeber der Übersetzung bestimmt - eingegeben wird.

Nord betont, dass alle Rahmenbedingungen (Auftrag/ Medium/Sprachfunktion) genauestens beschrieben sein müssen, bevor mit der Translation begonnen werden kann. Die zweite Phase, nämlich die Analyse des Ausgangstextes, wird laut Nord an erster Stelle von textexternen Faktoren bestimmt: Ort und Zeit der Entstehung des Textes, Anteil des Autors, etc.). Erst dann sollte der Analyse textinterner Faktoren Aufmerksamkeit gewidmet werden. (Stil, Thematik, Inhalt, Struktur, kulturspezifische Elemente) . Diese Analyse ist für Nord selbstverständlich translationsrelevant, aber auch auf den Skopos gerichtet: Änderungen können nur vorgenommen werden, wenn sie dem Ziel des Translats gerecht werden können. In der Phase der eigentlichen Translation steht wieder die Funktion des Textes an erster Stelle: Nicht der Ausgangstext bestimmt die gewählten Übersetzungsstrategien, sondern die Funktion, die das Translat in der empfangenden Kultur erfüllen soll.

Das Buch eröffnet mit einem Beitrag aus dem Jahr 1980, in dem anhand der kritischen Besprechung einer veröffentlichten Übersetzung der Kurzgeschichte *Don Payasito* der spanischen Schriftstellerin Ana Maria Matute ein Modell aufgestellt wird, das die Bedeutung der Textanalyse für die Qualität des Translats illustrieren soll. Es handelt sich hier um den ersten translationswissenschaftlichen Artikel Nords, der noch stark vom Äquivalenz-Modell Katharina Reiß' geprägt ist, für Nord jedoch "den Ausgangspunkt meiner übersetzungswissenschaftlichen Entwicklung markiert. (Nord, 2011, S. 11)

Meines Erachtens hantiert Nord hier einen fragwürdigen Begriff des "Literarischen". Sie rechnet literarische Texte generell "nicht zur Kategorie der pragmatischen Texte" (Nord, 2011, 15), untersucht jedoch den Text anhand ihres Kommunikationsmodells, wobei Sender, Empfänger, Kode, Senderintention und Empfängererwartung feste Kategorien sind. Den vorliegenden Text definiert sie als literarischen Text, der "durch seinen Inhalt/Gehalt die Leser ansprechen, nachdenklich machen, ihnen anhand eines – fiktiven oder autobiographischen – Kindheitserlebnisses ein allgemein menschliches Problem bewusst machen" möchte (Nord, 2011, S. 16). Ferner würden literarische Texte von einem "Stilwillen" (Nord, 2011, S.16), der bewussten Handhabung bestimmter sprachlicher Ausdrucksweisen bestimmt und seien sie so Äußerung eines einzigartigen Sprachgebrauchs, der dazu diene, den Inhalt zu unterstützen. Die Bestimmung des Texttyps aufgrund dieser Kriterien führe "zwingend" (Nord, 2011, S. 16) zur Translationsmethode.

In einem zweiten Beitrag "Übersetzungshandwerk – Übersetzungskunst" (1988), setzt Nord ihren Versuch, den Begriff 'literarisch' zu definieren, fort: sie bringt ihn in ein Kommunikationsmodell ein (Intention des Senders/Empfängers/Referenten/Code/Effekts) und stellt dieses Modell dann in einen Rahmen der interkulturellen Kommunikation und Translation. Schließlich beschreibt sie den daraus gewonnenen theoretischen Rahmen für die literarische Übersetzung. Das Fazit ist erstaunlich: Die Forderung nach Äquivalenz von Ausgangs- und Zieltext sei unvereinbar mit den Hypothesen der interkulturellen literarischen Kommunikation. Auf den ersten Blick sei die Übersetzung von literarischen Texten also eine unmögliche Handlung und werde von ihr eigentlich "die Quadratur des Kreises" verlangt. (Nord, 2011, S.60)

Den einzigen Ausweg aus dieser Sackgasse sieht Nord in der Formulierung einer klaren, wissenschaftlich untermauerten theoretischen Grundlage und Zielsetzung. Außerdem seien die Unterschiede zwischen literarischer und nicht-literarischer Kommunikation so gering, dass eine einzige theoretische Grundlage für beide Textsorten ausreiche. Um diese Argumentation zu unterstützen greift Nord auf die Skopostheorie von Reiß und Vermeer zurück. (Reiß/Vermeer, 1984, S.43)

In einem weiteren Beitrag behandelt sie den Diskussionspunkt, dass literarische Übersetzungen eine Kunst seien, die nichts mit Wissenschaft zu tun hätten. Nord setzt dem entgegen, dass gerade literarische Übersetzungen oft einen auffallenden Qualitätsmangel aufweisen und ihnen eher vom "Bauch" her als vom "Kopf" her begegnet wird. (Nord, 20011, S.65) Anhand einiger 'typischer' Translationsprobleme, die die Translationswissenschaft wohl lösen kann, versucht sie, eine theoretische Grundlage zu schaffen, die der literarischen Übersetzung dienlich sein kann. Diese Grundlage geht ihrerseits vom funktionalistischen Modell aus und berücksichtigt Faktoren aus der Translationswissenschaft, Rezeptionstheorie, Stiltheorie, Textanalyse, Soziologie und Phonologie.

In den nächsten Kapiteln werden Themen behandelt wie die Translation kulturspezifischer Unterschiede ("Alice im Niemandsland", S. 75-98); die Transkription paraverbalen Verhaltens ("Wer spricht wie und warum?" S. 99-115); der Mythos der treuen Übersetzung ("So treu wie möglich?" S. 117-143) und die Übersetzung von Anreden in literarischen Übersetzungen aus dem Spanischen ("Ja mein Herr – o nein, Señorito!" S. 145-165).

Der zweite Teil des Bandes ist der Übersetzung religiöser Texte aus funktionalistischer Sicht gewidmet und formuliert u.a. einen neuen "Skopos für alte Texte" (S. 169-185); das Verhältnis von Interpretation und Übersetzung: "Auslegung und Übersetzung" (S. 207-213) und ein Plädoyer, auch nach Luther die Bibel immer wieder neu zu übersetzen. Der Band schließt mit einem interessanten Kapitel über Translationskompetenz und Bibelübersetzung und Kreativität versus Methode.

Die Bündelung dieser eher erschienenen Beiträge weist eine gewisse Kohärenz auf, ohne allzu große Überschneidungen. Der Standpunkt Christiane Nords ist von Anfang an klar: Die Bedeutung der Übersetzungsmethode und der Analyse von sowohl Ausgangs- wie auch

Zieltext kann nicht überschätzt werden. Eine klare Betrachtungsweise der Funktion von Ausgangs- und Zieltext und die Ersetzung des Begriffs der 'getreuen Übersetzung' durch den Begriff 'Loyalität' müssen einfach bessere Übersetzungen hervorbringen.

Referenzen

Kohlmayer, R (1988): Der Literaturübersetzer zwischen Original und Markt. Eine Kritik funktionalistischer Übersetzungstheorien. In: *Lebende Sprachen* 33/4, 145-156.

Nord, Ch. (1989): Loyalität statt Treue. Vorschläge zu einer funktionalen Übersetzungstypologie. In: *Lebende Sprachen 3*. Langenscheid, 100-105.

Nord, Ch. (2011). *Funktionsgerechtigkeit und Loyalität. Die Übersetzung literarischer und religiöser Texte aus funktionaler Sicht.*, Berlin: Frank & Timme (In der Reihe: TransÜD Arbeiten zur Theorie und Praxis des Übersetzens und Dolmetschens.)

Reiß, K./Vermeer, J. (1984),43 *Grundlegung einer allgemeinen Translationstheorie. Tübingen: Niemeyer*

Patricia Linden, Department of Translators and Interpreters, Artesis University College Antwerp

Nord, C (2011). *Funktionsgerechtigkeit und Loyalität. Theorie, Methode und Didaktik des funktionalen Übersetzens.* Berlin: Frank & Timme. 331p. [TransÜD. Arbeiten zur Theorie und Praxis des Übersetzens und Dolmetschens 32.]

In diesem Band hat Christiane Nord auf Vorschlag von Hartwig Kalverkämper eine Auswahl ☐alter" d.h. eher veröffentlichter Aufsätze gesammelt. Sie bringt sie in drei Teilen unter und ordnet sie in jedem Teil chronologisch aufgrund ihrer Erstveröffentlichung. Nach einem I. Teil über die Theorie des funktionalen Übersetzens folgt im II. Teil ("Methode des funktionalen Übersetzens") die Anwendung des Funktionsbegriffs auf verschiedene Probleme und Aspekte des Übersetzens, z.B. auf die Einteilung von Zitattypen, die Unterscheidung von Übersetzungseinheiten und Einheiten kommunikativen Handelns und die Einteilung von Metakommunikation. Der III. Teil ist der Didaktik des funktionalen Übersetzens gewidmet. Nicht alle Aufsätze sind eine wörtliche Reproduktion der früheren Veröffentlichung. Da sich der Band ausschließlich aus deutschsprachigen Beiträgen zusammensetzen sollte, sind einige der Aufsätze aus dem Englischen übersetzt worden. Außerdem erwähnt die Autorin in ihrem Vorwort auch, dass sie bestimmte Artikel gekürzt hat und gelegentlich mit □C.N. 2010" gekennzeichnete Anmerkungen hinzugefügt hat.

Das große Verdienst der Translationswissenschaftlerin und der Translatorin Christiane Nord besteht wohl darin, dass sie der □rücksichtlosen Funktionsorientierung" ein □Korrektiv" geboten (S. 103) und den Funktionalismus für die Praxis des Übersetzens und die Übersetzerausbildung brauchbar gemacht hat. Und gerade dieses Verdienst spiegelt sich auch in dieser Sammlung wider. Im I. Teil sind drei der sechs Beiträge explizit dem Begriff der *Loyalität* gewidmet, der für Nord das Korrektiv zur Funktionsgerechtigkeit darstellt. Loyalität bedeutet, dass es zum ethischen Verhalten des Translators gehört, alle Beteiligten im Interaktionsprozess - das sind der Sender und der Ausgangstext, der Auftraggeber und der Auftrag sowie die Rezipienten - □nach bestem Wissen und Gewissen" (S. 105) zu berücksichtigen. Auf all diese Beteiligten im kommunikativen Interaktionsprozess, der die Translation ist, nimmt Nord auch Rücksicht in ihren Beiträgen zur Didaktik des Übersetzens: bei der Analyse des Übersetzungsauftrags, bei der Formulierung der Anforderungen an ein Übersetzungslehrbuch, bei der Klassifizierung von Übersetzungsfehlern und beim Vorschlagen neuer Arbeitsformen im Übersetzungsunterricht.

Eine solche Sammlung von eher veröffentlichten Beiträgen weist auch einige Nachteile auf. Die Autorin kündigt im Vorwort ausdrücklich an, dass sie "auf die Einbeziehung neuerer Publikationen" (S.8) verzichtet, was dazu führt, dass zeitgebundene Themen nicht aktualisiert werden, wie z.B. mit den Vertextungskonventionen von Packungsbeilagen der Fall ist (S. 93-99 und S. 308-309) und dass die in einem Artikel aus dem Jahr 2003 versprochenen Erweiterungen in diesem 2011 erschienenen Band noch immer in Aussicht gestellt werden (S. 225). Daneben ist bei einer Sammlung autonomer Aufsätze Wiederholung kaum zu vermeiden. Es ist nicht verwunderlich, dass gerade die Textfunktionen als Schlüsselbegriffe des funktionsorientierten Übersetzens in mehreren Aufsätzen erläutert werden. Das Vier-Funktionen-Modell wird zweimal ausführlich dargestellt (S. 161-164 und S. 213-216) und die Textfunktionen stehen auch im Mittelpunkt, wenn Probleme bei der Übersetzung von Titeln, Zitaten oder Werbetexten behandelt werden.

Bedauernswert ist, dass sich in diesen Band – vermutlich als Folge des Bearbeitungsprozesses - sehr viele Druckfehler eingeschlichen haben. Manche dieser Druckfehler sind möglicherweise dem Scannen des Manuskripts zuzuschreiben: z.B. □Hierarchier" statt □Hierarchie" (S. 35), □sodas" statt □sodass" (S.58), □la bruit" statt □le bruit" (S. 62). Andere Fehler tragen deutlich die Spuren von zwei Fassungen: z.B. „[…] auf die man *sich* beim Übersetzen […] *zurückgreifen* kann" (S. 29), □[…] *begrenzen* die Signale […] das Spektrum […] *ein*" (S. 49). Einmal wird derselbe Inhalt in zwei aufeinander folgenden Absätzen einfach in anderer Formulierung wiederholt (S.172-173). Es mag auch an der Textbearbeitung liegen, dass an zwei Stellen Inkongruenzen zwischen Fließtext und Abbildung entstehen. Gemeint sind: die Beschreibung der Abb. 7 (S. 94-96) und die Erläuterung der Abb. 1 (S. 162-163), in der auf □Wellenlinien" verwiesen wird, die es in der Abbildung nicht gibt.

Trotz der genannten Schwächen erfüllt dieser Band seine Zielsetzungen. Er dokumentiert die wesentlichen Aspekte von Christiane Nords wissenschaftlicher Arbeit, er stellt einen Überblick der funktionalistischen Ansätze und deren Anwendungsmöglichkeiten dar und enthält wichtige Hinweise für all diejenigen, die in der Übersetzerausbildung mit Translationsübungen beauftragt sind.

Leona Van Vaerenbergh, Department of Translators and Interpreters, Artesis University College Antwerp

Alphabetical list of authors & titles with keywords

Alphabetical list of contributors & contact addresses

Abekawa, Takeshi
Research and Development Center for Informatics of Association
National Institute of Informatics
2-1-2 Hitotsubashi, Chiyoda-ku
101-8430 Tokyo
Japan
e-mail: abekawa@nii.ac.jp

Albers, Frank
Artesis University College
Department of Translators and Interpreters
Schildersstraat 41
2000 Antwerp
Belgium
e-mail: frank.albers@artesis.be

DePalma, Donald A
Common Sense Advisory
100 Merrimack Street
Lowell, MA 01852-1708
USA
e-mail: Don@commonsenseadvisory.com

Désilets, Alain
Institute for Information Technology
National Research Council of Canada
1200, Montreal Road, Building M-50,
Ottawa, Ontario
Canada, K1A 0R6
e-mail: alain.desilets@nrc-cnrc.gc.ca.

Desjardins, Renée
School of Translation and Interpretation
Institute of Canadian Studies
University of Ottawa
70 Laurier Street
Ottawa, Ontario
Canada
e-mail: rdesjard@uottawa.ca

Drugan, Joanna
Centre for Translation Studies
Leeds University
Leeds LS2 9JT
UK
e-mail: j.drugan@leeds.ac.uk

Gough, Joanna
School of English and Languages
Faculty of Arts & Human Sciences
University of Surrey
Guildford
Surrey GU2 7XH
UK
j.gough@surrey.ac.uk

Jiménez-Crespo, Miguel A.
Department of Spanish and Portuguese
Rutgers, The State University of New Jersey
105 George St
New Brunswick, NJ, 08901
USA
e-mail: miguelji@rci.rutgers.edu

Kageura, Kyo
Graduate School of Education
University of Tokyo
7-3-1 Hongo, Bunkyo-ku
113-0033 Tokyo
Japan
e-mail: kyo@p.u-tokyo.ac.jp

Kapsaskis, Dionysios
Roehampton University
Department of Media, Culture and Language
Roehampton Lane
London SW4 6SZ
United Kingdom
e-mail: D.Kapsaskis@roehampton.ac.uk

Kelly, Nataly
Common Sense Advisory
100 Merrimack Street
Lowell, MA 01852-1708
USA
e-mail: nataly@commonsenseadvisory.com

Lievois, Katrien
Artesis University College
Department of Translators and Interpreters
Schildersstraat 41
2000 Antwerp
Belgium
e-mail: katrien.lievois@artesis.be

Linden, Patricia
Artesis University College
Department of Translators and Interpreters
Schildersstraat 41
2000 Antwerp
Belgium
e-mail: patricia.linden@artesis.be

McDonough Dolmaya, Julie
School of Translation
York University, Glendon Campus
2275 Bayview Ave
Toronto, Ontario M4N 3M6
Canada
e-mail: dolmaya@yorku.ca

O'Hagan, Minako
School of Applied Language and Intercultural Studies
Centre for Translation and Textual Studies
Dublin City University
Dublin 9
Ireland
e-mail: minako.ohagan@dcu.ie

Ray, Rebecca
Common Sense Advisory
100 Merrimack Street
Lowell, MA 01852-1708
USA
e-mail: rebecca@commonsenseadvisory.com

Sagara, Miori
Baobab, Inc.
3-14-4 Shiba, Minato-ku
105-0014 Tokyo
Japan
e-mail: sagara@baobab-trees.com

Secară, Alina
Centre for Translation Studies
School of Modern Languages and Cultures
University of Leeds
Leeds
LS2 9JT
UK
e-mail: a.secara@leeds.ac.uk

Stallaert, Christiane
Artesis University College
Department of Translators and Interpreters
Schildersstraat 41
2000 Antwerp
Belgium
e-mail: christiane.stallaert@artesis.be

Katholieke Universiteit Leuven
Faculty of Social Sciences, Department of Anthropology
Interculturalism, Migration and Minorities Research Centre
Parkstraat 45 box 3615
3000 Leuven
Belgium
e-mail: christiane.stallaert@soc.kuleuven.be

Sumita, Eiichir
Multilingual Translation Laboratory
National Institute of Information and Communications Technology
3-5 Hikaridai, Keihannna Science City
619-0289 Kyoto
Japan
e-mail: eiichiro.sumita@nict.go.jp

Ureel, Jimmy
Artesis University College
Department of Translators and Interpreters
Schildersstraat 41
2000 Antwerp
Belgium
e-mail: jimmy.ureel@artesis.be

Utiyama, Masao
Multilingual Translation Laboratory
National Institute of Information and Communications Technology
3-5 Hikaridai, Keihannna Science City
619-0289 Kyoto
Japan
e-mail: mutiyama@nict.go.jp

Van Poucke, Piet
University College Ghent
Faculty of Applied Language Studies
Groot-Brittanniëlaan 45
9000 GENT
Belgium
e-mail: piet.vanpoucke@hogent.be

Van Vaerenbergh, Leona
Artesis University College
Department of Translators and Interpreters
Schildersstraat 41
2000 Antwerp
Belgium
e-mail: leona.vanvaerenbergh@artesis.be

van der Meer, Jaap
TAUS
Oudeschans 85III
1011KW Amsterdam
Netherlands
e-mail: jaap@translationautomation.com